Learning Ext JS 4

Sencha Ext JS for a beginner

Crysfel Villa

Armando Gonzalez

[PACKT] open source*

PUBLISHING

community experience distilled

BIRMINGHAM - MUMBAI

Learning Ext JS 4

Copyright © 2013 Packt Publishing

First published: January 2013

Production Reference: 1180113

Published by Packt Publishing Ltd.
Livery Place
35 Livery Street
Birmingham B3 2PB, UK.

ISBN 978-1-84951-684-6

www.packtpub.com

Cover Image by Neha Rajappan (neha.rajappan1@gmail.com)

Credits

Authors
Crysfel Villa
Armando Gonzalez

Reviewers
Satyajith Bhat
Justin Beal
Bruce Sklar
JD Smith
Iwan van der Schoor

Acquisition Editor
Usha Iyer

Lead Technical Editor
Arun Nadar

Technical Editors
Ankita Meshram
Kaustubh S. Mayekar
Sharvari Baet

Project Coordinator
Shraddha Vora

Proofreader
Linda Morris

Indexers
Hemangini Bari
Tejal Daruwale

Graphics
Valentina D'silva
Aditi Gajjar

Production Coordinator
Nilesh R. Mohite

Cover Work
Nilesh R. Mohite

About the Authors

Crysfel Villa is a Software Engineer with more than 7 years of experience with JavaScript on a daily basis. He started his career as a Web Developer working with HTML and basic JavaScript in the late nineties, but then he started focusing on Server Side technologies, such as PHP and Java J2EE.

Before he started working with the Ext JS library he loved to work with MooTools, but in late 2007 he started learning about an awesome new library that was emerging as an Open Source project. At that time the version 2.0 of the Ext JS library was just coming out and Crysfel started using this new library for medium-large projects in the agency that he used to work with.

In early 2010 Crysfel started working as a freelancer, he began to train teams on Ext JS for private companies, writing a blog with tutorials, tips and tricks, developing custom components on Ext JS for his clients, and working on Open Source projects to share his knowledge with the world.

If you want to find more information about his work, you can follow him on Twitter (@crysfel) or download his Open Source projects from GitHub (crysfel).

Writing this book was very hard, especially when you are a busy person and really like to get involved in exciting things. I want to give special thanks to my wife Hazel, who supported me in every step of the process, without her this wouldn't have been possible. She read all the scripts before I submitted them; she usually found some mistakes or things to clarify, her work on this project is priceless.

Thanks to my parents and brothers, who used to keep asking me very often about the project and providing moral support to work and complete this dream. Also, I want to thank all my closest friends for the moral support that they gave me, special thanks to my best friends Carlos and Gina who usually pushed me to continue working on this project.

Armando Gonzalez is a Software Engineer with more than 4 years of experience in developing enterprise applications with Ext JS. He has plenty of experience in server-side technologies like PHP, Java J2EE, Node JS, and ROR. Before he started with Ext JS he was a Java and PHP developer.

Since he started using JavaScript and Ext JS he became a JavaScript Evangelist, and started training teams on JavaScript and Ext JS. He loves to teach and share his knowledge with other developers and is always trying to make them use this awesome library.

In early 2012 Armando started a software company, Codetlan, with some of his friends. This company focuses on developing enterprise applications using Sencha technologies. He is also a minor actionist in a Mexican startup called Cursame, where he developed the mobile version of the application and helped developing the main application using ROR technologies.

If you want to know more about his work, you can follow him on Twitter (@manduks) or can watch his Open Source projects on Github (manduks).

About the Reviewers

Satyajith Bhat is an engineer, who majored in computer science, and a Sun certified Java Developer. He has spent over 6.5 years designing, developing, and maintaining large enterprise systems in Java/J2EE and related technologies. He has a love for all things Java – a fascination that started during his days in college.

He was one of the early adopters of Ext JS and has worked extensively with Ext 2.0, using it to build complete enterprise web applications for over 3 years.

He currently works as a Java Developer for a major fashion retail company in New York.

Bruce Sklar has more than 28 years of software design and development experience. For the last 12 years of his career he has been designing and developing user interfaces for web-based applications. Recently, he has been designing and developing user interfaces for mobile websites and applications.

Bruce is a User Experience manager at HandySoft Global Inc. HandySoft is a provider of business process management software.

JD Smith is a UI developer, who loves to bring beautiful web interfaces to life.

Since writing his first BASIC program on an Apple IIe in 1986, he has been passionate about turning engineering into art. His passions also include theology, coffee, music, outdoor adventure, and his wife and children.

For more than 12 years, JD has been consulting on front-end web development projects. He has broad experience with web development and UX design for enterprises, small businesss, and mobiles. To know more about him, visit `jdsmith.pro`.

Iwan van der Schoor is a Software Engineer with over 15 years of web development experience. He holds a bachelor's degree in Higher Informatics from the Fontys University in Eindhoven (Netherlands) and has been working in software development in the Netherlands, United Kingdom, and is currently working as a Front-end Engineer at a small start-up company in Silicon Valley. His focus in the last couple of years has been building highly scalable management interfaces for complex infrastructure equipment, and all this using the latest web technologies.

www.PacktPub.com

Support files, eBooks, discount offers and more

You might want to visit www.PacktPub.com for support files and downloads related to your book.

Did you know that Packt offers eBook versions of every book published, with PDF and ePub files available? You can upgrade to the eBook version at www.PacktPub.com and as a print book customer, you are entitled to a discount on the eBook copy. Get in touch with us at service@packtpub.com for more details.

At www.PacktPub.com, you can also read a collection of free technical articles, sign up for a range of free newsletters and receive exclusive discounts and offers on Packt books and eBooks.

http://PacktLib.PacktPub.com

Do you need instant solutions to your IT questions? PacktLib is Packt's online digital book library. Here, you can access, read and search across Packt's entire library of books.

Why Subscribe?

- Fully searchable across every book published by Packt
- Copy and paste, print and bookmark content
- On demand and accessible via web browser

Free Access for Packt account holders

If you have an account with Packt at www.PacktPub.com, you can use this to access PacktLib today and view nine entirely free books. Simply use your login credentials for immediate access.

Table of Contents

Preface	**1**
Chapter 1: The Basics	**7**
Should I use Ext JS for my next project?	**8**
Getting started with Ext JS	**9**
Looking at the whole picture	10
Why so many files and folders?	11
Our first program	**12**
Editors	**17**
Sublime Text 2	18
Eclipse Web Tools Platform project	19
Aptana	20
Textmate	21
Sencha Architect	22
Building an application	**26**
Planning our application	26
Wireframing	27
Data structure	30
File structure	31
Summary	**32**
Chapter 2: The Core Concepts	**33**
The class system	**33**
Simple inheritance	37
Pre-processors and post-processors	39
Mixing many classes	42
Configurations	49
Statics methods and properties	51
Singleton	52
Alias	53

Loading classes on demand **54**
Enabling the loader 55
Dependencies 57
Synchronous Loading 60
Working with the DOM **61**
Getting elements 62
Query – How to find them? 63
Manipulation – How to change it? **66**
Summary **70**
Chapter 3: Components and Layouts **71**
The components lifecycle **71**
The creation phase 72
The rendering phase 75
The destruction phase 78
The lifecycle in action 79
About containers **82**
The panel 86
The Window component 90
The layout system **91**
Fit layout 92
Card layout 93
HBox layout 95
VBox layout 99
Border layout 101
Accordion layout 102
Summary **104**
Chapter 4: It's All About the Data **105**
Ajax **106**
Models **111**
Validations 113
Relationships 117
Dealing with the store **119**
Adding new elements 120
Looping through the elements 122
Retrieving the records 122
Removing records 125
Retrieving remote data **126**
Ajax proxy 126
JSON reader 128

XML reader   130
Mappings   132
Sending data   **134**
Summary   **138**
Chapter 5: Buttons and Toolbars   139
Event driven development   **139**
A simple button   **145**
Adding menus   **151**
Toolbars   **156**
The main menu for our application   **162**
Summary   **172**
Chapter 6: Doing it with Forms   173
The form component   **173**
Anatomy of the fields   182
Available fields   **182**
The Textfield class   183
The number field   185
The combobox field   188
The date field   192
The checkbox   196
The radio button   198
The field container   **201**
Submitting the data   **204**
Summary   **206**
Chapter 7: Give me the Grid   207
The data connection (models and stores)   **208**
Defining a model for the store of the grid   208
Defining a store for the grid   209
A basic grid panel   **210**
Columns   **213**
Columns renderers   **216**
Selection models   **218**
Grid listeners   **220**
Features   **223**
Ext.grid.feature.Grouping   223
Ext.grid.feature.GroupingSummary   227
Ext.grid.feature.RowBody   230
Ext.grid.feature.Summary   232

Plugins — **233**
  Ext.grid.plugin.Editing — 234
  Ext.grid.plugin.CellEditing — 234
  Ext.grid.plugin.RowEditing — 236
Grid paging — **239**
Infinite scrolling — **241**
Summary — **244**

Chapter 8: Architecture — **245**
  The MVC pattern — **245**
  Creating our first application — **246**
    The views — 250
    The controller — 253
      Listening events — 255
      Opening modules — 257
  Creating a module — **263**
    Adding functionality — 272
    References — 279
  Summary — **281**

Chapter 9: DataViews and Templates — **283**
  The data connection (models and stores) — **283**
    Defining our User Model — 284
    Defining the store — 285
  A basic dataview — **285**
    Getting all our code together — 286
  Handling events on the dataview — **287**
    Adding the listeners to the dataview — 288
  Templates — **289**
  A more complex dataview — **294**
  Summary — **297**

Chapter 10: The Tree Panel — **299**
  A basic tree panel — **300**
  The TreeStore — **303**
  Tree nodes — **305**
  Tree drag-and-drop — **306**
  Adding and removing nodes — **309**
  The check tree — **313**
  The grid tree — **315**
  Adding an invoices' categories tree panel — **320**
  Summary — **327**

Chapter 11: Drag and Drop   **329**

Make an item draggable   330
Hitting the drop zone   333
Drag and drop between Ext JS components   338
Enhancing our application with drag and drop   348
Summary   350

Chapter 12: Look and Feel   **351**

Setting up our environment   351
The resources folder   353
Variables   357
Advanced theming   358
   Adding new gradients   358
   Styles for the tabs   362
   Styling the panel   367
Different styles for the same component   370
Supporting legacy browsers   373
Summary   376

Chapter 13: From Drawing to Charting   **377**

Basic drawing   378
Adding interaction   382
Charts   384
   Legend   384
   Axis   385
   Gradients   385
   Series   386
   Theming   386
Series examples   386
   Area   387
   Bar   389
   Line   391
   Pie   394
   Radar   395
   Scatter   397
   Gauge   399
Enhancing our application with charts   400
Summary   406

Index   **407**

Preface

Before we started writing this book we thought about the issues we have faced when we started learning this framework. Over the years we have made many mistakes and faced a lot of troubles because of the lack of a good guide and unavailability of the proper documentation. We wrote this book thinking about the new developers, who want to dive into the library, and the way we would have liked to have a guide when we started.

Whether you are a beginner or a mid-level developer this book will take you to the next level. Ext JS 4 is one of the best JavaScript frameworks out there; with all its components, developing enterprise web applications is a breeze. The main power of the Ext JS 4 library is its class system. It has been so well designed and well implemented that the result is a really powerful set of JavaScript tools that will boost our development.

This book covers all the information you need to know when starting with this awesome framework.

What this book covers

Chapter 1, *The Basics*, covers an explanation for why there are so many folders and files when you download the library, the installation of the library, and a quick review of the Sencha Architect, a software to develop prototypes and applications faster.

Chapter 2, *The Core Concepts*, is about the awesome Class System. You will learn how to implement Object Oriented Programming with Ext JS. We will also cover the Loader System to define and require dependencies dynamically.

Chapter 3, *Components and Layouts*, talks about the component lifecycle and how to take advantage of it. We will also talk about the most important and commonly used layouts in the library.

Chapter 4, It's All About the Data, covers the data package and how to manipulate our data in order to display it on any widget or component.

Chapter 5, Buttons and Toolbars, talks about events and how to listen to your own events, we also cover some of the most popular configurations for buttons and toolbars.

Chapter 6, Doing it with Forms, provides information about forms and the types of input fields, which are available in the library, as well as how to submit the introduced user's data.

Chapter 7, Give me the Grid, covers the grid panel and its implementations, the column model, grid renderers, selection models, and listeners are explained here. It also covers two new concepts of Ext JS 4 features and plugins. Features like grouping row body and plugins like cell editing, row editing, and infinite scrolling are explained here.

Chapter 8, Architecture, is one of the most important chapters in the book. We describe how to define our folder structure and the way we should use the MVC pattern in order to distribute our code's application wisely.

Chapter 9, DataViews and Templates, covers how we can use DataViews to render our data and how to use Templates to give format to that data. This chapter shows how events can be implemented on DataViews and how we can add basic logic to Templates.

Chapter 10, The Tree Panel, covers the tree panel and its implementations, drag and drop, the tree store, the check tree, and the grid tree. This chapter also shows a real world example implementation of a tree panel.

Chapter 11, Drag and Drop, covers the basics of drag and drop in Ext JS 4. It covers how easy it is to implement the drag and drop behavior between Ext JS 4 components and how we can optimize our applications using drag and drop.

Chapter 12, Look and Feel, covers how we can create a custom design for the UI components. We can customize any of the available components using Compass and SASS.

Chapter 13, From Drawing to Charting, covers how the drawing and charting package works in Ext JS 4, how series like Area, Pie, Radar, Line, Bars, and more can be easily implemented, and how they can be used in a real world application. It is important to mention that these implementations are flash free.

Chapter 14, Finishing our Application, covers the Sencha Command, so we can prepare our application for a production environment. We also talk about some very useful plugins and extensions from the community.

Chapter 15, Ext JS 4 Next Steps, provides information to create the documentation of our applications using JSDuck, how we can use Sencha Touch 2 for mobile versions of the applications, and what other resources can help when developing applications with Ext JS 4.

Chapter 14, Finishing our Application, and *Chapter 15, Ext JS 4 Next Steps*, are not present in the book but are available for download at the following links:

http://www.packtpub.com/sites/default/files/downloads/6846OS_14_Final

http://www.packtpub.com/sites/default/files/downloads/6846OS_15_Final

Who this book is for

This book is for a beginner as well as a mid-level Ext JS 4 developer.

Conventions

In this book, you will find a number of styles of text that distinguish between different kinds of information. Here are some examples of these styles, and an explanation of their meaning.

Code words in text are shown as follows: "The build folder contains the descriptor files to create a custom version of the Ext JS library."

A block of code is set as follows:

```
<!DOCTYPE html>
<html>
<head>
<meta http-equiv="Content-Type" content="text/html; charset=utf-8">
<title>First program</title>
```

When we wish to draw your attention to a particular part of a code block, the relevant lines or items are set in bold:

```
    <!--  Importing our application -->
<script type="text/javascript" src="app.js"></script>

    </head>
    <body>
    </body>
```

Any command-line input or output is written as follows:

```
$ [sudo] gem install jsduck
```

New terms and **important words** are shown in bold. Words that you see on the screen, in menus or dialog boxes for example, appear in the text like this: "The previous screenshot shows the code editor region, where we can edit the code and see it in action just by clicking on the **Live Preview** button."

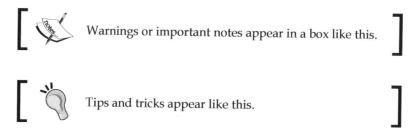

Warnings or important notes appear in a box like this.

Tips and tricks appear like this.

Reader feedback

Feedback from our readers is always welcome. Let us know what you think about this book—what you liked or may have disliked. Reader feedback is important for us to develop titles that you really get the most out of.

To send us general feedback, simply send an e-mail to feedback@packtpub.com, and mention the book title via the subject of your message.

If there is a topic that you have expertise in and you are interested in either writing or contributing to a book, see our author guide on www.packtpub.com/authors.

Customer support

Now that you are the proud owner of a Packt book, we have a number of things to help you to get the most from your purchase.

Downloading the example code

You can download the example code files for all Packt books you have purchased from your account at http://www.PacktPub.com. If you purchased this book elsewhere, you can visit http://www.PacktPub.com/support and register to have the files e-mailed directly to you.

Errata

Although we have taken every care to ensure the accuracy of our content, mistakes do happen. If you find a mistake in one of our books—maybe a mistake in the text or the code—we would be grateful if you would report this to us. By doing so, you can save other readers from frustration and help us improve subsequent versions of this book. If you find any errata, please report them by visiting http://www.packtpub.com/support, selecting your book, clicking on the **errata submission form** link, and entering the details of your errata. Once your errata are verified, your submission will be accepted and the errata will be uploaded on our website, or added to any list of existing errata, under the Errata section of that title. Any existing errata can be viewed by selecting your title from http://www.packtpub.com/support.

Piracy

Piracy of copyright material on the Internet is an ongoing problem across all media. At Packt, we take the protection of our copyright and licenses very seriously. If you come across any illegal copies of our works, in any form, on the Internet, please provide us with the location address or website name immediately so that we can pursue a remedy.

Please contact us at copyright@packtpub.com with a link to the suspected pirated material.

We appreciate your help in protecting our authors, and our ability to bring you valuable content.

Questions

You can contact us at questions@packtpub.com if you are having a problem with any aspect of the book, and we will do our best to address it.

1
The Basics

When learning a new technology such as Ext JS it's complicated to find good material. We have to go from the library documentation to blogs and forums looking for answers, trying to figure out how the library and all the components work together. Even though there are tutorials in the official learning center, it would be great to have a guide to learn the library from the basics to a more advanced level; this is the main goal for this book.

Ext JS is a state of the art framework to create **Rich Internet Applications (RIAs)**. The framework allows us to create cross-browser applications with a powerful set of components and widgets. The idea behind the framework is to create user-friendly applications in rapid development cycles.

This book will walk you through the very beginning, explaining to you why there are so many files when you download the library for the first time, and showing you the meaning of all the files and folders. We will learn when and how to use the library in every stage of the process of creating our first application and how we can make the components work together. We will also learn about architecture and how to use the **Model-View-Controller (MVC)** pattern in order to write maintainable and scalable code.

We will define layers to delegate specific responsibilities to each of them in order to have reusable code. Finally, we will learn how to prepare our code to deploy our application in a production environment, we will compress and obfuscate our code to be delivered faster.

Ext JS is not just a library of widgets anymore; the brand new version is a framework full of new exciting features for us to play with. Some of these features are the new class system, the loader, the new application package, which defines a standard way to code our applications and many more awesome stuff.

The company behind the Ext JS library is SenchaInc., they are working on great products that are based on web standards.

In this chapter, we will cover the basic concepts of this new framework. We'll learn how to import the library, the available tools to write our code, and we'll define the application that we'll build through the chapters of this book:

- Should I use Ext for my next project?
- Getting started with Ext JS
- Our first program
- Editors
- Building an application

Should I use Ext JS for my next project?

Ext JS is a great library to create RIAs that require a lot of interactivity with the user. If you need complex components to manage your information then Ext is your best option because it contains a lot of widgets such as the grid, forms, trees, panels, and a great data package and class system.

Ext JS is best suited for enterprise or intranet applications; it's a great tool to develop an entire CRM or ERP software. One of the more appealing examples is the Desktop sample (`http://dev.sencha.com/deploy/ext-4.1.0-gpl/examples/desktop/desktop.html`), it really looks and feels like a native application running in the browser; in some cases this is an advantage because the users already know how to interact with the components and we can improve the user experience.

Ext JS 4 came out with a great tool to create themes and templates in a very simple way. The framework for creating the themes is built on top of Compass and Sass, so we can modify some variables and properties and in a few minutes we can have a custom template for our Ext JS applications. If we want something more complex or unique we can modify the original template to suit our needs. This might be more time consuming depending on our experience with Compass and Sass.

Compass and Sass are extensions for CSS. We can use expressions, conditions, variables, mixins, and many more awesome things to generate well formatted CSS. We can learn more about Compass on their own website at `http://compass-style.org/`.

The new class system allows us to define classes incredibly easily. We can develop our application using the object-oriented programming paradigm and take advantage of the single and multiple inheritance. This is a great advantage because we can implement any of the available patterns such as the MVC, Observable, or any other. This will improve our code.

Another thing to keep in mind is the growing community around the library, there are lot of people around the world that are working with Ext JS right now. You can even join the meeting groups that have local reunions frequently to share knowledge and experiences, I recommend you to look for a group in your city or create one.

The new loader system is a great way to load our modules or classes on demand. We can load only the modules and applications that the user needs just in time. This functionality allows us to bootstrap our application faster by loading only the minimal code for our application to work.

One more thing to keep in mind, is the ability to prepare our code for deployment. We can compress and obfuscate our code for a production environment using the Sencha Command, a tool that we can run on our terminal to automatically analyze all the dependencies of our code and create packages.

Documentation is very important and Ext JS has a great documentation, very descriptive with a lot of examples, and code so that we can see it in action right on the documentation pages, we can also read the comments from the community or even help by commenting and extending the API content.

We should know that Ext JS has a dual license option for us. If we want to develop an open source project, we need to use the GPLv3 license for our own project, this way we don't need to pay a license for Ext. But, if we want to develop a commercial project and we don't want to share our code with the world, we have to buy a license for Ext JS on Sencha's website at `http://www.sencha.com`.

Getting started with Ext JS

Enough talking, let's start our journey! The first thing we should do is download the framework from the official website, `http://www.sencha.com/products/extjs/`. The version available at the time of writing this book is 4.1.1.

There are two types of licenses. The commercial license that you need to buy if you are planning to develop a closed source project, usually used for corporations, banks, or enterprises. The other available license is the GPLv3 for open source projects. Choose the license that meets your needs.

When you download and extract the library for the first time, probably you will get overwhelmed by the size of the zip and by the number of files and folders, but don't worry, the purpose of each file and the content of each folder will be explained shortly.

We can also use the available **Content Delivery Network (CDN)** so we don't need to store the library in our own computer or server:

- The CSS file: http://cdn.sencha.io/ext-4.1.0-gpl/resources/css/ext-all.css

- The JavaScript file: http://cdn.sencha.io/ext-4.1.0-gpl/ext-all.js

Looking at the whole picture

Before we start writing code we need to learn and understand a few concepts first. Ext JS is divided in three layers, as shown in the following screenshot. The purpose of these layers is to share code with Sencha Touch, a framework to create mobile web applications:

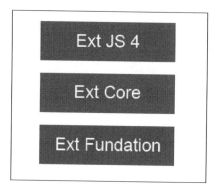

In the **Ext Foundation** layer the Ext object is created, as well as some useful utilities and the class system that allows us to extend classes, override methods and properties, add mixins and configurations to classes, and many more things.

The **Ext Core** layer contains the classes that manage the **Document Object Model(DOM)**, setting and firing events, support for Ajax requests, and classes to search the DOM using CSS selectors.

Finally the **Ext JS 4** layer contains all the components, widgets, and many more features that we're going to be learning in this book.

Why so many files and folders?

This is a natural question when you look at the downloaded files and folders for the first time, every file and folder is there for a purpose and now you're going to learn it:

- The `build` folder contains the descriptor files to create a custom version of the Ext JS library. In here, we can find the JSB3 files that describe the files and packages to build the library from the source code. These JSB3 files will be used by the JavaScript Builder utility that we will learn to use later in this book.

- The `builds` folder contains the minified version of the library; we find the foundation, the core, and the Ext JS sandboxed version of the library. The sandboxed version allows us to run Ext 4 and any older version of the Ext library on the same page.

- The `docs` folder contains documentation of the API. Just open the `index.html` file and you're going to see the packages and classes with all the configuration, properties, methods and events available, guides and tutorials, links to watch videos online, and examples.

- The `examples` folder contains a lot of examples of the components, layouts, and small applications that are built to show what we can do with the library. Open the `index.html` file and explore the samples and demos by yourself. It's important to say that some of them need to run on a web server, especially those that use Ajax.

- The `locale` folder has the translations of 45 languages. By default the components are displayed in English, but you can translate them to any other language.

- The `jsbuilder` folder contains the tool to build and compress our source code; the tool is written in Java and uses the YUI Compressor to improve file minification. The minification process allows us to create packages with all the classes and files that are needed in our application, this is an important step before deploying our application in production.

- The `src` folder contains all the classes of the framework. Each class is in its own file so we can read it easily, and every folder corresponds to the namespace assigned to the class. For example, the class `Ext.grid.Panel` is in a file called `Panel.js` that is in a folder called `grid` (`src/grid/Panel.js`).

- The `resources` folder is where the styles and images are located; also we can find the Sass files to create our custom theme in here. Sass is an extension of CSS3 to improve the language; we can use variables, mixins, conditionals, expressions, and more with Sass.

- The `welcome` folder contains the styles and images that are shown when we open the `index.html` file in the `root` folder.

  If you look at the `root` folder you can also see other JavaScript files. Basically, they are the compressed, debug, and development versions of the library.

- The `ext-all.js` file is the complete library with all the components, utilities, and classes. This file is minified so we can use it for a production environment.

- The `ext-all-debug.js` file is the same as the `ext-all.js` file, but it is not minified so we can use this file to debug our application.

- The `ext-all-dev.js` file is similar to the `ext-all-debug.js` file but contains additional code to show more specific errors and warnings at development time; we should use this file when developing our application.

- The `ext.js` file is the core and foundation layer for Ext JS. If we use this file, we're not loading the whole library; this file contains only the class system, the loader, and a few other classes. We can use the `Ext.Loader` class to load just the required classes and not the entire framework; we should use this file only in development environments.

- The `ext-debug.js` and `ext-dev.js` files follow the same concept as mentioned with the `ext-all` files. The `ext-debug.js` file is an exact version of the `ext.js` file but is not minified. The `ext-dev.js` file contains extra code to log more specific errors in a development environment.

Now that we have a basic understanding of the downloaded files and folders we can go to the next step and get our hands on some code.

Our first program

We need to setup our workspace to write all the examples of this book. Let's create a folder named `learning-ext-4`. For now we don't need a web server to host our examples, but in the following chapters we are going to use Ajax; therefore, it's a good idea to use our favorite web server to host our code from these first examples.

In our new folder we are going to create folders that contain the examples for each chapter in this book. At this point we have a folder called `01-basics` that corresponds to this chapter and other called `extjs-4.1.1` that contains the Ext JS framework. Both folders are located at the same level.

Inside the `01-basics` folder we're going to create a file called `installation.html`, where we need to import the Ext library and create a JavaScript file called `app.js` that will contain our JavaScript code:

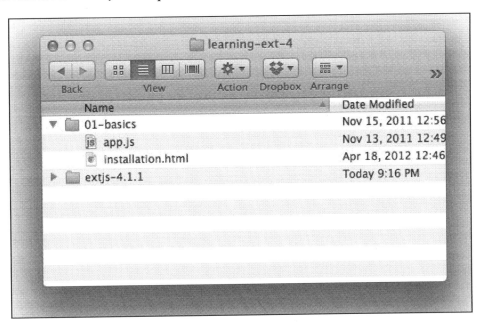

Let's open the `installation.html` file in our favorite editor and type the following code:

```
<!DOCTYPE html>
<html>
<head>
<meta http-equiv="Content-Type" content="text/html; charset=utf-8">
<title>First program</title>

<!-- Importing the stylesheet for the widgets -->
<linkrel="stylesheet" type="text/css" href="../extjs-4.1.1/resources/
css/ext-all.css">
<!-- Importing the Ext JS library -->
<script type="text/javascript" src="../extjs-4.1.1/ext-all-dev.js"></
script>

<!-- Importing our application -->
<script type="text/javascript" src="app.js"></script>

</head>
<body>
</body>
</html>
```

Downloading the example code

You can download the example code files for all Packt books you have purchased from your account at http://www.packtpub.com. If you purchased this book elsewhere, you can visit http://www.packtpub.com/support and register to have the files e-mailed directly to you.

The previous code shows how to import the library for a development environment. First we import the stylesheet that is located at extjs-4.1.1/resources/css/ext-all.css, the second step is to import the whole library from extjs-4.1.1/ext-all-dev.js. Now we're ready to write our code in the app.js file.

Before we can start creating widgets we need to wait until the DOM is ready to be used. Ext JS provides a function called Ext.onReady, which executes a callback automatically when all nodes in the tree can be accessed. Let's write the following code in our app.js file:

```
Ext.onReady(function(){
alert("We're ready to go!");
});
```

One of the advantages of using Ext JS is that the library only uses one single object in the global scope called Ext to allocate all the classes and objects within the framework.

If you open the HTML file in your favorite browser you will see something like the following screenshot:

Feel free to use your favorite browser to work through the examples in this book. I recommend you to use Google Chrome because it has more advanced developer tools and it's a fast browser. If you are a Firefox fan, you can download the Firebug plugin, it's a powerful tool that we can use for debugging on Firefox.

If for some reason we can't see the alert message in our browser, it's because we haven't defined the correct path to the `ext-all-dev.js` file. If we look at the JavaScript console, we'll probably see the following error:

`Uncaught ReferenceError: Ext is not defined`

That means that the `ext-all-dev.js` file is not imported correctly. We need to make sure everything is correct with the path and refresh the browser again.

Now that we know how to execute code when the DOM is ready, let's send an alert message from the Ext library. Using the `Ext.Msg` object we can create different types of messages such as an alert, confirmation, prompt, progress bar, or even a custom message:

```
Ext.onReady(function(){
//alert("We're ready to go!");
Ext.Msg.alert("Alert","We're ready to go!");
});
```

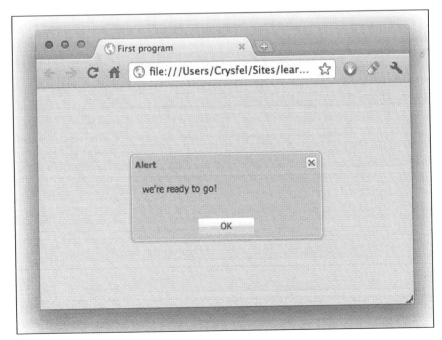

If you're not getting any errors in the JavaScript console, but still you can't see the message on the screen, as seen in the preceding screenshot, make sure you have inserted the stylesheet correctly.

In this case we're using the `alert` method of the `Ext.Msg` object. The first parameter is the title of the message and the second parameter is the content of the message. That was easy, right? Now let's create a confirmation dialog box:

```
Ext.onReady(function(){
//alert("We're ready to go!");
Ext.Msg.alert("Alert","We're ready to go!");
Ext.Msg.confirm("Confirm","Do you like Ext JS?");
});
```

We use the `confirm` method to request two possible answers from the user. The first parameter is the title of the dialog box and the second parameter is the question or message we want to show to the user:

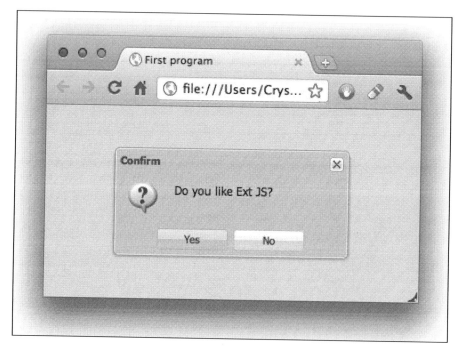

Before the confirmation dialog box appeared there was an alert that didn't show up. One important thing to keep in mind is that the messages and alerts from the Ext library don't block the JavaScript loop, unlike the native browser dialog box. This means that if we add another alert or custom message after the `confirm` method is called, we shall not see the confirmation dialog box anymore.

So far we have shown a confirmation dialog box requesting two possible answers to the user, but how can we know the user's response in order to do something according to the answer? There's a third parameter in the confirmation dialog box that is a callback function that will be executed when the user clicks on one of the two answers:

```
Ext.onReady(function(){
//alert("We're ready to go!");
Ext.Msg.alert("Alert","We're ready to go!");

Ext.Msg.confirm("Confirm","Do you like Ext JS?",
function(btn){
if(btn === "yes"){
Ext.Msg.alert("Great!","This is great!");
}else{
Ext.Msg.alert("Really?","That's too bad.");
}
});
});
```

The callback function is executed after the user clicks on the **Yes** or **No** button or closes the confirmation dialog box. The function receives as a parameter the value of the clicked button which is **Yes** or **No**; we can do whatever we want inside of the callback function. In this case we're sending a message depending on the given answer. Let's refresh our browser and test our small program to watch our changes. Confirmations are usually asked when a user wants to delete something, or maybe when he/she wants to trigger a long process, basically anything that has only two options.

Editors

Before we move on it's important to use the right tools in order to be more productive when building applications. There are many editors we can use to write our code. Let's review some of them.

Sublime Text 2

The **Sublime Text 2** editor is a very light and fast editor. We can add many plugins to have a powerful development environment. The team behind this software is actively working on new improvements and new features; we have updates almost every day (if we compile the editor from the source code at `github`). The package manager for plugins works greatly to install new software from third-party developers.

We can use an evaluation version that never expires, but it's really worth buying the license for this great editor.

If we decide to work with this editor, we should use the JavaScript Lint plugin to validate our code every time we save our file (`https://github.com/Kronuz/SublimeLinter`). Code completion is always welcome, we have a plugin for that too, which is available at `https://github.com/Kronuz/SublimeCodeIntel`. And, of course, a snippet package for writing common Ext JS 4 code can be found at `https://github.com/rdougan/Sencha.sublime`:

```
     js app.js — learning-ext-4
FOLDERS
▼ learning-ext-4
   ▼ 01-basics
      app.js                  1
      installation.html       2   Ext.onReady(function(){
   ▶ extjs-4.1.1              3       //alert("We're ready to go!");
                              4       Ext.Msg.alert("Alert","We're read
                              5
                              6       Ext.Msg.confirm("Confirm","Do you
                              7          if(btn == "yes"){
                              8             Ext.Msg.alert("Great!","T
                              9          }else{
                             10             Ext.Msg.alert("Really?","
                             11          }
                             12       });
                             13   });
                             14

Line 1, Column 1                              Tab Size: 4      JavaScript
```

Eclipse Web Tools Platform project

The **Eclipse** editor is one of the most used editors out there. If you add the web tools plugin into the platform, you can get a JavaScript syntax validation, an Ext JS class `autocomplete`, HTML and CSS validation. The downside of these tools is that they require a lot of resources from your computer, but if you have enough RAM, this is a good option for writing your code:

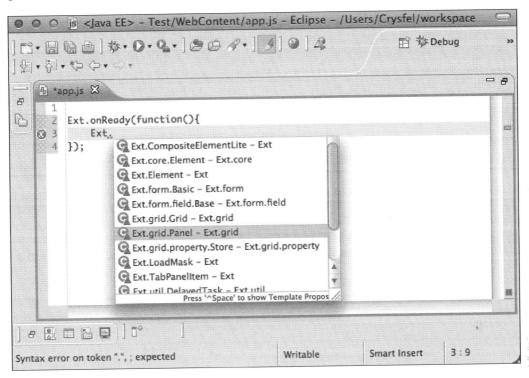

The previous screenshot shows the `autocomplete` class in action. As you can see when you type `Ext` you can select a class from the list. If you keep typing, it filters the classes that match your text.

You need to use the Spket plugin for adding the autocomplete functionality for Ext JS or any other JavaScript library. We can find the required steps to setup the Spketplugin at `http://www.spket.com/extjs.html`.

Aptana

The **Aptana** editor is an IDE from Appcelerator. It's based on Eclipse but optimized for web applications. It's an open source project and free of charges.

Among other things, Aptana contains an autocomplete functionality for JavaScript and Ext JS, a JavaScript validator, CSS and HTML validator, a JavaScript debugger, Bundles, and so on:

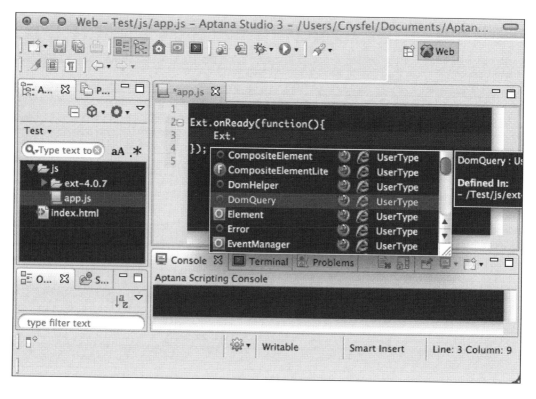

Aptana is a great tool when working with Python, Ruby, or PHP as the backend of our projects. It contains tools to work with those out-of-the-box languages and also contains tools to deploy your application in the cloud using Heroku or Engine Yard.

Textmate

The **Textmate** editor is a light and fast editor for Mac OS. It's not free, but it's worth what you pay for. Textmate doesn't have an autocomplete functionality like Aptana or Eclipse, but it contains bundles to automate some repetitive tasks such as creating classes, documenting methods, properties, and things like that. I suggest you download the available bundles for Ext JS from `https://github.com/edspencer/Sencha.tmbundle` or create a custom bundle to automate these tasks:

```javascript
Ext.onReady(function(){
    //alert("We're ready to go!");
    Ext.Msg.alert("Alert","We're ready to go!");

    Ext.Msg.confirm("Confirm","Do you like Ext JS?",function(btn){
        if(btn == "yes"){
            Ext.Msg.alert("Great!","This is great!");
        }else{
            Ext.Msg.alert("Really?","That's too bad.");
        }
    });
});
```

Line: 5 Column: 6   JavaScript   Tab Size: 4

Sencha Architect

The **Sencha Architect** desktop application is a tool that will help you design and develop an application faster than coding it by hand. The idea is to drag-and-drop the components into a canvas and then add the functionality. The Sencha Architect desktop application is a product from Sencha Inc. that aims to help developers to define components with a few clicks. We can create an Ext JS or Sencha Touch project. We can get a free trial from the official website of Sencha, we can also buy the license there.

To start our application we need to create a project for Ext 4. The Sencha Architect desktop application will show an empty canvas in the center, the available components and classes on the left-hand side, a project inspector and a configuration panel in the right-hand side:

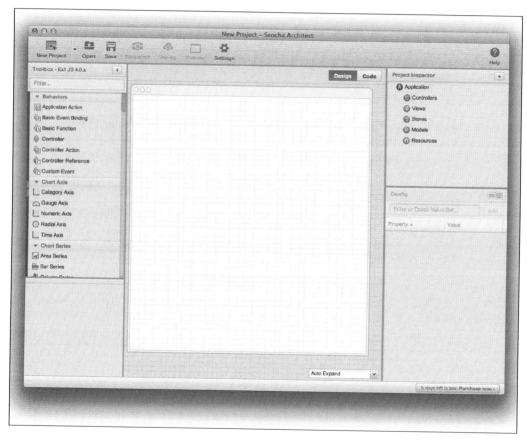

Now let's create a simple application with this tool. First we need to drag a viewport component from the left-hand side panel into the canvas; the width and height are set automatically. The viewport always takes all the available space on our browser.

The next step is to add a **Tab Panel** section inside the viewport. To do this let's drag the component to the viewport. We can change the title of the tabs by clicking in the text and typing the new title; in this case we're going to set **General**, **Groups**, and **Contacts** for each tab. At this point we haven't set the height of the Tab Panel section; we can set the height in the **Property** panel at the right-hand side or by dragging the border of the panel. Another option is to set the **layout** property of the viewport to **fit**, this will expand the **Tab Panel** section to fit the viewport. Just select the viewport and in the **Property** panel, look for the **layout** property and select **fit** from the combobox:

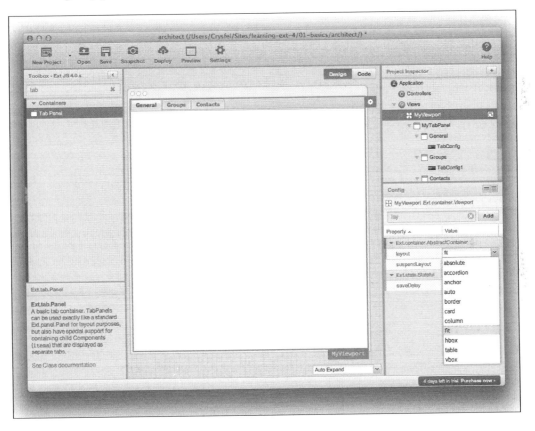

Let's add a form to the **General** tab by dragging the form panel component to the tabs container. We will see an empty form with the title **MyForm**. Let's look for the **title** property in the **Property** panel at the right-hand side and delete the title. We can also set the **border** property to zero in order to get rid of the border.

So far we have an empty form in the **General** tab, let's add some text fields to the form by dragging them to the empty form. For this example let's set the label of these fields to **Name** and **Last name**. Now let's add a field date and a text area for the **Birthdate** and **Comments** field:

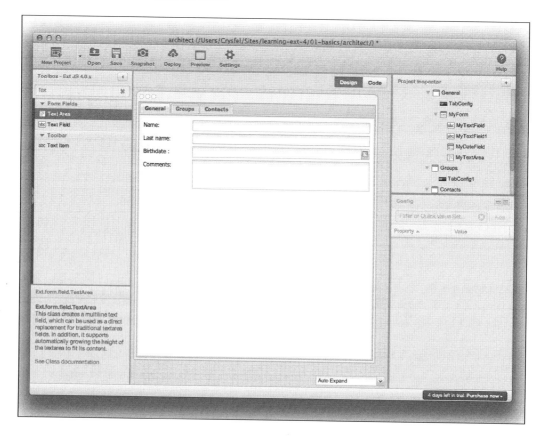

As we can see it's pretty simple and fast to create prototypes or interfaces with this tool. Now that we have our application let's see it in action, we just need to save our project and then click on the **Preview** button at the top bar. A prompt dialog box will appear asking us for the prefix of our application where our project is located. In here we can use `http://localhost/learning-ext-4/01-basics/architect/`, if we are using a web server. A new window of our default browser will open with a working example of the components that we have designed; we can play with it and see how it is working:

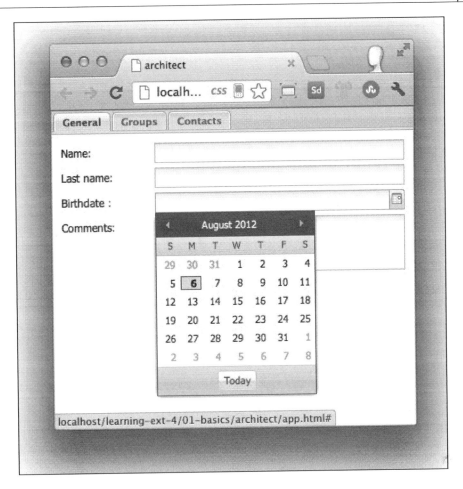

If we want to see the code that is generated, we need to go to the folder where we save our project. In there we will see all the files and classes that have been created for this small example.

The Sencha Architect desktop application is a great tool to build our interfaces. At the time of writing this book the application allows us to modify the code directly in the Architect, but this is not as easy as using a text editor or IDE.

Throughout the chapters of this book we're not going to use the Sencha Architect desktop application. I believe it's a good idea to understand how to create the components by code and once we know the basics we can use the Sencha Architect desktop application even better. If you are interested in using this tool, you should read the documentation that is available online on Sencha's official website.

Building an application

In this book we're going to be building a small invoice application. This will help us learn the most commonly used components in the library and the way they interact with each other. Most of the code and examples presented in this book are used to create the UI for the final application.

There are two approaches when we develop an application with Ext JS. We can use only a few widgets and render them within the HTML page in a specific `div` element along with other things and load as many pages as the system needs just like any other traditional web application. This is the first approach.

The second approach is to create a single web page application and only load data using Ajax and REST to transfer our data using JSON or XML. There's no need to create multiple views or pages in our project. We only need one and then we will dynamically create the required Ext JS components.

In this book we will go for the second option. We're going to develop a single web page application, loading our data using JSON. We're going to compress and minify our source code using the Sencha tools in order to deploy our application in a production environment.

The downside of this approach is that we lost the browser history. When the user clicks on the back button of the browser he/she will be redirected to the last visited page. Gmail, Twitter, and some other sites that use this approach usually append a hash tag to the URL in order to simulate and keep track of the user history. Ext JS comes with a solution for these issues and we can take advantage of that by implementing the required utilities.

Planning our application

We're going to build an application to handle clients and categories of invoices. The client's module should display a list of clients with the basic information about them. The application should allow the user to see and edit the details of the selected client in the list.

The categories module should allow the user to manage the invoices categories in a tree. The user should create children nodes from any existing category. If the user deleted a category that has invoices, then the category and its invoices should be deleted as well. We will be able to drag-and-drop invoices to any of the categories on the tree. We will allow the user to re-order the categories by dragging them with the mouse.

Wireframing

Before we start coding we should define the requirements about how we are going to do our application using wireframes, so we can have a better idea of the final product.

 A wireframe is just a sketch of how we will create the layout of our modules. I'm using a free tool at `mockflow.com`, but we can even use a piece of paper and pen.

First we define the main menu using a toolbar at the top of the viewport. This menu will contain the modules that we need and also it will display the name of the logged user in the right-hand side of the toolbar. The viewport is a component that takes all the available space on the browser, therefore we should have only one viewport in our application:

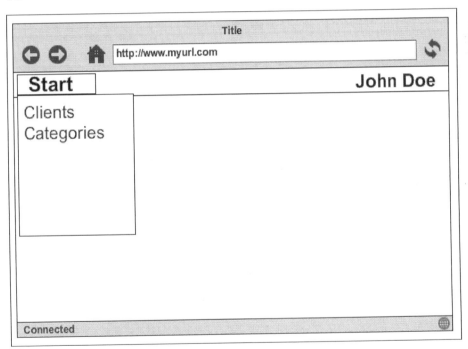

For the main content we're going to use tabs to display each module. When the user clicks on any option of the main menu a new tab will be opened. The user should be able to close the tab when he/she finishes his/her tasks.

The **Clients** module, in the left-hand side, will contain a grid with the current clients in the application and in the right-hand side will be the form to create or edit a client. The module should look as the following screenshot:

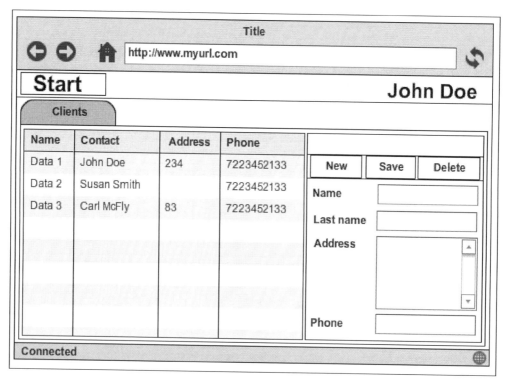

When the user clicks on one of the clients of the grid, the form will be filled with the information of the selected client to be edited or deleted.

The **New** button will clear the form so the user can start filling the form with the information of a new client.

The **Save** button will submit the form data to the server in order to be saved. The server will create a new record or update the existing client in the database based on the sent ID.

The **Delete** button will remove the client from the database. Before sending the request the application should ask for confirmation. After the server responds with a success message, the form should be cleared and a feedback message should be displayed informing that the client has been deleted successfully. If an error occurs while deleting, an error message should be shown.

The second module manages the categories; we need to show a tree in order to display the categories correctly. Each time the user expands a category the application will make a request to the server asking for the children of the selected category:

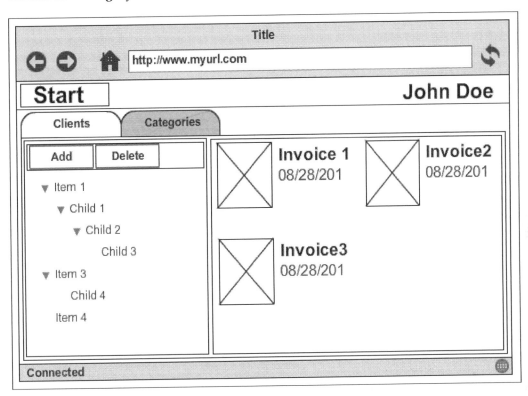

The **Add** button will create a new node in the tree panel as a child of the selected category. If there's no selected category then the new category will become a child of the root node.

The **Delete** button will delete the category and all its children. For this action the application should ask for confirmation from the user.

The user will be able to drag-and-drop any of the invoices on the right-hand side panel to any of the categories on the left-hand side tree. We will also allow the user to re-order the categories on the tree by dragging them on the position they want.

Data structure

We need to define our models and how they are related to each other. According to the given requirements we need only three models, each of them are described as follows, as well as their fields:

- Client: This describes a client entity.

  This model contains ID, name, contact, address, and phone fields.

- Category: This is used to classify many invoices.

  This model contains ID, owner, name, created at fields.

- Invoice: This belongs to one category and describes an invoice entity.

  This model contains ID, category ID, name, date fields.

The following diagram represents the relationships between the models:

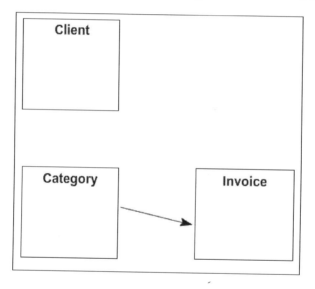

Ext JS 4 came with a great data package. We can define each of the previous models in a class that represents each entity; for now we're just defining and preparing things to start developing our application.

File structure

We are going to use Ajax to load and send data. In order to start developing we're going to need a web server. I suggest you use Apache because it's easy to install using some of the all-in-all packages such as XAMP or WAMP. If you are using a Mac OS you already have an installed Apache server, just turn it on by going to the **Settings and Sharing** configurations.

It's important to note that programming the services that manage the requests on the server side, to save and delete the information in the database, are out of the scope of this book. We're going to focus our attention on Ext JS programming and defining the JSON format to transfer the data. You can use whatever server-side language you want such as PHP, Python, Ruby, and so on to deal with the database.

Once you have your web server up and running create a `learning-extjs-4` folder in the public content of your server. Inside that folder we will copy the Ext JS framework with all the files and folders that we have downloaded before. We are going to create a folder for each chapter of this book where we will create our examples. At the end we will have something like in the following screenshot:

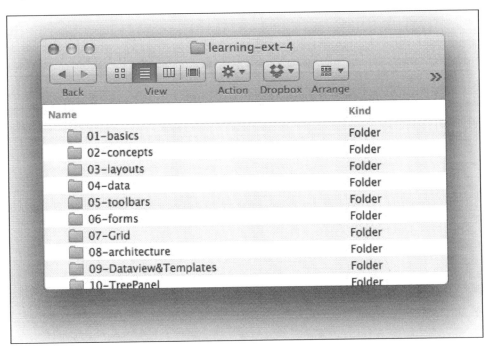

Summary

In this chapter, we learned important concepts about the Ext JS library, such as the three layers in which the library is divided. We also learned the meaning of the files and folders that the Ext library has, importing the library, and the troubles we may have. We also have reviewed a few editors that will help us to be more productive in doing our job. Feel free to use your favorite editor.

Throughout the course of the book we're going to learn about the components and at the same time we're going to build an application using what we have defined in this chapter. In the next chapter, we're going to learn about how to create object-oriented JavaScript using the amazing class systems that come with the latest version of the Ext JS library; also we'll learn about DOM manipulation and events.

The Core Concepts

2

In this chapter we're going to learn about the new class system that version four introduces. There are a lot of new features to take advantage of in this version. We are also going to learn how to load classes dynamically and how to interact with the **Document Object Model (DOM)** to modify the structure of the tree to our convenience.

We should know that in JavaScript, classes don't exist; however we can emulate them using the `prototype` object and other techniques. One of the major features about Ext JS is the way we can emulate object-oriented programming.

It's important to mention that you should know and understand the concepts of object-oriented programming. In this chapter we are not going to explain the concepts, but instead we are going to learn how to implement those concepts using Ext JS.

The following are the main topics in this chapter. We need to understand these concepts well before moving on to other parts of the library.

- The class system
- Loading classes on demand
- Working with the DOM

The class system

Since the beginning, Ext JS has been an object-oriented library. In the latest version the class system was completely redesigned and new features were added. It became more powerful for extending and creating classes.

In order to create classes Ext JS uses the `Ext.ClassManager` object internally to manage the associations between the name we defined and the actual class object in the whole framework. It's not recommended to use this class directly; instead we should use the following shorthand:

- `Ext.define`: This shorthand internally calls the `create` method from the class manager in order to create a new class. In addition we can override methods and properties from an existing class.

- `Ext.create`: This shorthand is an alias for the `instantiate` method from the class manager. We can use this shorthand to create objects from an existing class.

- `Ext.widget`: This shorthand calls the `instantiateByAlias` method to create instances of the given alias. An alias is a short name for a class.

Let's create our first class using the first shorthand in the preceding list. In a new file called `Client.js` we need to write the following code:

```
Ext.define("MyApp.Client",{      //Step 1
  name      : "John",       //Step 2
  lastName  : "Doe",

  constructor  : function(config){   //Step 3

Ext.apply(this,config || {}); //Step 4

    console.log("I'm a new client!");
  }
});
```

In the first step we defined the name of our class by passing a string as the first parameter of the `Ext.define` function. In this case we're defining `MyApp.Client` class.

The second step is to define the properties and methods for our new class. We pass an object as the second parameter of the `define` method. In this case we are defining the name and the last name for the client.

Step three defines a special method. The manager class looks for a `constructor` method that will be used when the class is created. If we don't define this method, an empty function will be used instead.

In the last step we are setting the new values to the new instance that is being created. The `config` object should have the properties that we can modify; this way we can set different values for the new objects that will be created. If we don't pass any parameters when we create a new instance the default values will be applied.

When working on real world applications we should always use a namespace to create our classes. In this example we've used MyApp but that wouldn't be enough for a big application, something like MyApp.modules.accounting. Client would be better. A namespace allows us to group classes or objects and avoid collisions.

Once we have defined our class we can create instances by using the Ext.create method as follows:

```
//creating an instance of Client
var client = Ext.create("MyApp.Client");

console.log(client.name); //Print the default value: John
```

The create method receives, as a first parameter, the name of the class that we want to instantiate, in this case MyApp.Client.

If we want to change the default values of the name and last name properties, we should create an object containing the new value for each property.

```
//creating an instance of Client
//with params
var client2 = Ext.create("MyApp.Client",{
name      : 'Susan',
lastName: 'Smith'
});

console.log(client2.name); //Print the new value: Susan
```

In order to run the example, we need to create an HTML page, import the Ext JS library and the client class, after that we can execute the preceding code.

```
<!DOCTYPE html>
<html>
<head>
<meta http-equiv="Content-Type" content="text/html; charset=utf-8">
<title>First class</title>

<!-- Importing the stylesheet for the widgets -->
<linkrel="stylesheet" type="text/css" href="../extjs-4.1.1/resources/
css/ext-all.css">
<!-- Importing the Ext JS library -->
<script type="text/javascript" src="../extjs-4.1.1/ext-all-dev.js"></
script>
```

```
<!--  Importing the client class -->
<script type="text/javascript" src="js/Client.js"></script>

  <script type="text/javascript">
    //creating an instance of Client
    var client = Ext.create("MyApp.Client");

    console.log(client.name);

  </script>

</head>
<body>
</body>
</html>
```

Let's open the HTML file in our favorite browser and the JavaScript console by pressing *Ctrl* + *Shift* + *I* (shortcut for Windows users) or *Cmd* + *Option* + *I* (shortcut for Mac users) to open the developer tools in Google Chrome. If you're using Firefox, the shortcut to show the JavaScript console is *Ctrl* + *Shift* + *K* (for Windows users) or *Cmd* + *Option* + *K* (for Mac users). If you are using Internet Explorer 8 or above, press *F12* key to open the developer tools, where the JavaScript console is present. If you are using a different browser, the key shortcuts would be different. We should see in the JavaScript console two log messages as in the following screenshot:

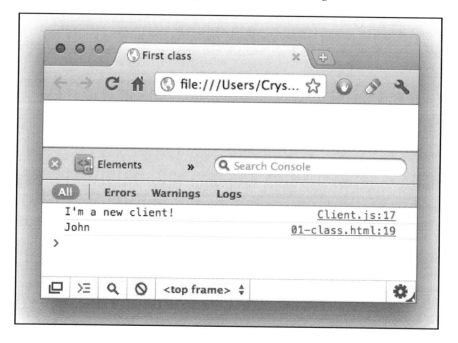

The first message is printed in the constructor method that is executed when the Client class is created. The second message is printed when we have the instance and we have accessed the name property.

Once we have the instance of the Client class, we can modify its properties by assigning the new value.

```
client.name = "Carl";

console.log(client.name);
```

If we refresh our browser we shall see a new message in the console and with the new value. We can create as many instances as we want from our class and everyone would have the same properties and methods. However, we can change their values individually or even pass an object to the constructor with the properties that we want to change.

Simple inheritance

When we create a class using the Ext.define method we're extending from the Ext.Base class. This class contains abstract methods that will be inherited to all the subclasses so we can use them to our convenience.

In our previous example the Client class extends from the Base class. We didn't have to do anything special to accomplish that. By default, if we don't configure a class to extend from any other class, it extends from the Base class. We should keep this in mind.

Most of the classes in the Ext library extend from the Ext.Base class, however there are a few core classes that don't. The following screenshot shows the inheritance tree for the button and model components:

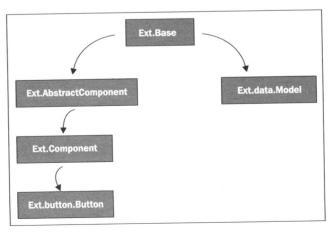

As we can see the root of the tree is the `Ext.Base` class, which means that the button and model components share the same methods defined in the `Base` class.

In order to extend from any other class we need to define the `extend` property to our new class; this will allow us to inherit all the methods and properties from the parent.

```
Ext.define("MyApp.Category",{
    extend   : "Ext.data.Model", //Step 1

    fields   : [ //Step 2
      "id",
      "name",
      "description"
    ]

});
```

In the first step we have created a class that extends from the `Ext.data.Model` class just by adding the `extend` property and assigning the name of the superclass.

In the second step we defined the `fields` of the category, in this case `id`, `name`, and `description`. We can define as many fields as needed just by adding more entries to the list of fields.

Once we have our class, let's create instances to hold our data. First we need to create an HTML file that includes the Ext library and the category class.

```
<!DOCTYPE html>
<html>
<head>
<meta http-equiv="Content-Type" content="text/html; charset=utf-8">
<title>Inheritance</title>

<!-- Importing the stylesheet for the widgets -->
<linkrel="stylesheet" type="text/css" href="../extjs-4.1.1/resources/
css/ext-all.css">
<!-- Importing the Ext JS library -->
<script type="text/javascript" src="../extjs-4.1.1/ext-all-dev.js"></
script>

<!-- Importing the category class -->
<script type="text/javascript" src="js/Category.js"></script>

  <script type="text/javascript">
    var category = Ext.create("MyApp.Category",{
      id       : 1,
      name     : "Entertainment",
```

```
        description    : "Expenses to have some fun"
    });

  console.log(category.get("name"));
    console.log(category.get("description"));
  </script>

</head>
<body>
</body>
</html>
```

We used the `Ext.create` method to create an instance of the `Category` class. In this example we're passing two parameters. The first one is the name of the class and the second one is an object with the fields we want to assign a value.

Let's open the HTML file in our browser and look at the JavaScript console. We should see the **name** and **description** fields we have entered when creating the instance.

One important thing to highlight in the previous code is the use of the `get` method. We didn't write any line of code to define this method, however because we are extending from the `Ext.data.Model` class we can use any method or property from this class or even overwrite an existing method.

Pre-processors and post-processors

Every class in Ext JS is an instance of the `Ext.Class` class. When we use the `Ext.define` method to define a class we are in fact creating an instance of the `Ext.Class` class.

According to the documentation the `Ext.Class` class is a factory. It doesn't mean that our classes extend from the `Ext.Class` class. As mentioned before all classes extend from the `Ext.Base` class. What this really means is that when we use the `Ext.create` method Ext runs processes behind the scenes. Each process is a task with a specific purpose in the whole process of creating the class.

A process may be asynchronous or not, for example, we have a pre-processor that loads all the dependencies for our new class if they are not already loaded. When the pre-processor finishes its tasks, the next process is executed until the list is empty and our new class is created.

A **pre-processor** is a process that runs before the instance of an `Ext.Class` class is created, or in other words, before our new class is created. Each of the processes defined will change the behavior of our class, if needed.

A **post-processor** is a process that runs after our new class is created. There is a process to make our class as singleton, to define alternative names to our class, and a few other processes.

There are a few processes defined by the Ext library, but we can define our own and add them to the process queue if we want.

The question now is, what processes are we talking about? And what do they do? If we want to see the list of registered processes, we can execute the following lines of code:

```
var pre = Ext.Class.getDefaultPreprocessors(),
post = Ext.ClassManager.defaultPostprocessors;

console.log(pre);
console.log(post);
```

By running the previous code in a browser we should see in the JavaScript console the following messages:

```
["className", "loader", "extend", "statics", "inheritableStatics",
"config", "mixins", "xtype", "alias"]
["alias", "singleton", "alternateClassName", "uses"]
```

The following screenshot represents the flow of the class creation with the pre-processors and post-processors:

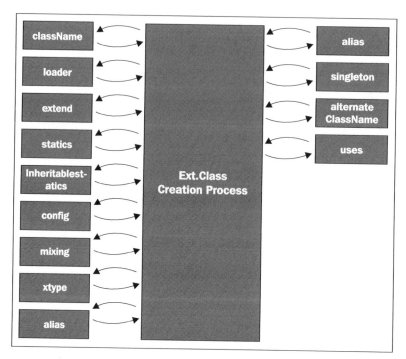

This is what happens when we create a class. All the pre-processors run before the class is ready, modifying the result. The post-processors on the other hand run when the class is ready to be used.

For example, the `loader` process looks for the dependencies and if they are not present, it tries to load them synchronously. After all the dependencies are ready, it passes the control to the `Ext.Class` class in order to continue with the next process. The following process in the queue is `extend`, which is responsible for copying all the prototype methods and properties from the superclass to the subclass.

The following table shows a brief description of all the pre-processors that may be executed to create a new class:

className	This defines the namespace and the name of the class.
loader	This looks for the dependencies and if they don't exist already then it tries to load them.
extend	This inherits all the methods and properties from the superclass to the new class.
statics	This creates the defined static methods or properties for the current class.
inheritableStatics	This inherits the static methods or properties from the superclass, if applicable.
config	This creates the getters and setters for the configurations properties.
mixins	This inherits all the methods and properties from the mixin classes.
xtype	This defines the xtype for the new class.
alias	This sets the alias for the new class.

Once the class is created the following post-processors are executed:

alias	This registers the new class to the class manager and its alias.
singleton	This creates a single instance of the new class.
alternateClassName	This defines alternative names for the new class created.
uses	This imports the classes that will be used, along with the new class.

There will be times when some processes won't run; this depends on how we configure or define our classes. Probably we didn't define dependencies or statics properties, so then those processes will be ignored.

Now that we have a basic understanding on how the class system works, we can continue learning how we can define our classes using the available processes and take advantage of them.

Mixing many classes

So far we have learned about simple inheritance, but we can also mimic multiple inheritance using the mixins processor. The concept is really simple; we can mix many classes into one. As a result, the new class will have access to all the properties and methods from the mixed classes.

Let's suppose we need to create an application that represents a competition program for figure skaters and ice dance skaters. A competition program is a sequence of jumps, spins, and footwork; the judges qualify the technique and the moves for each executed element in the program.

Single figure skaters are required to jump, spin, and do some footwork on the ice but for dancing skaters only spin and footwork is required, they don't jump.

We're going to separate the required elements in jumps, spins, and footwork classes. This way we would have three different classes with the elements that skaters can perform for their competition programs.

First we need to define a Jump class with a few types of jumps. If later on we need to add another jump we just define a new method in this class.

```
Ext.define("MyApp.skating.Jump",{

  waltz  : function(){
    console.log("Waltz: a one-half rotation jump that forms the basis
  for the axel jump.");
  },

  axel  : function(){
    console.log("Axel: A single axel actually has 1.5 rotations");
  },

  split  : function(){
    console.log("Split: With either a flip, lutz, or loop entry and
  split or straddle position in the air.");
  }
});
```

For the sake of simplicity we're just sending a log message to the console on each method. But we can do anything else if needed.

Now let's define the Spin class which contains a few methods representing the types of spins that a skater can do.

```
Ext.define("MyApp.skating.Spin",{

  scratch    : function(){
     console.log("Scratch: With the free leg crossed in front of the
  skating leg.");
     },

  crossfoot   : function(){
     console.log("Crossfoot: Is a back upright spin in which the free
  leg is crossed...");
     },

  camel     : function(){
     console.log("Camel: Is a spin in which the free leg is held
  backwards with the knee higher than the hip level");
     }
  });
```

Our last class will represent the steps sequence that a skater can perform on the ice for a competition.

```
Ext.define("MyApp.stepsequence.Footwork",{

  mohawk   : function(){
     console.log("Mohawk: This sequence is usually done in the counter-
  clockwise direction and on a circle or curve");
     },

  spreadeagle   : function(){
     console.log("Spread eagle: The skater glides on both feet");
     },

  twizzles   : function(){
     console.log("Twizzles: multirotational one-foot turns done in
  figure skating.");
     }
  });
```

So far we have represented the abilities for the skaters in three classes. We need to add the specific abilities to each type of skater. Let's start with the figure skater who will jump, spin, and do some footwork in his program.

```
Ext.define("MyApp.single.Skater",{
    extend  : "Ext.util.Observable",    //Step 1
    mixins  : {      //Step 2
      jump   : "MyApp.skating.Jump",
      spin   : "MyApp.skating.Spin",
      footwork: "MyApp.stepsequence.Footwork"
    },

    constructor  : function(options){
      Ext.apply(this,options);   //Step 3
    },

    compete  : function(){  //Step 4
      var me = this;

      console.log(me.name+" from "+me.nationality+" starts the program!
Good luck!");
      me.waltz();
      me.mohawk();
      me.camel();
      me.axel();
      me.spreadeagle();
      me.scratch();
      console.log(me.name+" ends the program and gets the first
place!");
    }
});
```

- **Step 1**: We have extended from the `Observable` class, this will allow us to implement events and listeners. We will explore more about events in future chapters, for now we will use the class as an example.

- **Step 2**: We have defined an object with the mixins we want to apply to our class. This will allow us to use all the methods and properties from those classes in our `Skater` class. We're mixing all the classes to have one with all the functionality from all of them.

- **Step 3**: We've created the `constructor` method. This receives a parameter that should be an object to be applied to the instance at runtime. This will allow us to configure our instance easily.

- **Step 4**: We created the `compete` method. This method defines the skater's program for the competition. Note that this method contains calls to the methods defined in the mixed classes. We can call all the `Jump`, `Spin`, and `Footwork` methods! We're also using the `name` and `nationality` properties, which should be set at runtime when we create instances.

Let's create an instance of the single `Skater` class. In order to do that we need to create an HTML file, import the Ext library, and all the classes we have created before.

```
var taky = Ext.create("MyApp.single.Skater",{
    name        : "Taky",
    nationality : "Japan"
});
taky.compete();
```

We're setting the `name` and the `nationality` properties and then calling the `compete` method, which internally executes all the needed calls. We should see something such as the following screenshot:

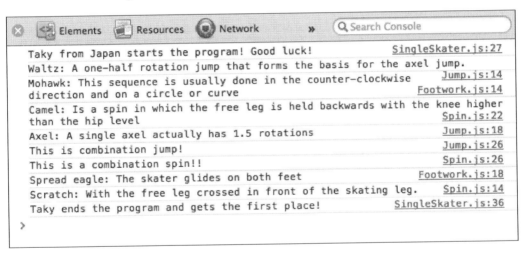

We'll see the jumps, spins, and footwork that Taky did in his program.

Now we need to create the class for the ice dance skater. These skaters are not required to jump but they perform more complicated footwork and spins. The class for representing an ice dance skater should look like the following:

```
Ext.define("MyApp.dancing.Skater",{
    extend  : "Ext.util.Observable",
    mixins  : { //Step 1
        spin    : "MyApp.skating.Spin",
        footwork: "MyApp.stepsequence.Footwork"
    },
```

```
constructor  : function(options){
  Ext.apply(this,options);  //Step 2
},

compete  : function(){  //Step 3
  var me = this;

  console.log(me.name+" from "+me.nationality+" starts the program!
Let's see how it goes...");
  me.camel();
  me.scratch();
  me.spreadeagle();
  me.twizzles();
  me.camel();
  console.log(me.name+" ends the program but with no good results
:(");
  }
});
```

- **Step 1**: We're mixing the classes for our ice dance skater, we only need the Spin and Footwork classes in this case, but we can define as many as we need.

- **Step 2**: We're creating the constructor method for our class. If you notice, it's the same as the single Skater class.

> Usually there's something wrong when we are repeating code. We should create an abstract class that contains the constructor method and then extend it for both of our types of skaters. This way we won't repeat code and it will be easy to maintain.

- **Step 3**: We have created the compete method which only calls the methods from the Spin and Footwork classes.

We can test our class by creating an instance in the main HTML file we already have. Let's add the following code:

```
var susan = Ext.create("MyApp.dancing.Skater",{
  name     : "Susan",
  nationality  : "USA"
});
susan.compete();
```

If we refresh our browser we should see something such as the following screenshot in the JavaScript console:

```
Susan from USA starts the program! Let's see how it goes...
Camel: Is a spin in which the free leg is held backwards   DancingSkater.js:26
with the knee higher than the hip level                          Spin.js:22
Scratch: With the free leg crossed in front of the skating leg.   Spin.js:14
Spread eagle: The skater glides on both feet                  Footwork.js:18
Twizzles: multirotational one-foot turns done in figure skating.
Camel: Is a spin in which the free leg is held backwards with  Footwork.js:22
the knee higher than the hip level                               Spin.js:22
Susan ends the program but with no good results :(        DancingSkater.js:32
>|
```
```
 🖵  >≡  Q  ⊘  <top frame> ⇕  <page context>        ⇕  All   Errors  War✖
```

The important thing about the mixins is that we can create classes to do specific tasks and then mix those classes into one. This way we can reuse the same classes over and over again.

In the Ext library classes such as Ext.util.Observable, Ext.util.Floating, Ext.state.Stateful, and others are treated like mixins, each class knows how to do specific things. This is something great for big applications and we should think wisely how we're going to structure our big application before we start coding.

Let's suppose that in our previous example we would have one jump and spin with the same name, what is going to happen when we mix them together? Which of them is going to be added to the resulting class?

In order to answer these questions we need to know that the mixins pre-processor do not override existing methods or properties in the resulting class. The configured classes in the mixins object are iterated in the order we have defined them and its methods and properties are applied to the resulting class.

In order to avoid collisions, the first class that applies the method wins and the other class just ignores the repeating method. For example let's add a combination method to the Jump and Spin classes.

```
Ext.define("MyApp.skating.Jump",{

    //...
    combination  : function(){
      console.log("This is a combination jump!");
    }
});
```

```
Ext.define("MyApp.skating.Spin",{

  //...
  combination  : function(){
    console.log("This is a combination spin!!");
  }
});
```

We have a method with the same name in the two classes; this means the skater can do a combination jump and a combination spin. Same name but different functionality.

When we mix them into the `Skater` class we need to know which of the methods will be applied to the resulting class. As mentioned before, the first class defined wins, in this case the `Jump` class will set the `combination` method to the resulting class and the `combination` method in the `Spin` class will be ignored.

Let's try our changes by calling the `combination` method with our `Taky` instance:

```
var taky = Ext.create("MyApp.single.Skater",{
  name      : "Taky",
  nationality  : "Japan"
});
taky.compete();
taky.combination();
```

We should see in the JavaScript console the following message:

This is a combination jump!

But what if we actually want to call the `combination` method from the `Spin` class? How can we achieve that? When our instance is created Ext defines an object called `mixins`, which contains an instance of each class we have defined. We can access those instances by the key we've set when configuring our class in the mixins pre-processor. In this case we defined the spin and jump keys, so we should access the `combination` method in the `Spin` class as follows:

```
var taky = Ext.create("MyApp.single.Skater",{
  name      : "Taky",
  nationality  : "Japan"
});
taky.compete();
taky.combination();//Defined in Jump class

taky.mixins.spin.combination(); //Defined in Spin class
taky.mixins.jump.combination(); //Defined in Jump class
```

We can access any method and property using the `mixins` object with the key that we need. We can even access the `mixins` object within the class members, for example, let's modify the `compete` method of the single `Skater` class.

```
Ext.define("MyApp.single.Skater",{

//...
compete   : function(){
    var me = this;

        console.log(me.name+" from "+me.nationality+" starts the program!
Good luck!");
    me.waltz();
    me.mohawk();
    me.camel();
    me.axel();
    me.mixins.jump.combination();
    me.mixins.spin.combination();
    me.spreadeagle();
    me.scratch();
        console.log(me.name+" ends the program and gets the first
place!");
    }
});
```

This way we can avoid collisions and we can make sure we're always calling the right method.

Configurations

Another great feature in this new version of Ext is the addition of configurations. Usually when we create a class we set configurations so we can change the values and behavior of our class depending on the input parameters. Ext 4 makes this process really easy by adding a pre-processor to handle the configurations for us.

```
Ext.define("MyApp.data.Invoice",{
config : {
    client   : '',
    tax      : 0.083,
    subtotal : 0,
    total    : 0
}
    constructor  : function(config){
      var me = this;

        me.initConfig(config);    //Step 2
    }
});
```

- **Step 1**: We have defined the pre-processor config, which allows us to define an object with the properties we need. We can set a default value for each configuration.

- **Step 2**: We have initialized the configurations by executing the initConfig method and passing the configuration's parameter. This is a really important step and it's required if we want to use the configuration feature. The initConfig method is defined in the Base class. We need to keep in mind that every class in Ext JS extend from the Ext.Base class.

Now we can create a test HTML file, importing the Ext library and our previous class, then we create an Invoice instance as follows:

```
var invoice = Ext.create("MyApp.data.Invoice",{
  client  : "Tuxtux Inc",
  subtotal  : 100,
  total    : 108.3
});

console.log(invoice.getClient());
console.log(invoice.getSubtotal());
console.log(invoice.getTax());        // 0.83
console.log(invoice.getTotal());

invoice.setTax(0.16);

console.log(invoice.getTax());        // 0.16
```

When using the config pre-processor, Ext automatically creates the getters and setters for our configurations. We can use them to read or change the value of any property defined in the config object.

Let's suppose we need to change the value of the subtotal property at runtime. We should calculate the new total property based on the tax property. The Ext generates an apply method for every property defined in the configuration. The auto generated setter method calls internally the apply method before it sets the new value to the property. If we need to add a custom logic, we need to override the apply method as follows:

```
Ext.define("MyApp.data.Invoice",{

  //...
  applySubtotal  : function(value){  //Step 1
    var me = this;
    me.setTotal(value + value * me.getTax());//Step 2
    return value; // Step 3
  }
});
```

- **Step 1**: We override the `applySubtotal` method. We can add our custom logic here; in this case we will calculate the new value for the `total` property.

- **Step 2**: We read the `tax` property in order to calculate the new `total` property.

- **Step 3**: We returned the new value for the `subtotal` property. If we don't return a value then nothing will be set for the property.

Now we can test our changes by modifying the HTML file by adding the following lines of code:

```
invoice.setSubtotal(1000);

console.log(invoice.getTotal());
```

Everything should work now. We should see number **1160** in our JavaScript console, which is the subtotal plus the tax.

Statics methods and properties

The `statics` methods belongs to the class and not to the instance, therefore we can use `statics` methods without an instance.

```
Ext.define("MyApp.data.Client",{
  statics   : {   //Step 1
    sequence   : 0,
    nextId     : function(){
      return ++this.sequence;
    }
  },

  constructor  : function(){
    this.id = this.self.nextId();   //Step 2

    console.log(this.id);
  }
});
```

- **Step 1**: We have defined the `statics` configuration, this will fire the `statics` pre-processor when creating an instance. We have defined the `sequence` property and the `nextId` method; these properties will be added to the class as statics properties. We can define as many properties and methods as we need.

- **Step 2**: We are using the `self` reference to access the class. The Ext defines this reference in the `statics` pre-processor for each instance.

In order to test our class we need to create an HTML file, import the Ext library, the class we have defined previously, and the following code to create instances:

```
Ext.create("MyApp.data.Client");
Ext.create("MyApp.data.Client");
Ext.create("MyApp.data.Client");

console.log(MyApp.data.Client.nextId()); //prints 4
```

We created three instances; by doing this we should see in the JavaScript console the IDs for each instance. We can even execute the nextId method statically.

Singleton

By definition a singleton class can't be instantiated more than once. It should be the same instance all the time. The Ext allow us to create singleton classes very easily with one post-processor.

If we want a class to be singleton we only need to set the singleton property to true. This will fire the correct post-processor:

```
Ext.define("MyApp.Constants",{
    singleton     : true,         //Step 1

    BASE_PATH  : "/myapp", //Step 2
    ATTEMPTS   : 5,
    TIMEOUT    : 6000
});
```

- **Step 1**: We set the singleton property to true, this is all we need to do in order to create a singleton class.
- **Step 2**: Define some properties for our singleton class, we can define as many properties and methods as needed.

Let's create a test HTML file, import the Ext library and the previous class, then we can access the properties from the class.

```
console.log(MyApp.Constants.BASE_PATH);
Ext.create("MyApp.Constants"); //Throws an error
```

We should see in our JavaScript console the value for the BASE_PATH property. We'll see an error too, telling us that we can't create instances from a singleton class.

The singleton classes are commonly used for holding constants or configuration for our application such as the base path of our application, the path where the images are located, and things like that.

Alias

An alias is a short name for a class. The class manager maps the alias name with the actual class object. This feature is really useful when using the xtype property to create widgets.

```
Ext.define("MyApp.abstract.Panel",{
  extend  : "Ext.panel.Panel",
  alias   : "widget.mypanel",

  title   : "Abstract panel",
  html  : "Main content"
});
```

In the previous code we're setting the alias property with a short name. We're also using the widget prefix to indicate we're creating a component. A component is a class such as the window, grid, or panel.

Let's create our class by the alias name. We have a few options to do that. We need to create an HTML file, import the library and the previous class.

```
Ext.onReady(function(){

  Ext.create("widget.mypanel",{ //Option 1
    renderTo  : Ext.getBody()
  });

//Option 2
  Ext.ClassManager.instantiateByAlias("widget.mypanel",{
    renderTo  : Ext.getBody()
  });

//Option 3
  Ext.ClassManager.instantiate("widget.mypanel",{
    renderTo    : Ext.getBody()
  });

  var win = Ext.create("Ext.window.Window",{
    title  : "Window",
    width    : 350,
    height   : 250,
    items    : [{
      xtype : "mypanel"  //Option 4
    }]
  });
  win.show();

});
```

The explanation for the preceding code is as follows:

- **Option 1**: We can use the `create` method, which accepts the alias too. As configuration we set the `renderTo` property to the body of the page.

- **Option 2**: We use the `instantiateByAlias` method, we define the `renderTo` property again.

- **Option 3**: We use the `instantiate` method from the `ClassManager` class, which actually is the same as using the `Ext.create` method. We have discussed this in *Chapter 1, The Basics*.

- **Option 4**: Create an instance of the class by its alias using the xtype property when the main window is created. We don't need to define the `widget` prefix. The Ext identifies that we're trying to create a component so it assumes the given `xtype` property should be prefixed by `widget`.

It's important to note we can use the `xtype` property only within the components or widgets.

Loading classes on demand

When we develop large applications, performance is really important. We should only load the scripts we need; this means that if we have many modules in our application, we should separate them in packages so we would be able to load them individually.

The Ext JS allows us to dynamically load classes and files when we need them, also we can configure dependencies in each class and the Ext will load them for us.

We need to understand that using the loader is great for development, that way we can easily debug the code because the loader includes all the classes one by one. However, it's not recommended to load all the Ext classes in production environments. We should create packages of classes and then load them when needed, but not class by class.

In order to use the loader system we need to follow some conventions when defining our class.

- Define only one class per file.

- The name of the class should match the name of the JavaScript file.

- The namespace of the class should match the folder structure. For example, if we define a class `MyApp.customers.controller.Main`, we should have the `Main.js` file in the `MyApp/customers/controller` path.

Enabling the loader

The loader system is enabled or disabled depending on the Ext file that we import to our HTML file. If we import the `ext-all`, `ext-all-debug`, or `ext-all-dev` file, the loader is disabled because all the classes in the Ext library are loaded already. If we import the `ext`, `ext-debug`, or `ext-dev` file, the loader is enabled because only the core classes in the Ext library are loaded.

If we need to enable the loader, we should do the following:

```
Ext.Loader.setConfig({
    enabled   : true
});
```

The previous code will allow us to load the classes when we need them. Also there's a pre-processor that loads all the dependencies for the given class if they don't exist.

In order to start loading classes we need to set up the paths where the classes are, we can do that in two different ways. We can use the `setConfig` method defining a paths property as follows:

```
Ext.Loader.setConfig({
    enabled   : true,
    paths   : {
        MyApp : "loader"
    }
});
```

The `paths` property receives an object containing the root namespace of our application and the folder where all the classes are located in this namespace. We can add as many objects as needed.

```
Ext.Loader.setConfig({
    enabled   : true,
    paths   : {
        MyApp   : "loader",
        Ext     : "../extjs-4.1.1/src"
    }
});
```

In the previous code we have defined the `Ext` path, which is located in the `src` folder. Every time the loader finds a namespace starting with `MyApp` or `Ext` it will know where to look in order to load the missing class.

We can also use the `setPath` method to add a new path to the loader, for example:

```
Ext.Loader.setPath("MyApp.models","loader/models");
```

This way we can load classes in the `MyApp.models` namespace at runtime, this method is useful for adding paths dynamically at any time.

Once we have enabled and configured the loader correctly we can start loading our classes using the `require` method.

```
Ext.require("MyApp.models.Movie");

Ext.onReady(function(){
  var movie = Ext.create("MyApp.models.Movie",{
    title   : "Zoombies attack!",
    director: "Johnny Doe"
  });

  console.log(movie.get("title"));
});
```

The `require` method creates a script tag behind the scenes. After all the required files are loaded the `onReady` event is fired. Inside the callback we can use all the loaded classes.

If we try to load the classes after the `require` call, we'll get an error because the class won't exist until it's downloaded and created. This is why we need to set the `onReady` callback and wait until everything is ready to be used.

We can also set a callback directly in the `require` call. We can pass a second parameter with a function to be executed after the class is imported correctly.

```
Ext.require("MyApp.music.Song",function(){

  var song = Ext.create("MyApp.music.Song",{
    title    : "The next thing",
    autor    : "John Doe",
    duration : 3.55
  });

  console.log(song.get("title"));

});
```

Dependencies

Once we have the loader system up and running we can take advantage of a pre-processor to load automatically the class dependencies. This is really useful when we create a class. We can define which classes are needed in order to instantiate our classes.

```
Ext.define("MyApp.models.Book",{
  extend   : "Ext.data.Model",

  fields   : ["id","title","author","description","pages"]
});
```

First we create a class that represents a book; the class extends from a `models` class and contains a few fields that describe a book. Now let's create another class that depends on the book.

```
Ext.define("MyApp.library.bookshelf.Bookshelf",{
  requires   : ["Ext.util.MixedCollection"],//Step 1
  uses       : ["MyApp.models.Book"], //Step 2

  constructor  : function(){
    this.books = Ext.create("Ext.util.MixedCollection");
  },

  getBook    : function(index){
    return this.books.get(index);
  },

  addBook    : function(data){
    var book = Ext.create("MyApp.models.Book",data);
    this.books.add(book);
  }
});
```

- **Step 1**: The `Bookshelf` class depends on the `MixedCollection` class in order to work properly. In the first step we're using the `requires` property to define a list of classes that are needed to be imported to the document. We can define as many classes as needed. The pre-processor's loader will see if the class is already imported, if it is not then the loader will import it.

- **Step 2**: We're defining the `uses` property. This is a list of classes that needs to be imported too.

The difference between `requires` and `uses` is that `requires` is a pre-processor and `uses` is a post-processor.

If our class needs other classes in order to be constructed, we need to use the `requires` property. The Ext will import all the classes before our class is created. In the previous example we required `MixedCollection` because we created an instance of that class in our constructor.

On the other hand if our class needs other classes that may or may not be used, we can import them after the class is created. In the previous example we don't know for sure if the `Book` class is going to be used or not, it depends if the method `addBook` is called at some point.

> As a rule of thumb we need to identify which classes are used to create or construct our component and those classes that may or may not be used later depending on the user's interaction.

Once we have settled up the dependencies we can test our example. Let's create an HTML file, but this time we're going to include the `ext-dev.js` file. If you remember from *Chapter 1, The Basics,* this file contains only the core classes and not the whole Ext library, we're going to load only the needed Ext classes.

```
Ext.Loader.setConfig({
    //enabled     : true,
    paths    : {
      MyApp   : "loader",
      Ext    : "../extjs-4.1.1/src"
    }
});
```

If we use the `ext.js`, `ext-debug.js`, or `ext-dev.js` files, it's not necessary to enable the loader because by default it is enabled. We only need to set the right paths for our application classes and for the Ext classes.

Then we need to require only the `Bookshelf` class, the loader will detect that this class contains dependencies and will try to include them.

```
Ext.require("MyApp.library.bookshelf.Bookshelf");
```

After we require the class we need to wait until all the dependencies are ready. We can achieve this by using the `onReady` method.

```
Ext.onReady(function(){

    var bookshelf = Ext.create("MyApp.library.bookshelf.Bookshelf");

    bookshelf.addBook({
```

```
    id    : 1,
    title: "Steve Jobs",
    author: "Walter Isaacson",
    pages : 562
});

console.log(bookshelf.books.getCount()); // 1

});
```

We are creating the `Bookshelf` class as usual and then we add a book to the bookshelf and get the count of the books in the instance. We should see the number one in the JavaScript console, because we have only added one book to the collection.

If we look at the network traffic tab in the development tools in Chrome, we should see all the files included when we required only the `Bookshelf` class. Internally the Ext figured out which classes it needs to import in order to run our example:

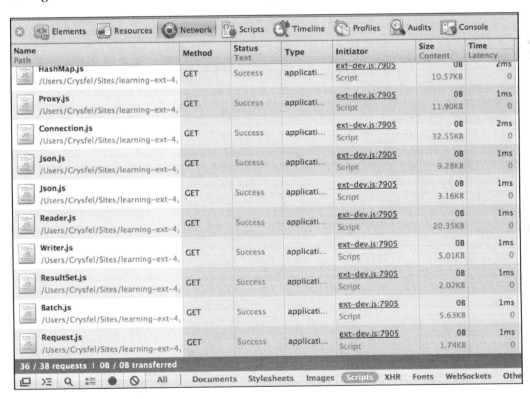

Name Path	Method	Status Text	Type	Initiator	Size Content	Time Latency
HashMap.js /Users/Crysfel/Sites/learning-ext-4,	GET	Success	applicati...	ext-dev.js:7905 Script	0B 10.57KB	2ms 0
Proxy.js /Users/Crysfel/Sites/learning-ext-4,	GET	Success	applicati...	ext-dev.js:7905 Script	0B 11.90KB	1ms 0
Connection.js /Users/Crysfel/Sites/learning-ext-4,	GET	Success	applicati...	ext-dev.js:7905 Script	0B 32.55KB	2ms 0
Json.js /Users/Crysfel/Sites/learning-ext-4,	GET	Success	applicati...	ext-dev.js:7905 Script	0B 9.28KB	1ms 0
Json.js /Users/Crysfel/Sites/learning-ext-4,	GET	Success	applicati...	ext-dev.js:7905 Script	0B 3.16KB	1ms 0
Reader.js /Users/Crysfel/Sites/learning-ext-4,	GET	Success	applicati...	ext-dev.js:7905 Script	0B 20.35KB	1ms 0
Writer.js /Users/Crysfel/Sites/learning-ext-4,	GET	Success	applicati...	ext-dev.js:7905 Script	0B 5.01KB	1ms 0
ResultSet.js /Users/Crysfel/Sites/learning-ext-4,	GET	Success	applicati...	ext-dev.js:7905 Script	0B 2.02KB	1ms 0
Batch.js /Users/Crysfel/Sites/learning-ext-4,	GET	Success	applicati...	ext-dev.js:7905 Script	0B 5.63KB	1ms 0
Request.js /Users/Crysfel/Sites/learning-ext-4,	GET	Success	applicati...	ext-dev.js:7905 Script	0B 1.74KB	1ms 0

36 / 38 requests | 0B / 0B transferred

All   Documents   Stylesheets   Images   Scripts   XHR   Fonts   WebSockets   Othe

As we can see there are 38 files included, this is because we're using the `models` class. It's important to mention that we didn't define a `require` property in our `Book` model we just defined the `extend` property. The Ext also checks if the superclass exists. If it doesn't, it tries to import it. The same applies to the mixins.

Synchronous Loading

We use the `Ext.create` method to create an instance of a specific class; if the given class doesn't exist, the loader tries to load synchronously using an Ajax call. Let's modify our latest example by removing the require line.

```
//Ext.require("MyApp.library.bookshelf.Bookshelf");
```

If we reload our browser, we should see an error, telling us that the `Bookshelf` class could not be loaded. This is because an Ajax call is made so we need to use a web server in order to make this work:

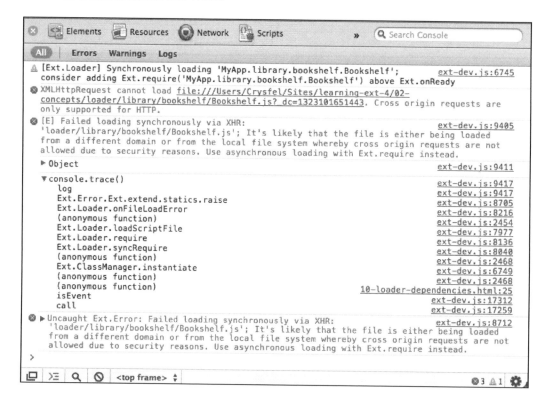

Since we're using the `ext-dev.js` file, we're getting a warning and a very descriptive error. If we are using any other version of the `ext` file, we will get a generic error that will be harder to understand.

 We should always use the `ext-all-dev` or `ext-dev` files when importing the Ext library in our development environment. This way we'll get meaningful warnings and errors. For production environments we should use the compressed versions.

Let's use a web server such as Apache (`http://httpd.apache.org/`) to run our previous example. We can use whatever web server we feel comfortable with or have previous experience of. We only need to copy our example with all our dependencies to the public folder in our web server. Let's open the browser and navigate to the URL where our example is present:

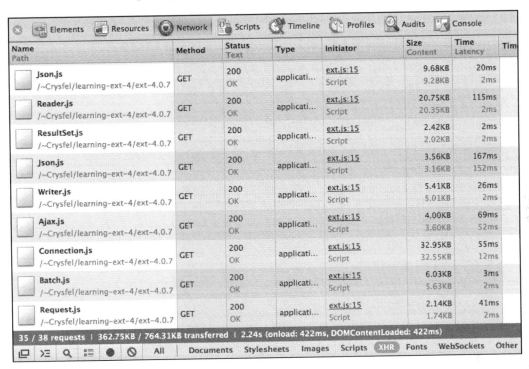

If we notice, the example takes a lot more time to run our code than before. This is because the 38 classes are getting imported using Ajax calls, one after another, this makes the loading process really slow. This is why we should use the `require` method instead.

Working with the DOM

The Ext JS provides an easy way to deal with the DOM. We can create nodes, change styles, add listeners, and create beautiful animations, among other things without worrying about the browsers implementations. The Ext JS provides us with a cross-browser compatibility API that will make our lives easy.

The responsible class for dealing with the DOM nodes is the `Ext.Element` class. This class is a wrapper for the native nodes and provides us with many methods and utilities to manipulate the nodes.

Getting elements

We can use the `get` method from the `Ext.Element` class to get a node by its ID and then manipulate the node using the `Element` wrapper.

```
<!DOCTYPE html>
<html>
<head>
<title>The DOM</title>

<!-- Importing the Ext JS library -->
<script type="text/javascript" src="../extjs-4.1.1/ext-all-dev.js"></
script>

  <script type="text/javascript">


    Ext.onReady(function(){

      var div = Ext.Element.get("main");


    });

  </script>

</head>
<body>
  <div id="main"></div>
</body>
</html>
```

We can also use the `Ext.get` alias to do the same. In the `div` variable we have an instance of the `Ext.Element` class containing a reference to the node that has `main` as its ID.

We may use the `setStyle` method in order to assign some CSS rules to the node. Let's add the following code to our example:

```
div.setStyle({
    width    : "100px",
    height   : "100px",
    border   : "2px solid #444",
    margin   : "80px auto",
    backgroundColor : "#ccc"
});
```

We're passing an object with all the rules that we want to apply to the node. As a result we should see a gray square in the center of our screen:

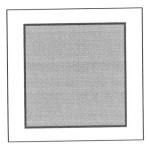

If we want to add a CSS class to the node we can use the addCls method. We can also use the removeCls if we want to remove a CSS class from the node.

```
div.addCls("x-testing x-box-component");

div.removeCls("x-testing");
```

There are a lot of methods we can use to manipulate the node element. Let's try some animations with our element.

```
div.fadeOut()
.fadeIn({
duration:3000
});
```

The fadeOut method slowly hides the element by changing the opacity progressively. When the opacity is zero percent the fadeIn method is executed by changing the opacity by 100 percent in three seconds.

We should take a look at the documentation (http://docs.sencha.com/) in order to know all the options we have available, there we can find examples of code to play with.

Query – How to find them?

The Ext JS allows us to query the DOM to search for specific nodes. The query engine supports most of the CSS3 selectors specification and the basic XPath.

The responsible class that does the job is the Ext.DomQuery class; this class contains a few methods to perform a search.

The following code is an HTML document which contains a few tags so we can search for them using the DomQuery class:

```html
<!DOCTYPE html>
<html>
<head>
<meta http-equiv="Content-Type" content="text/html; charset=utf-8">
<title>The DomQuery</title>

<!-- Importing the Ext JS library -->
<script type="text/javascript" src="../extjs-4.1.1/ext-all-dev.js"></
script>

  <script type="text/javascript">

    Ext.onReady(function(){

        //code here...

    });

  </script>

</head>
<body>
  <div id="main">
    <div class="menu">
      <ul>
        <li>Home</li>
        <li>About us</li>
      </ul>
    </div>
    <div class="content">
      <h1>Welcome to Ext JS 4!</h1>
      <p>This is an example for the DomQuery class.</p>
    </div>
  </div>
</body>
</html>
```

In order to perform the search we'll use the select method from the DomQuery class; we'll pass a CSS selector as the only parameter.

```javascript
//Step 1
varlis = Ext.DomQuery.select("#main .menu ulli");

lis = Ext.get(lis); //Step 2

lis.setStyle({  //Step 3
  display       : "inline",
```

```
    backgroundColor : "#003366",
    margin        : "3px",
    color         : "#FFCC00",
    padding       : "3px 20px",
    borderRadius  : "10px",
    boxShadow     : "inset 0 1px 15px #6699CC"
});
```

- **Step 1**: We define our selector. This is a simple CSS rule, but we can create more advanced selectors. We should have a look at the documentation so we can know all the selectors, attribute filters, and pseudos that we can use to construct our selectors.

- **Step 2**: The `select` method returns an array of nodes that match our selector. In this step we use the `Ext.get` method and pass the array of nodes as a parameter. This will allow us to wrap the nodes into an `Ext.CompositeElementLite` collection; this way we can modify all the nodes at once using the `Ext.Element` APIs.

- **Step 3**: In the last step we set some styles to the list of elements. We define colors, margins, and borders, but we could do anything we want, even an animation or whatever we need:

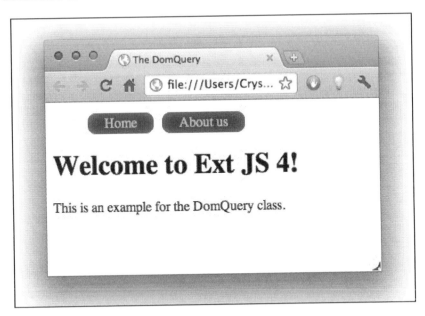

The previous screenshot shows the nodes that have been modified. Those nodes are a list of elements with the styles that we have applied to them.

If we would like to change the color of the title, we should use the selector and apply the styles that we need.

```
var h1 = Ext.select("#main div[class=content] h1");

h1.setStyle("color","#003399");
```

In the previous code we have created a selector to match the title of the page. One interesting thing about the code is the use of the `Ext.select` method. This method uses the `Ext.DomQuery` class internally and also returns an `Ext.CompositeElementLite` collection so we can modify all the nodes at once:

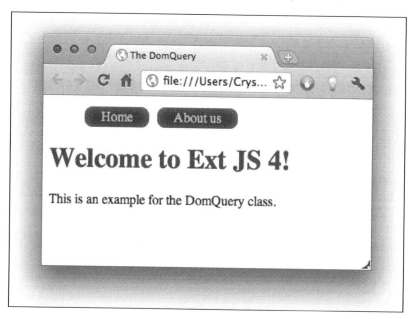

Manipulation – How to change it?

We can create and remove nodes from the DOM very easily. The Ext contains a `DomHelper` object, which provides an abstraction layer and give us an API to create DOM nodes or HTML fragments.

Let's create an HTML file, import the Ext library, and then use the `DomHelper` object to append a `div` element to the document's body.

```
Ext.onReady(function(){

  Ext.DomHelper.append(Ext.getBody(),{
    tag     : "div",
    style   : {
      width   : "100px",
      height  : "100px",
      border  : "2px solid #333",
      margin    : "20px auto"
    }
  });

});
```

We used the `append` method; the first parameter is where we want to append the new element. In this case we're going to append it to the document's body.

The second parameter is the element that we want to append; the `tag` property defines the type of element that we want to create. In this case we define a `div` element, but we can define any of the available tags in the HTML specification:

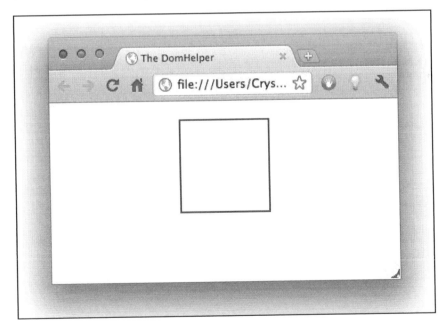

We can define styles, classes, children, and any other property that an HTML element supports. Let's add some children to our previous example.

```
Ext.DomHelper.append(Ext.getBody(),{
    //...
children  : [{
        tag           : "ul",
        children  : [{
          tag : "li",
          html  : "Item 1"
        },{
          tag : "li",
          html  : "Item 2"
        }]
    }]
});
```

We have added an unordered list to the main `div`. The list contains two children that are list elements. We can have as many children as needed:

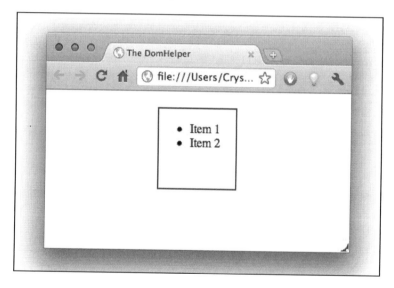

There's another method that we can use if we want to create a node, but we want to insert it into the DOM later.

```
var h1 = Ext.DomHelper.createDom({
    tag   : "h1",
    html  : "This is the title!"
});

Ext.getBody().appendChild(h1);
```

When we use the `createDom` method we create a new node in the memory. We probably append this node to the DOM later on, or maybe not. In this example we have appended it to the document's body:

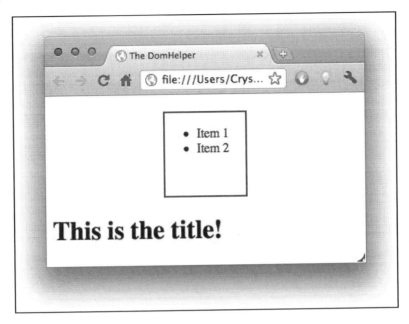

We know how to create and append nodes to the DOM, but what if we want to remove elements from the DOM? In order to remove the element from the DOM we need to use the `remove` method from the `Ext.Element` class.

```
Ext.fly(h1).remove();
```

The previous code is calling the `Ext.fly` method. This method is similar to the `Ext.get` method; it returns an instance to the `Ext.Element` class containing a reference to the node element. Once we have the node in the wrapper we can call the `remove` method and the node will be removed from the DOM.

Summary

When using Ext JS we need to change our mind and see everything as an object or class. We need to think carefully how we're going to model our objects and data. We have learned how to work with object-oriented programming with the new class system.

We also learned about the new loader system to import our classes dynamically, managing dependencies for us, and only loading what we need. At the end of this chapter we learned about the DOM and how to perform a search in order to manipulate the nodes easily.

In the next chapter we'll learn about the layout system, a powerful way to create and manage our layouts. There are several types of layouts that we can use and combine to create unique interfaces.

3
Components and Layouts

One of the greatest features in Ext JS is the ability to create complex layouts to arrange our components in different ways using a container. Since the early versions of the library, Ext has had a great layout system. In the latest version, new layouts have been added and some others have been redesigned.

In this chapter, we're going to learn about containers, how the components work, and how we can create nested layouts to achieve complex designs.

We're going to cover the following topics in this chapter:

- Components
- Containers
- The Layout system
- Available layouts

The components lifecycle

Before we move into the layout systems and widgets, we should know a few concepts about how components work.

Every widget in the Ext framework extends from the `Ext.Component` class. This class extends from the `Ext.AbstractComponent` class, which provides shared methods for components across the Sencha products.

When we create a component such as windows, grids, trees, and any other, there's a process called **The component lifecycle** that we should understand.

It is important for us to know the things that occur during each of the phases in the lifecycle process. This will help us to create custom components or extend the existing ones.

Basically, there are three phases in the component's lifecycle: the creation process, the rendering process, and the destruction process.

The creation phase initializes our new instance and it gets registered on the component manager, the rendering phase will create all the needed nodes on the DOM, and the destruction phase will be executed when the component is destroyed, removing listeners and nodes from the DOM:

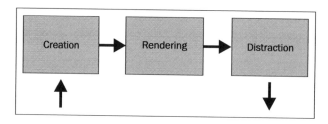

The Ext.AbstractComponent and Ext.Component classes directs the lifecycle process. Every class that extends from the Component class will participate in the lifecycle automatically. All the visual widgets extend from these two classes and if we're planning to create our own custom components, we should extend from those classes too.

In order to have a better understanding of all three phases, let's create a panel component and see what's going on in each phase step by step.

```
var panel = Ext.create("Ext.panel.Panel", {
    title   : "First panel",
    width   : 400,
    height  : 250,
    renderTo : Ext.getBody()
});
```

The creation phase

The main purpose of this phase is to create the instance of the component according to the configurations that we defined. It also registers our new component on the component manager and a few other things. The following screenshot shows all the steps in this phase:

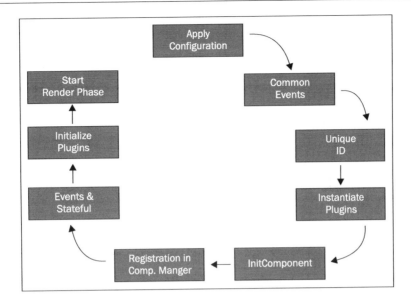

1. The first step is to apply the configuration properties to the generated instance of the class that we are creating. In the previous code, the `title`, `width`, `height`, and `renderTo` properties will be copied to the instance of the panel, as well as any other property that we decide to define.

2. The second step is to define common events such as enable, disable, or show. These are common events for every component.

3. The next step is to assign an ID to the instance. If we define an ID in the configuration object, then the instance will use that ID. In our example, we didn't specify an ID. In this case, an auto generated ID is assigned.

> Assigning IDs to our components is considered a bad practice. We should avoid doing that because they should be unique. If we work in a big project with other developers, there's a big chance that we will repeat IDs. Duplicating IDs will drive us to unexpected behaviors, because the component's ID is used in the DOM elements when rendering the component.

4. In the fourth step, the creation process verifies if we have defined plugins in our configuration and tries to create all the needed instances for those plugins. A plugin is an additional functionality for our instances. In our previous example, we didn't define any plugin, so this step is skipped.

5. In the fifth step, the `initComponent` function is executed. We should override this method in our subclasses if we want to execute code when the instance is being created.

 There are many more methods that are defined by the Component class. These template methods are intended to be overridden in the subclasses to add specific functionality in different phases of the lifecycle.

6. In this step, the new instance is added to the `Ext.ComponentManager` object. This means that every component that we create will be stored in the component manager allowing us to get any reference by using the `Ext.getCmp` method and passing the `ID` as a parameter.

```
//getting a component by it's ID
var panel = Ext.getCmp("panel-1234");

console.log(panel);
```

 The `getCmp` method is great for debugging applications. We can get the ID of any component by looking at the DOM elements. Then, we can get the instance and inspect the state of our object, but we shouldn't use this method in our code.

7. The Component class contains two mixins, one for the event management and the other for the state of our components. In this step, the two mixins are initialized by calling their constructor.

8. If we have defined plugins, they should be already instantiated in the previous step and now they have to be initialized by calling the `init` method of each plugin and passing our component instance as a parameter. We will learn how plugins work and how to create one from scratch later in this book.

If the `renderTo` property has been defined in the configurations, the rendering phase starts in this step, which means that all the needed nodes that visually represent our component will be inserted into the DOM. If we don't define this property, nothing happens and we are responsible to render our instance whenever we need.

```
var panel = Ext.create("Ext.panel.Panel",{
    title   : "First panel",
    width    : 400,
    height   : 250
});

panel.render(Ext.getBody());
```

If we want to render our component later on, we can call the `render` method of our instance and pass the place where we want to add our new component as a parameter. In the previous code, we are rendering our panel on the body of our document, but we can also set the ID of the node where we want to place our component, for example:

```
panel.render("some-div-id");
```

The rendering phase

The rendering phase only occurs if the component is not rendered already. In this phase, all the required nodes will be inserted to the DOM, the styles and listeners will be applied, and we will be able to see and interact with our new component. The following diagram shows the steps that are executed during this phase:

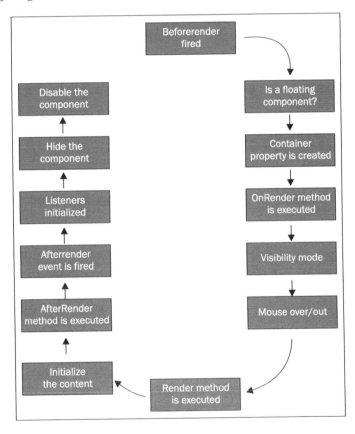

1. In the first step, the `beforerender` event is fired. If some of the listeners return `false`, then the rendering phase is stopped.

2. In the second step, the process checks if the component that is being rendered is a floating component, such as a menu or a window, to assign the correct `z-index` property. The `z-index` is a CSS property that specifies the stack order of an element. The greater number assigned will be always in front of the other elements.

3. The third step is to initialize the container by creating the `container` property which refers to the DOM element, where the new component will be rendered. The `container` property is an `Ext.Element` instance.

4. In the fourth step, the `onRender` method is executed. The `el` property is created which contains the main node element of the component. We can define a template for our components; if we do that then the template will be created and appended to the main node in this step. We can override the `onRender` method in our subclasses to append specific nodes to the DOM.

5. The next step is to set the visibility mode. There are three modes for hiding the component's element (display, visibility, or offset).

6. If the `overCls` property is set, then a listener for the mouse over and mouse out is set to add or remove the `css` class for each state. We can set some CSS rules to these classes to modify the look of our components.

7. In the sixth step, the `render` event is fired. The component's instance is passed as a parameter to the listeners.

8. The seventh step is to initialize the content. There are three ways to set the content of the component:

    i. We can define an `html` property with tags and nodes that will be added to the content of our new component.

    ii. We can define the `contentEl` property that should be the ID of an existing DOM element. This element will be placed as the component content.

    iii. We can define a `tpl` property with a template to be appended to the content. Also, we should define a `data` property with an object containing the replacements in our template. We will talk about templates in future chapters.

9. The following code shows the three ways to add HTML content to a component. We should use only one way at a time.

```
//Using the html property
Ext.create("Ext.Component",{
   width  : 300,
   height : 150,
   renderTo : Ext.getBody(),
   html   : "<h1>Hello!</h1><p>This is an <strong>example</strong>
of content</p>"
```

```
});

//Using an existing DOM element with an ID content
Ext.create("Ext.Component",{
  width   : 300,
  height  : 150,
  renderTo  : Ext.getBody(),
  contentEl: "content"
});

//Using a template with data
Ext.create("Ext.Component",{
  width   : 300,
  height  : 150,
  renderTo   : Ext.getBody(),
  data    : {name:"John"},
  tpl    : ["<h1>Content</h1><p>Hello {name}!</p>"]
});
```

10. Returning to the render phase, the next step is to execute the `afterRender` method. If the component contains children, these are rendered in this step too. We're going to talk about containers shortly.

11. In the ninth step, the `afterRender` event is fired. We can listen to this event in our subclasses to perform some actions when all the needed nodes are rendered in the DOM.

12. In the tenth step, all the listeners that depend on the new nodes are initialized.

13. The eleventh step is to hide the main component node if the `hidden` property is set to `true` in our configurations parameter.

14. Finally, if the `disabled` property is set to true, then the component executes the `disable` method, which adds some CSS classes to the main node to make the components appearance disabled and mark the `disabled` flag as `true`.

The following code shows an example of how the rendering phase works. We are starting the whole process by calling the `render` method:

```
varcmp = Ext.create("Ext.Component",{
  width   : 300,
  height  : 150,
  data   : {name:"John"},
  tpl    : ["<h1>Content</h1><p>Hello {name}!</p>"]
});

//The rendering phase starts for this component
cmp.render(Ext.getBody());
```

By knowing the steps that are executed inside of the render phase, we will be able to overwrite the methods such as the onRender, render, or afterRender in our own classes. This is very useful when creating new components or widgets.

The destruction phase

The main idea of this phase is to clean the DOM, remove the listeners, and clear the used memory by deleting objects and arrays. It's very important to destroy all our components when we don't want them anymore. The destroy phase will be executed when the user finishes the task with our component, for example, if we create a window the destroy phase will be invoked when the user closes the window.

The following diagram shows the steps that are executed in this phase:

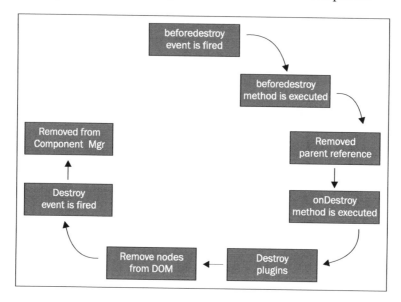

1. The destruction phase starts by firing the beforedestroy event. If any listener returns false, then the destruction is stopped.

2. The second step executes the beforeDestroy method. Some subclasses use this method to remove their children or to clear memory.

3. In the third step, if the component that is being destroyed is a child of another component, then the parent reference to this component is removed.

4. In the fourth step, the `onDestroy` method is executed. We should override this method in order to destroy our component properly.

5. The fifth step tries to destroy all the plugins if there are any.

6. If the component is rendered, then in the sixth step, all nodes from the DOM are removed.

7. In the next step, the `destroy` event is fired. We can listen for this event and perform some actions if needed.

8. The last step is to unregister the instance of the component from the component manager and clear all the events.

One important thing to keep in mind is that we should always remove and clear the memory that we're using in our components, as well as the nodes in the DOM that we have added before. We should override the appropriate methods in order to destroy our components correctly.

If we want to eliminate a component, we can execute the `destroy` method of the component. This method will trigger the destroy phase and all the previous steps will be executed.

```
//The destroy phase starts for this component
cmp.destroy();
```

The lifecycle in action

Now that we know the process of the creation of a component, we can create our own component, taking advantage of the lifecycle to customize our component. The following example shows the methods that we can override to add the functionality that we need in any of the available steps of the lifecycle:

```
Ext.define('MyApp.test.LifecycleExample',{
extend        : 'Ext.Component',

initComponent    : function(){
var me = this;

me.width = 200;
me.height = 100;
me.html = {
tag    : 'div',
html   : 'X',
style : {
                'float'             : 'right',
                'padding'           : '10px',
                'background-color': '#e00',
                'color'             : '#fff',
```

```
                              'font-weight'        : 'bold'
                  }
            };

    me.myOwnProperty = [1,2,3,4];

    me.callParent();

    console.log('1. initComponent');
        },

    beforeRender : function(){
    console.log('2. beforeRender');

    this.callParent(arguments);
        },

    onRender : function(){
    console.log('3. onRender');

    this.callParent(arguments);

    this.el.setStyle('background-color','#ccc');
        },

    afterRender : function(){
    console.log('4. afterRender');

    this.el.down('div').on('click',this.myCallback,this);

    this.callParent(arguments);
        },

    beforeDestroy : function(){
    console.log('5. beforeDestroy');

    this.callParent(arguments);
        },

    onDestroy : function(){
    console.log('6. onDestroy');

    delete this.myOwnProperty;
    this.el.down('div').un('click',this.myCallback);

    this.callParent(arguments);
        },

    myCallback : function(){
    var me = this;
```

```
Ext.Msg.confirm('Confirmation','Are you sure you want to close this
panel?',function(btn){
if(btn === 'yes'){
me.destroy();
            }
        });
    }
});
```

The previous class overrides the **template methods**. This term is used for the methods that are automatically executed during the lifecycle. From the previous code, we can see how to add content using the `html` property, how to add listeners to the elements that we create, and more importantly how to destroy and clear our events and custom objects.

In order to test our class, we need to create a `.html` file, include the Ext JS library, and our class, then we need to create the instance of our class as follows:

```
Ext.onReady(function(){
    Ext.create('MyApp.test.LifecycleExample',{
        renderTo : Ext.getBody()
    });
});
```

As a result, we will see something like the following screenshot in our browser:

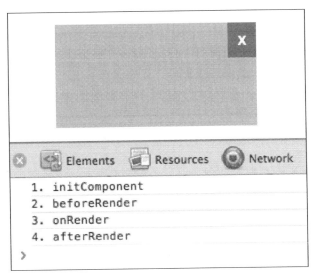

As we can see, there are four messages in the JavaScript console. These messages were sent by each of the methods that we have overridden. We can also see the order of the execution based on the lifecycle. Now, if we want to destroy this component, we need to click the red button at the top-right. This action will call the `destroy` method that is responsible for clearing the nodes from the DOM, events, and objects from memory.

About containers

At this point, we know all the steps of the lifecycle. If you remember in the rendering phase there's a step where the children of the components are rendered too. Now we're going to learn how we can add children to a component.

The `Ext.container.Container` class is responsible to manage children and to arrange those using layouts. If we want our class to contain other components, we should extend from this class. It's worth saying that this class extends from `Ext.Component`, so we'll be able to use the component lifecycle in our subclasses too:

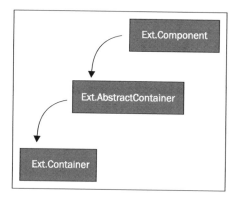

All classes that extend from `Ext.Container` will be able to have children using the `items` property or the `add` method to append a new component as a child.

```
Ext.define("MyApp.container.MyContainer",{
    extend  : "Ext.container.Container",   //Step 1

    border  : true,
    padding : 10,

    initComponent  : function(){
      var me = this;

      Ext.each(me.items,function(item){   //Step 2
        item.style = {
          backgroundColor:"#f4f4f4",
          border:"1px solid #333"
```

```
    };
    item.padding = 10;
    item.height = 100;
  });

  me.callParent();
},

onRender   : function(){
  var me = this;

  me.callParent(arguments);

  if(me.border){  //Step 3
    me.el.setStyle("border","1px solid #333");
  }
}
});
```

1. The previous class extends from the `Ext.container.Container` class. Now we can use the layout system to arrange the children of the container.

2. When extending from the `Container` class, we can use the `items` property to define the children of the main container. We're looping the `items` property, which is an array, to add some basic styles. We're using the `initComponent` method that is executed automatically in the creation phase. We shouldn't forget to call the super class by executing the `callParent` method.

3. The last step overrides the `onRender` method. After executing the `callParent` method, we can have access to the `el` property that is a reference of the main node of our component. If the `border` property is set to `true`, we will add CSS styles to display a border around the main element's node.

4. Once we have defined our class, we can create an instance of it. Let's create an HTML page including the Ext library and our class in order to execute the following code:

```
Ext.onReady(function(){

  Ext.create("MyApp.container.MyContainer",{
    renderTo: Ext.getBody(),
    items  : [{
      xtype  : "component",
      html   : "Component one"
    },{
      xtype  : "component",
      html   : "Component two"
    }]
  });

});
```

We're creating the instance of our class as usual. We added the `items` property as an array of components. We can define as many components as we need because our class is a container.

In this example, we are using the `xtype` property to define each inner component, but we could also create an instance of the component's child and then pass the reference into the `items` array.

 Using the `xtype` property allows us to create components with a few lines of code. When the main container is created, all their children are created as well. We'll find all the available `xtype` properties in the documentation under the `Ext.Component` class.

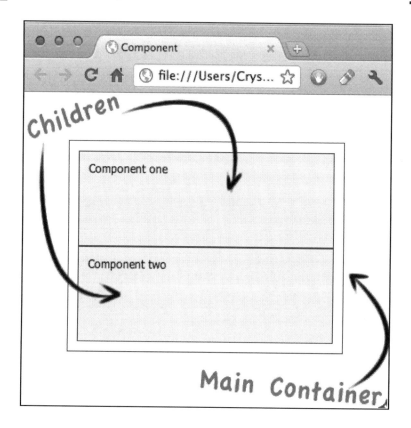

The previous screenshot shows three components. One is the main component that contains two children. We have achieved this by extending from the `Container` class and using the `items` property.

When using containers, we can define a property called `defaults` that allows us to apply the same properties to all of the children in the main container. Let's add some default values to our previous example:

```
Ext.create("MyApp.container.MyContainer",{
    renderTo: Ext.getBody(),
    defaults: {
        xtype   : "component",
        width   : 100
    },
    items   : [{
        //xtype   : "component",
        html    : "Component one"
    },{
        //xtype   : "component",
        html    : "Component two"
    }]
});
```

The `defaults` property receives an object containing all the configurations that we want to apply to the components inside the `items` array. In this case, we have added the `width` and `xtype` properties. This way we don't have to repeat the same lines of code for each component:

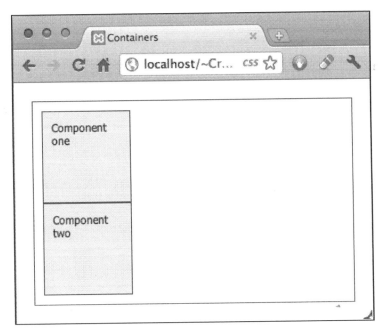

As we can see in the previous screenshot the size of the two children are the same. We can also override a default property by simply adding the property that we want to be different to the specific child.

 Every time we find properties that are repeated in each child component. We should use the `defaults` property to apply all these properties at once. This will reduce the lines of code and will prevent code duplication. If we define the same property in any of the children, the default value will be overridden.

The panel

A panel is a container that can be placed as a block in a given space. A panel can contain other panels or even other components because it extends from the `container` class.

A panel contains a few regions where we can add content. Let's create our first panel, by instantiating the `Ext.panel.Panel` class. We need to create an HTML page, import the Ext library, and then execute the following code when the DOM is ready to be used:

```
Ext.onReady(function(){

    var panel = Ext.create("Ext.panel.Panel",{
        renderTo: Ext.getBody(),
        title   : "My first panel",
        width     : 300,
        height  : 200,
        html     : "The content"
    });

    panel.center();

});
```

We have created the instance of the `Panel` class in the same way we created a component in previous examples. The only difference is that we have added a new configuration called `title` with the text we want to show as the title of our panel.

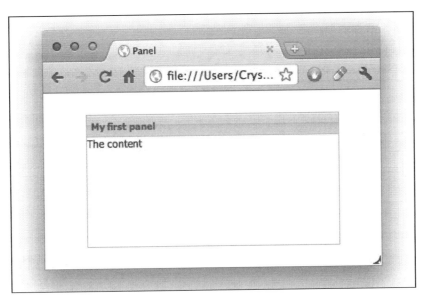

The previous screenshot shows the header area on top of the panel. We can move the header to the bottom, left-hand, or right-hand side of the panel by using the `headerPosition` configuration and setting the side we want.

We can also see the content area. In this example, we use the `html` property, but we could also use the `items` array to set other components as children.

Another area where we can add content is the tools region. We can define small buttons in the top-right of the title bar by using the `tools` configuration.

```
Ext.onReady(function(){

  var panel = Ext.create("Ext.panel.Panel",{
    renderTo: Ext.getBody(),
    title  : "My first panel",
    width  : 300,
    height : 200,
    html   : "The content",
    tools  : [
        {type   : "help"},
        {type   : "search"},
        {type   : "gear"},
        {type   : "print"}
    ]
```

```
    });

  panel.center();

});
```

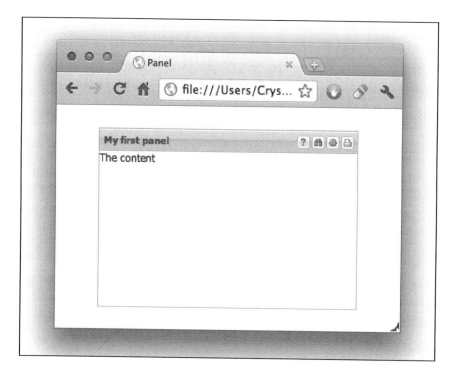

We have a set of 25 icons available that can be specified by using the `type` property for each button. We can consult the documentation in order to see all available icons under the `Ext.panel.Tool` class.

If we want our panel to be collapsible or closable, we can set the `collapsible` and `closable` configuration to `true`. This will add two buttons in the tools region.

The last region, where we can place components, is the docked items region. We can place components in the top, bottom, left-hand, or right-hand side of the content area. The typical component that we place in these regions is a toolbar with buttons, but we can place any other if we want.

```
    var panel = Ext.create("Ext.panel.Panel",{
      //...
      dockedItems : [{
        xtype  : "toolbar",
        dock   : "top",
        items  : ["Top toolbar!"]
```

```
      },{
        xtype   : "toolbar",
        dock    : "bottom",
        items   : ["Bottom toolbar!"]
      },{
        xtype   : "toolbar",
        dock    : "left",
        items   : ["Left<br /> toolbar!"]
      },{
        xtype   : "toolbar",
        dock    : "right",
        items   : ["Right<br /> toolbar!"]
      }]
    });
```

We can define an array of components to be placed in different positions. In this case, we're placing toolbars in four different places using the dock property. We can add two or more components in the same position and they will be placed one over each other.

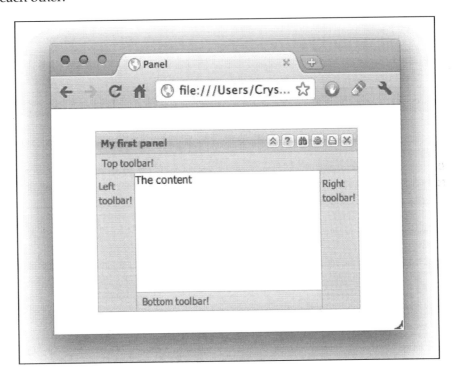

We can also use a short way to add our toolbars. For example, if we want to add a toolbar to the top of the container, we can use the tbar property that receives an array of buttons or other components that will conform the toolbar.

There's also the bbar property to place a toolbar on the bottom, the lbar property to place a toolbar on the left-hand side, the rbar property to place it on the right-hand side, and the fbar property to place it in the footer of the container.

We use panels to create blocks of content and to define our layouts. We can create nested panels and arrange the children with one of the available layouts.

The Window component

A window is basically a floating panel with more features. The Window component extends from the Panel class. This means we can use all the methods and properties that the panel has.

We can drag a window from the header bar, close it, and maximize it among other things. Let's create a .html file importing the Ext library and running the following code when the DOM is ready.

```
var win = Ext.create("Ext.window.Window",{
    title      : "My first window",
    width      : 300,
    height     : 200,
    maximizable : true,
    defaults: {
      xtype      : "panel",
      height     : 60,
      collapsible : true
    },
    items   : [{
      title  : "Menu",
      html   : "The main menu"
    },{
      title  : "Content",
      html   : "The main content!"
    }]
});

win.show();
```

The only difference in our previous code and the panel's code is the maximizable property that allows us to maximize the window. We've removed the renderTo property too and used the show method to render and display the window.

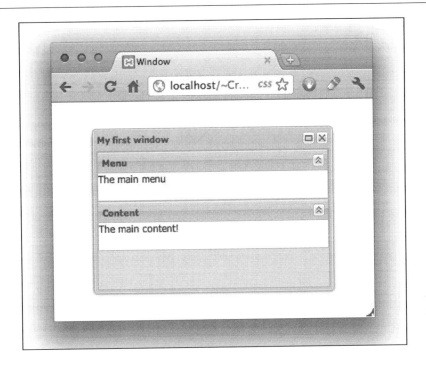

The previous screenshot shows a window with two panels inside. By default, the window is closable, but we can make it unclosable by setting the `closable` property to `false`.

We can move the window across the screen by dragging the header. We can also resize the window with the mouse for each of the four sides.

There are many more options for the window component. We should take a look at the API documentation and play around with this component. Go to the following link: `http://docs.sencha.com/ext-js/4-1/#!/api/Ext.window.Window`.

The layout system

One of the greatest features of the Ext JS library is the ability to create layouts in an easy way. We can define fixed layouts or fluid layouts using the right classes.

At this point, we know how a container works. We can arrange the children of a container by setting a layout. If we don't define a layout to our containers, by default the `auto` layout will be used. In our previous examples, we've used the `auto` layout and as we could see the children are displayed one after another.

There are many available layouts we can use to arrange our components, such as `accordions`, `cards`, `columns`, `regions`, and so on.

We can find all available layouts in the `Ext.layout.container` package. If we go to the documentation and look into the layouts package, we will see many classes, each representing a type of layout.

Fit layout

This layout is intended to be used for only one child. It allows us to expand the inner component to the size of the container. The child component takes all the available space in the container component. When the parent is resized, the child size is updated too to fit the new dimensions.

Let's modify our previous window example and add a `fit` layout to the main container.

```
var win = Ext.create("Ext.window.Window",{
    title      : "My first window",
    width      : 300,
    height     : 200,
    maximizable : true,
    layout     : "fit",
    defaults: {
        xtype    : "panel",
        height   : 60,
        border   : false
    },
    items   : [{
        title  : "Menu",
        html   : "The main menu"
    },{
        title  : "Content",
        html   : "The main content!"
    }]
});

win.show();
```

In the previous code, we have only added the `layout` property. In this case, we're setting a string with the name of the layout, but we can also set an object and define some configurations for the selected layout. In fact, every layout is a class that accepts configurations. We'll see an example of this shortly.

The following screenshot shows how the `fit` layout arranges the children of the container component:

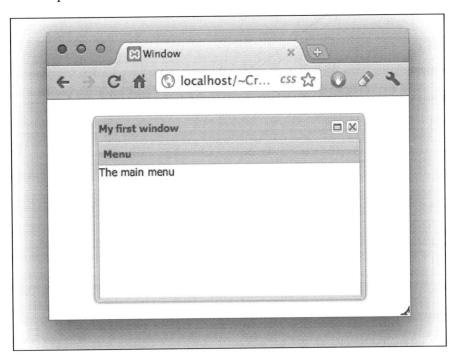

Even if we define two children components to the window, it only appears as one. If we resize the main window, we should see that the **Menu** panel is expanded to fit the new size of the window.

Card layout

If we need to create a wizard or display only one component at a time, we should use the `card` layout. It extends from the `fit` layout which means only one component will be shown and expanded to fill all the available space in the container.

The difference with the `card` layout is that we can move the components easily by calling the `next` or `prev` method. We can also set the displayed component by its index in the items array.

```
var win = Ext.create("Ext.window.Window",{
    title     : "My first window",
    width     : 300,
    height    : 200,
    maximizable : true,
    layout    : "card",   //Step 1
```

```
    defaults: {
       xtype     : "panel",
       height    : 60,
       border    : false
    },
    items   : [{
       title : "Menu",
       html  : "The main menu"
    },{
       title : "Content",
       html  : "The main content!"
    }]
});

win.show();

setTimeout(function(){
   win.getLayout().setActiveItem(1);   //Step 2
},2000);
```

The previous code creates a window component with two panels. We have set the layout of the window to card in step one.

In step two, we get the layout instance by calling the getLayout method after 2 seconds. Now, we can display any of the components we have in the items array. In this example, we have executed the setActiveItem method, passing the index of the component to be shown. We can also use the prev and next methods from the layout instance to show the next and previous card.

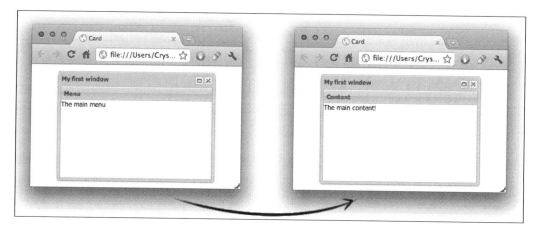

The previous image shows how the card layout works, first we displayed the **Menu** panel and after 2 seconds, the **Content** panel is displayed.

HBox layout

When using this layout, we can arrange our inner components horizontally. We can assign a flexible width for each component and even align the components to the top, center, or stretch them to fit the container's height.

```
var win = Ext.create("Ext.window.Window",{
    title     : "My first window",
    width        : 300,
    height     : 200,
    maximizable : true,
    layout     : {
        type  : "hbox",
        align  : "top" //middle, top, stretch, stretchmax
    },
    defaults: {
        xtype      : "panel",
        height   : 60
    },
    items   : [{
        title: "Menu",
        html  : "The main menu"
    },{
        title: "Content",
        html  : "The main content!"
    }]
});
```

In our previous code, we have defined an object to the layout property. The object contains a type property that receives the layout we want to use, in this case hbox. We have also set an align property that allows us to define four ways to align our components.

By default, the `align` property is set to `top`. This way all the children will be aligned vertically to the top of the container.

We can also set the `align` property of the children to `middle` of the container. If we want to make the children's components fit the height of the container, we can use the `stretch` value as follows:

```
var win = Ext.create("Ext.window.Window",{
    //...
    layout    : {
      type  : "hbox",
      align : "stretch"
    },
    //...
});
```

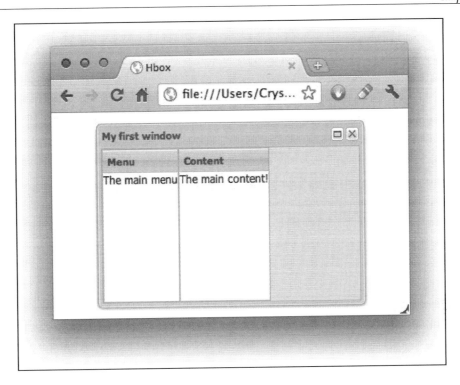

Even if we resize the window, the two panels will be resized to fit the new height. We can also make our **Menu** and **Content** panels have flexible width size too just by adding the `flex` property.

```
var win = Ext.create("Ext.window.Window",{
    //...
items   : [{
    title: "Menu",
    html  : "The main menu",
    flex  : 1
  },{
    title: "Content",
    html  : "The main content!",
    flex  : 2
  }]
});
```

Now both components are flexible. When we resize the main window, the two panels are resized too, maintaining their proportions.

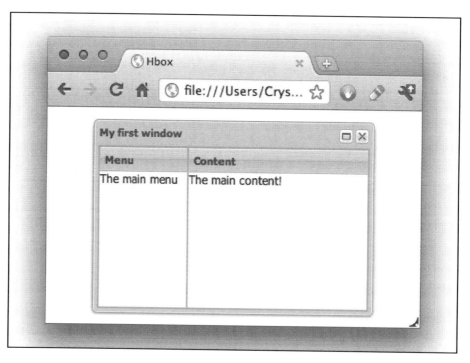

The **Content** panel is twice the size of the **Menu** panel. This is because we have defined the `flex` property to 2.

The `hbox` layout calculates the width size of each component according to the available space in the container. To set the right size, the layout counts the components that are configured with a `flex` property and adds their values. In our previous example, the sum of the two components is three; this means that all the available space will be divided in three equal portions as shown in the following screenshot:

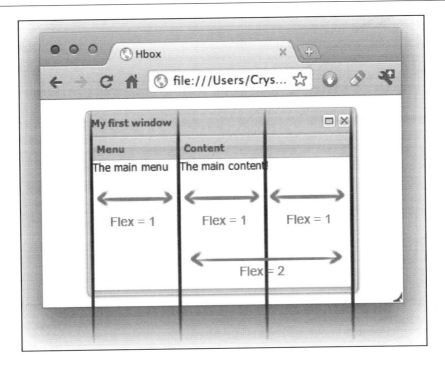

The **Content** panel is taking two spaces because we configured its `flex` property to `2` and the **Menu** panel is taking just one portion of the available space.

Every time we resize the window, the proportions are maintained. The width may vary depending on the width of the container, but the proportions are always the same. We can configure as many components as we want with a `flex` property.

VBox layout

This layout is very similar to the `hbox` layout. The difference is that this layout makes the children vertically flexible. We can also align them to the left, center, or stretch.

The following code shows how to make the two panels vertically flexible, one using only one space of the available height and the other one using two spaces:

```
var win = Ext.create("Ext.window.Window",{
    title     : "My first window",
    width     : 300,
    height    : 200,
    maximizable : true,
```

```
layout    : {
   type   : "vbox",
   align  : "stretch" //center, left, stretchmax
},
defaults: {
   xtype     : "panel",
   height    : 60
},
items   : [{
   title : "Menu",
   html  : "The main menu",
   flex  : 1
},{
   title : "Content",
   html  : "The main content!",
   flex  : 2
}]
});

win.show();
```

Even if we have defined a height to the two panels, the vbox layout is setting the appropriate height to each component. If we resize the window, the proportions of the two panels is kept.

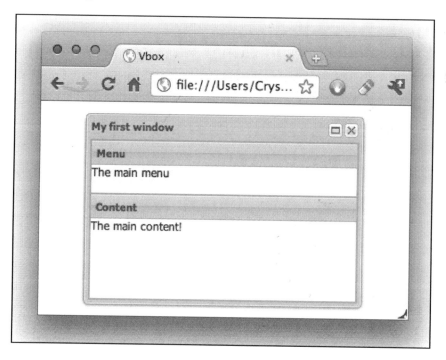

The **Menu** panel is smaller than the **Content** panel. This is because we have defined the `flex` twice as the **Menu** panel.

In our previous example, we have used the `stretch` alignment, but can try other types such us the `center` alignment or the `left` alignment depending on our requirements.

Border layout

The border layout divides the container space into five regions: `north`, `south`, `west`, `east`, and `center`. We can place our children in any of the regions, but we are required to use the center region.

```
var win = Ext.create("Ext.window.Window",{
    title     : "My first window",
    width     : 300,
    height    : 200,
    maximizable : true,
    layout    : "border",
    defaults: {
        xtype    : "panel",
        height   : 60
    },
    items    : [{
        title  : "Menu",
        html   : "The main menu",
        region : "west",
        width  : 100,
        collapsible : true,
        split  : true
    },{
        title  : "Content",
        html   : "The main content!",
        region : "center"
    }]
});
```

In the previous code, we have defined the layout as `border`. We have also defined the `center` region and the `west` region:

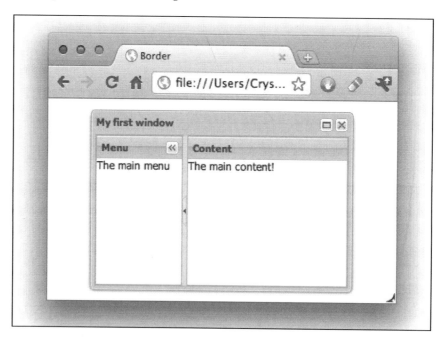

We have made the **Menu** panel collapsible. If we click in the small arrow located in the header or in the division bar, we'll see that the panel will collapse to the left-hand side. Also, we have defined our **Menu** panel to be split. This allows us to resize the **Menu** panel by dragging the separation bar with our mouse.

We can add more panels in the other regions.

Accordion layout

This layout allows us to show one component at a time. We will see the header of the inner components and we're going to be able to expand and collapse the components by clicking in their title bars.

```
var win = Ext.create("Ext.window.Window",{
    title      : "My first window",
    width      : 300,
    height     : 200,
    maximizable : true,
    layout     : {
        type     :"accordion"
    },
```

```
defaults: {
    xtype    : "panel",
},
items   : [{
    title: "Menu",
    html   : "The main menu"
},{
    title: "Content",
    html   : "The main content!"
},{
    title: "3rd Column",
    html   : "Content!"
}]
});
```

In the previous code, we have only defined the `accordion` layout and added a new panel to the `items` array. We'll see something as shown in the following screenshot:

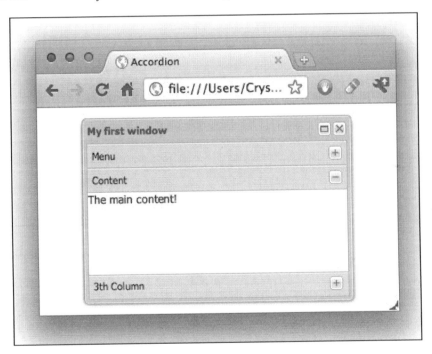

When using the `accordion` layout, we'll see only one panel expanded at a time. The expanded panel will take the available height to be displayed. It doesn't matter if we resize the container.

Summary

In this chapter, we have learned about the component's lifecycle. We don't need to remember every step that is executed in each phase, but we should know the methods that we can override in our subclasses, so we can add specific functionality in one of the three phases. When creating our custom components, it's very important to remember that we need to destroy all our references and internal components that we have created. This way we'll free memory. We've also learned about the containers and layouts. Now we know how to add other components to a container and arrange them according to our needs.

In the next chapter, we're going to talk about the data package. We'll learn about the models, stores, associations, and so many more exciting things.

4
It's All About the Data

In this chapter we're going to learn about the new data package in Ext JS 4. There are lot of changes and differences between Ext JS 4 and Ext JS 3 and a lot of new features. We'll talk about Ajax, Models, Stores, and the available readers and writers that we can use in order to store our data locally.

It's important to have a solid understanding of the data package so we can work with the widgets without problems. Ext JS creates an abstract layer with a lot of classes and configurations; the idea is to use these classes when dealing with information. All the widgets and components that show information use the data package to manipulate and present the data easily.

The topics that we will cover in this chapter are the following. It's important to mention that a web server is required for this chapter and the following chapters. It doesn't matter which one you decide to use because we are not using any specific server-side technology.

- Ajax
- Creating a model
- A collection to store our models
- Working with the store
- The available proxies
- The readers and writers to parse our data

Ajax

Before we start learning about the data package it's important to know how we can make an Ajax request to the server. The Ajax request is one of the most useful ways to get data from the server asynchronously. This means that the JavaScript loop is not blocked while the request is being executed and an event will be fired when the server responds; this allows us to do anything else while the request is being performed.

If you are new to Ajax, I recommend you read more about it. There are thousands of tutorials online, but I suggest you to read this simple article at `http://thomashunter.name/blog/simple-ajax/`.

The Ext JS provides an object that is responsible for dealing with all the required processes to perform a request in any browser. There are a few differences in each browser, but Ext JS handles all the troubles and gives us a cross browser solution to make Ajax requests.

The responsible class to make asynchronous requests to the server is the `Ext.data. Connection` class. We can instantiate this class to start making requests to the server, however Ext comes with an instance of this class called `Ext.Ajax`, we can use this object to our convenience.

Let's make our first Ajax call to our server. First we need to create an HTML file and import the Ext library. Then we can add the following code inside the `script` tag:

```
Ext.Ajax.request({
    url            : "serverside/data.json"
});

console.log("Next lines of code...");
```

Using the `request` method we can make an Ajax call to our server. The `request` method receives an object containing the configurations for the Ajax call. The only configuration that we have defined is the URL where we want to make our request.

It's important to note that Ajax is asynchronous. This means that once the `request` method is executed the JavaScript engine will continue executing the following lines of code and it doesn't wait until the server responds.

In the previous code we are not doing anything when the server responds to our request. In order to get the response date we need to configure a callback function to execute when the server responds with success or failure. Let's modify our previous example to set up those callbacks:

```
Ext.Ajax.request({
    url     : "serverside/data.json",
    success : function(response,options){

    },
    failure : function(response,options){

    }
});
```

The `success` function will be executed only when the server responds with a 200-299 status, which means that the request has been made successfully. If the response status is 403, 404, 500, 503, and any other error status, the `failure` callback will be executed.

Each callback receives two parameters. The first parameter is the server response object, where we can find the response text and headers. The second parameter is the configuration option that we used for this Ajax request, in this case the object will contain three properties: the URL, the `success` and `failure` callbacks.

At this point we have our callbacks set, but we're not doing anything inside them. Normally we need to get the data response and do something with it, let's suppose we get the following JSON in our response:

```
{
    "success"    : true,
    "msg"     : "This is a success message"
}
```

> One of the preferred formats, in the Ext JS community, to send and receive data to the server, is JSON, but we can also use XML. JSON stands for JavaScript Object Notation. If you are not familiar with JSON, I recommend you visit http://www.json.org/.

If we want to show the message, we need to decode that JSON and convert the text to an object so we can access easily the `msg` property. Let's add the following code to our `success` callback:

```
Ext.Ajax.request({
    url     : "serverside/data.json",
    success : function(response,options){
        var data = Ext.decode(response.responseText);
```

```
        Ext.Msg.alert("Message", data.msg);
    },
    failure  : function(response,options){

    }
});
```

First we get the server response as a text using the `responseText` property from the `response` object. Then we use the `Ext.decode` method to convert the JSON text into JavaScript objects and save the result in a `data` variable.

After we have our data object with the server response we will show an alert message accessing the `msg` property from the data object. Let's keep in mind that if we want to show something using the DOM, we need to put our code inside the `onReady` method that we have learned in the previous chapter.

If we refresh our browser to execute the code we have modified, we should see something like the following screenshot:

Now, let's assume that we want to use XML instead of JSON, we will create the request in a very similar way as in our previous code. The following code should be saved in a new file at `serverside/data.xml`:

```xml
<?xml version="1.0" encoding="UTF-8"?>
<response success="true">
<msg>This is a success message in XML format</msg>
</response>
```

We only need to change the URL and the code in the `success` callback as follows:

```
Ext.Ajax.request({
    url      : "serverside/data.xml",
    success : function(response,options){
```

```
    var xml = response.responseXML,
node = xml.getElementsByTagName('msg')[0];

Ext.Msg.alert('Message',node.firstChild.data);
    },
failure : function(response,options){


    }
});
```

We use the `responseXML` property to get the tree of nodes, and then we get the node with a `msg` tag. After that we can get the actual text using the `firstChild.data` property from the previous node. If we execute the code we will see something very similar to our previous example with JSON.

As we can notice, it is easier to work with JSON, we just need to decode the text and then we can use the objects. XML is a little bit complicated, but we can also use this format if we feel comfortable with it.

We can also send parameters in our request; we only need to set a new configuration property to our request as follows:

```
Ext.Ajax.request({
    url     : "serverside/data.json",
    params  : {x:1,y:2,z:3},
    success : function(response,options){
      var data = Ext.decode(response.responseText);

      Ext.Msg.alert("Message",data.msg);
    },
    failure : function(response,options){


    }
});
```

Using the `params` property we can set an object of parameters, in this case we will send only three parameters: x, y, and z, but we can send as many as we need. We can also pass a string of parameters to the `params` property as follows:

```
Ext.Ajax.request({
    url     : "serverside/data.json",
    params  : "x=1&y=2&z=3",
    success : function(response,options){
      var data = Ext.decode(response.responseText);
```

```
        Ext.Msg.alert("Message",data.msg);
      },
      failure   : function(response,options){

      }
    });
```

 We can assign an object with an array or other objects to the params property. Basically we can assign any structure that we need.

There are times when the server takes too long to respond, so by default the Ajax request is configured to wait 30 seconds. We can increase or decrease that time by setting the timeout property in our configurations request as shown in the following code:

```
    Ext.Ajax.request({
        url     : "serverside/data.json",
        params  : {x:1,y:2,z:3},
        timeout : 50000,
        success : function(response,options){
          var data = Ext.decode(response.responseText);

          Ext.Msg.alert("Message",data.msg);
        },
        failure   : function(response,options){

        }
    });
```

We have increased the timeout property to 50 seconds, now our request will be dropped after 50 seconds of waiting for the response.

If we look into the documentation, we will find some other configurations, such as the scope of the callbacks, headers, cache, and so on. We should read the docs and play with those configurations too, but the ones that we have covered here are the most important ones to learn.

Now we know how to get data using Ajax, but we need a way to deal with that data. Ext JS provides us with a package of classes to manage our data in an easy way; let's move forward to our next topic.

Models

A model is a representation of the information in our application domain. We define objects that hold our data, so we can easily access performance specific tasks such as writing and reading. We can define as many models as we need. Each model represents an entity such as User, Invoice, Client, or whatever we need in our project.

A model may contain fields, validations, and relationships between other models. We can also set a proxy to persist and pull our data.

Let's create a new file located at js/MyApp/model and we will call it Invoice.js. In this file we're going to create our Invoice class as follows:

```
Ext.define('MyApp.model.Invoice',{
extend    : 'Ext.data.Model',  // Step 1

   idProperty  : 'idInvoice',//Step 2
fields   : [  // Step 3
    {name:'IdInvoice'},
    {name:'taxId'},
    {name:'dateIssued',type:'date',dateFormat:'Y-m-d h:i:s'},
    {name:'name'},
    {name:'address'}
    ]
});
```

We're defining a model the same way we defined a class, but in step one we extend from the Ext.data.Model class, which is the one responsible for adding all the functionality to our models.

In the second step we are defining the property in our JSON response that will contain the ID of each record instance. In this case we are going to use the idInvoice field, but if we don't define the idProperty configuration, the model will use a property called id by default.

In the third step we define the fields for our model. This is an array of fields; each field is an object containing the name of the field.

We can also define the type of information that the property will have. In our previous code the dateIssued field will contain a Date object. When using dates we need to define the date format that our model is expecting in order to parse the given string to a date object correctly. We do this by using the dateFormat property.

The available types of data are string, int, float, boolean, and date. If we define a type, the received value will be converted to the selected type of data.

Once we have defined our model we can create an HTML file. Let's import the Ext library and our `Invoice` class file to test our model as follows:

```
var invoice = Ext.create("MyApp.model.Invoice",{
  taxId       : '12345',
  dateIssued  : '2012-01-25 11:55:21',
  name        : 'Mr. Doe',
  address     : '123 ST 987 LA. USA'
});


console.log(invoice);
```

Using the `create` method we can instantiate our model class, the second parameter is an object with the data that our model will contain. Now we can use the `get` and `set` methods to read and write any of the defined fields.

```
var name = invoice.get('name');

//Modifying one field
invoice.set('name','Mr. Smith');

console.log('Old name:',name);
console.log('New name:',invoice.get('name'));

//Setting many values
invoice.set({
  taxId    : 54321,
  address  : '10th ST, McAllen TX'
});
```

The previous code shows how to read and write our data. The `set` method allows us to modify one field or even many fields at the same time by passing an object containing the new values.

If we inspect the `invoice` instance, we'll find that all the information is held in a property called `data`. We should always use the `get` and `set` methods to read and write our models, but if for some reason we need to have access to all the data in our model, we can use the `data` object as follows:

```
//reading
console.log(invoice.data.address);

//writing
invoice.data.address = "Main Avenue 123, Manassas VA";

console.log(invoice.get('address'));
```

We can read and write any fields in our model. However, setting a new value in this way is not a good practice at all. The `set` method performs some important tasks when setting the new value, such as marking our model as dirty, saving the previous value so we can reject or accept the changes later, and some other important steps.

> The advice is to avoid setting values using the `data` object directly.

Validations

One of the new features in this new version of Ext is the ability to validate our data directly in the model. We can define rules on each field and run the validations when we need it.

In order to define validations into our models we only need to define a property called `validations` that contains an array of rules that will be executed when the validator engine runs.

Let's modify our previous `Invoice` class to set the `taxId` as required and its value should have 5-7 characters. Also, we set the name as required and its format should be alphanumeric.

```
Ext.define('MyApp.model.Invoice',{
extend   : 'Ext.data.Model',

  //...

validations   : [
    {type:'presence',field:'taxId'},
    {type:'length',field:'taxId',min:5,max:7},
    {type:'presence',field:'name'},
    {type:'format',field:'name',matcher:/^[\w ]+$/}
  ]
});
```

When adding validations we use objects to define each rule. The `type` property defines the type of rule that we want to add and the `field` property defines to which field this rule will be applied.

There are a few types built within the library such as inclusion, exclusion, presence, length, format, and e-mail; these are very common validations. We can also add new types of validations as needed.

When defining a rule, it is required to always use the `type` and `field` properties, but some rules require the use of other extra parameters. The `type` property represents a function within the `Ext.data.validations` object; we can read the documentation of this object to see what are the specific parameters needed for each rule.

Now let's create an HTML file by importing the Ext library and our `Invoice` model to test our previous class as follows:

```
//Step 1
var invoice = Ext.create("MyApp.model.Invoice",{
    taxId   : '12345',
    date    : '2012-01-25 11:55:21',
    name    : 'Mr John',
    address : '123 ST 987 LA. USA'
});


if(invoice.isValid()){ //Step 2
    console.log('Everything is fine!');
}else{
    var errors = invoice.validate(); // Step 3

    errors.each(function(error){
        console.log(error.field,error.message);
    });
}
```

The steps are explained as follows:

- **Step 1**: We instantiated our `Invoice` model using some data.
- **Step 2**: We executed the `isValid` method, which returns true if all the validations were correct and false if any validation failed. By using this method we don't know which validation failed.
- **Step 3**: This step is executed only if there are any errors. The `validate` method will get a collection with the failed validations or will be empty if everything was correct. We can iterate this collection to know the fields and error messages.

> The collection returned by the `validate` method is an instance of the class `Ext.data.Errors`, which extends from `Ext.util.MixedCollection`. Therefore, we can use the `each` method to iterate in a simple way.

When we execute the previous example we will see in the console a message saying that all validations were successful. Let's change the value of some properties to see how the validations fail. For example, let's remove some characters from the `taxId` property and execute the example again. We will see a message in the JavaScript console saying that the length of the `taxtId` property is incorrect:

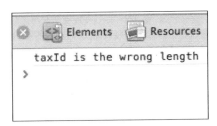

The message displayed in the previous screenshot is a generic description, but we can customize the message to our needs. To do this, we only have to override the property `lengthMessage`.

```
Ext.data.validations.lengthMessage = 'Please correct the length';
```

If we want to change the message of another rule, we only have to concatenate the name of the rule with `Message`. For example, `presenceMessage`, `includeMessage`, and so on.

We usually have a lot of custom validations when we develop applications. If we want to add a new validation we simply add a new function to the `Ext.data.validations` object, for example, take a look at the following code:

```
Ext.define('MyApp.data.validations', {
  override  : 'Ext.data.validations',
  singleton : true,

  creditcardMessage : 'Invalid credit card number',

  creditcardRe    : /^[\d]{16}$/,

  creditcard : function(config,value){
    return Ext.data.validations.creditcardRe.test(value);
  }
});
```

In the previous code we created a new class that overrides the `Ext.data.validations` object. We can add here as many validations as we need. In this example we added a credit card rule.

In order to create a rule we need to define a function with the name of the type of the rule, in this case it is called `creditcard`. This function receives two parameters, the first is the configuration that we defined in the model and the second one is the assigned value of the field.

It's necessary to define the error message for our new rule, in this case `creditcardMessage`. As it was previously mentioned we only need to concatenate the name of the new rule with the word `Message`.

If we want to test our new validation, we need to modify our `Invoice` class to add a new field and the new validation rule.

```
Ext.define('MyApp.model.Invoice',{
extend   : 'Ext.data.Model',

fields   : [

    //...

   {name:'creditCard'}
   ],

validations  : [
    {type:'creditcard',field:'creditCard'},
    //...
  ]
});
```

In the previous code we only added a new field called `creditCard`, now we add the new validation rule to the array of validations.

Once we have modified our `Invoice` class we need to modify our HTML file, where we're testing the validations, and add information to the new credit card field.

```
var invoice = Ext.create("MyApp.model.Invoice",{
    taxId   : '12345',
    date    : '2012-01-25 11:55:21',
    name    : 'Mr John',
    address : '123 ST 987 LA. USA',
    creditCard: '1234567890'
});
```

If we run the test, we'll see the validation error because the credit card number is invalid. We should set a 16 characters value to the credit card field if we don't want the error message to appear:

There are a few other built-in validations in the `Ext.data.validations` object such as inclusion, exclusion, and e-mail. Most of the time those validations are not enough, but now we know how to add more.

Relationships

We can create relationships between models to relate our data. For example, an invoice contains items, each item is an object with properties such as price, quantity, and description.

Ext JS 4 adds support to create one-to-many and many-to-one associations in a very easy way. Let's modify our `Invoice` class to create a one-to-many association:

```
Ext.define('MyApp.model.Invoice',{
extend   : 'Ext.data.Model',

//...

  hasMany   : [
    {model:'MyApp.model.Item',name:'getItems'}
    ]
});
```

Using the `hasMany` property we can define the association. In this example, we're assigning an array of objects because we can create as many associations as we need. Each object contains a `model` property, which defines the model with the `Invoice` class that will be related.

Additionally, we may define the name of the function that will be created in our `Invoice` class to get the items related. In this case we used `getItems`; if we don't define any name, Ext will pluralize the name of the child model, for this example it would be `items`.

Now we need to create the `Item` class. Let's create a new file located at `js/MyApp/model` called `Item.js` with the following content:

```
Ext.define('MyApp.model.Item',{
    extend  : 'Ext.data.Model',
    fields  : [
        {name:'quantity',type:'int'},
        {name:'description',type:'string'},
        {name:'unitPrice',type:'float'},
        {name:'subtotal',type:'float'}
    ]
});
```

There's nothing new in the previous code, just a regular model with a few fields describing an item of an invoice.

In order to test our relationship we need to create an HTML file importing the Ext library and our two models. Then we can test our models as follows:

```
//Step 1
var invoice = Ext.create("MyApp.model.Invoice",{
    taxId  : '12345',
    date   : '2012-01-25 11:55:21',
    name   : 'Mr John',
    address : '123 ST 987 Los Angeles, CA. USA'
});

invoice.getItems().add(  // Step 2
    {quantity:10,description:'Development services',unitPrice:65,subtot
al:650},
    {quantity:20,description:'Design services',unitPrice:55,subtot
al:1100}
);

//Step 3
invoice.getItems().each(function(item){
    console.log(item.get('description'));
});
```

The steps are explained as follows:

- **Step 1**: We have created the `Invoice` class with some data such as the `taxId`, `date`, `name`, and `address`.

- **Step 2**: We execute the `getItems` method. When we define our relationship we set the name of this method using the `name` property in the association configuration. This method returns an `Ext.data.Store` instance; this class is a collection to manage models in an easy way. We are also adding two objects to the collection using the `add` method, each object contains the data for the `Item` model.

- **Step 3**: We are iterating the items collection from our `invoice` object. Using the `get` method we are printing the description for each model to the console, in this case we have only two models in our store.

Dealing with the store

As mentioned before a store is a collection of models that acts as a client cache to manage our data locally. We can use this collection to perform some tasks such as sorting, grouping, and filtering the models in a very easy way. We can also pull data from our server using one of the available proxies and a reader to interpret the server response and fill the collection.

A store is usually added to the widgets to display data. Components such as the grid, tree, combobox, or data view use a store to manage the data. We will learn about these components in future chapters. If we create a custom widget, we should use a store to manage the data too. This is why this chapter is really important, we use models and stores to deal with the data.

In order to create a store we need to use the `Ext.data.Store` class. The following example will use the `Invoice` model that we already have and will extend the store to create a collection of invoices:

```
Ext.define('MyApp.store.Invoices',{
extend  : 'Ext.data.Store',     //Step 1
model   : 'MyApp.model.Invoice'  //Step 2
});
```

The steps are explained as follows:

- **Step 1**: To define a store we need to extend from the `Ext.data.Store` class. This class is responsible for dealing with the models.

- **Step 2**: We associated the model that our store will be using. It is required to specify a valid `model` class; in this case we're using our `Invoice` class that we have been working on in our previous examples.

Once we have our store class defined we are going to create an HTML page to run our test, let's import the Ext library, our `Invoice` model, and our `Invoices` store.

```
var store = Ext.create("MyApp.store.Invoices");

//counting the elements in the store
console.log(store.count());
```

We can use the `create` method to instantiate our `store` class, in this example we don't need to pass any parameter, but we could do it as any other class.

If we would like to know the number of items that are contained in our store, we can use the `count` method. In this case we're printing the number returned on the JavaScript console, which will be zero because our store is empty at this moment.

Adding new elements

Adding elements to the collection is very simple, we need to create an `Invoice` model with data and we will use the `add` or `insert` methods to add the new item to our store as shown in the following code:

```
var invoice = Ext.create("MyApp.model.Invoice",{   //Step 1
    taxId   : "32FG83",
    name    : "John Doe",
    address : "123 ST, TN USA",
    creditCard  : "1234567890123456"

});

store.add(invoice); //Step 2

console.log(store.count());
```

The steps are explained as follows:

- **Step 1**: We created the model that we want to add to our store, we are also setting values to some of the fields.
- **Step 2**: We executed the `add` method to append our model to the collection. It's important to know that using the `add` method will always insert the model in the last position of the collection.

Finally, we count our items again and we will see a number **1** in our JavaScript console.

We can also add a new item by just sending an object containing the data and the `add` method will create the `model` instance for us.

```
store.add({
  taxId  : "NT629Y",
  name   : "Susan Smith",
  address  : "312 ST, CA USA",
  creditCard  : "1234567890123456"

});

console.log(store.count());
```

When running the previous code we will see a number **2** in the JavaScript console. We can even add many items at once by passing an array of models to the `add` method as shown in the following code:

```
var model1 = Ext.create("MyApp.model.Invoice",{
  taxId  : "3E72KO",
  name   : "Carl Jr",
  address  : "789 ST, TX USA",
  creditCard  : "1234567890123456"

});
var model2 = Ext.create("MyApp.model.Invoice",{
  taxId  : "897HG56",
  name   : "Hazel Doe",
  address  : "987 ST, CA USA",
  creditCard  : "1234567890123456"

});

store.add([model1,model2]);

console.log(store.count());
```

We have added two models in the same method call, but we can pass whatever models we need in the array.

If we see the console, there will be a number **4** printed because we have four elements in our collection. As mentioned before if we use the `add` method, the new element will be placed in the last position of the collection, but what if we want to add the new element to the first position or maybe somewhere else? We can use the `insert` method to add the new element wherever we need.

The following example shows how to add a new item to the first position of the collection:

```
store.insert(0,{
    taxId   :"L125AP",
    name    : "John Smith",
    address   : "159 ST, TX USA",
    creditCard   : "1234567890123456"
});


console.log(store.count());
```

The `insert` method accepts two parameters. The first parameter should be the position where we want to add the new element. In this case we are using 0 because we want the new record to be inserted in the first position, but we can use any position we want. The second parameter should be an object containing the data for our model; it could also be a model or even an array of objects.

Looping through the elements

So far we know how to retrieve the number of elements in the existing store, but we're not sure if the `insert` method added the new record in the first position. We can iterate through the elements of the store by using the `each` method as follows:

```
store.each(function(record,index){
    console.log(index,record.get("name"));
});
```

The `each` method receives a function as the first parameter. This function will be executed for every record of the store; the anonymous function receives two parameters for our convenience, the `record` and `index` parameters of each iteration.

We can also set the scope where the anonymous function will be executed by passing a second parameter to the `each` method with the object where the anonymous function will be executed.

In our previous example we only printed the `index` and `name` properties in our model, but we can access any property or method defined in our `Invoice` class.

Retrieving the records

Once we have content in our store we can retrieve objects or perform a search of the collection of models. There are several ways of retrieving models. We are going to look at the most common ways.

If we only want to get a model at a specific position, we can use the `getAt` method as follows:

```
var model3 = store.getAt(2);

console.log(model3.get("name"));
```

In our previous example we get the model that is in the third position of the collection. The first position in the store uses the index 0, so if we want to get the third element we use the index 2. In our example the name printed should be **Susan Smith**.

There are also methods to retrieve the first element of the collection and the last element; for this we can execute the `first` and `last` methods as shown in the following code:

```
var first = store.first(),
    last = store.last();

console.log(first.get("name"),last.get("name"));
```

Our previous code will print the name of the first and last element in our store; in this case we will see the name of **John Smith** and **Hazel Doe**.

There are times when we need to get many records at once, so there's a method called `getRange` to retrieve a list of records. We may define the limits or we can even get all the records in the collection as shown in the following code snippet:

```
var list = store.getRange(1,3);

Ext.each(list,function(record,index){
    console.log(index,record.get("name"));
});
```

In the previous code we are retrieving records from the index number 1 to the index number 3. We are going to see three elements in our JavaScript console.

We have been adding records to the store, but we didn't assign an ID for any of the models we have in our store. If we don't assign an ID, the model will be marked as **phantom**, this means that the model is a new record and it's not present in our database.

We can get all the new records in order to send them to the server and save them as shown in the following code:

```
var newelements = store.getNewRecords();

Ext.each(newelements,function(record,index){
    console.log(record.getId(),record.get("name"));
});
```

Using the `getNewRecords` method we can get an array containing all the new records that don't exist in our database. This method looks for every record that's a phantom and contains valid data.

 It's important to see that even if the model is marked as phantom, but if it doesn't pass the validations then it will not be returned in the collection of new records.

We can also get the modified records. Let's add a new model to the store containing the ID property so it won't get marked as phantom, and then let's modify the content of one of their fields as shown in the following code:

```
//Step 1
store.add({
   idInvoice   : 672,
   taxId       : "VI8732",
   name        : "Eddy Smith",
   address     : "961 ST, NY USA",
   creditCard  : "1234567890123456"
});

//Step 2
var model4 = store.last();
model4.set("name","EddyMcFly");


var updated = store.getUpdatedRecords(); //Step 3
Ext.each(updated,function(record,index){
   console.log(record.getId(),record.get("name"));
});
```

The steps are explained as follows:

- **Step 1**: We added a new record with the `idInvoice` property, this way the record is not marked as phantom.

- **Step 2**: We got the last record in our store and modified the name of our model. When we modify the original information the record is marked as **dirty**.

- **Step 3**: We called the `getUpdatedRecords` method to get all the records marked as dirty. In this case we only have one record updated, but the method returns an array with all modified records.

Removing records

We have been adding and accessing records in our store, but if we would like to remove records from the store, we have three ways of doing this task.

```
store.remove(model1);
store.each(function(record,index){
  console.log(index,record.get("name"));
});
```

We executed the `remove` method and passed the model from where we want to delete the record. In our previous code we are passing the `model` variable that we created before. If we look at the JavaScript console, we will see that the **Carl Jr** record does not exist anymore.

We can also remove many records at once. We only need to pass an array of models to the `remove` method and those models will be removed from the store, as shown in the following code:

```
store.remove([first,last]);
store.each(function(record,index){
  console.log(record.get("name"));
});
```

When we execute the code we will see that the **John Smith** and **Hazel Doe** records are gone, we should not see those names in the JavaScript console.

There are times when we may not have the reference to the model that we want to delete. In those cases we can remove a record by its position in the store, as shown in the following code:

```
store.removeAt(2);
store.each(function(record,index){
  console.log(index,record.get("name"));
});
```

The `removeAt` method accepts an index; the record located at this position will be removed. Now we can only see two names in the JavaScript console.

If we want to remove all the records in our store, we only need to call the `removeAll` method and the store will be cleared.

```
store.removeAll();
console.log("Records:",store.count());
```

At this moment our store is empty. If we execute the `count` method, we will get zero as a result. Now we know how to add, retrieve, and remove records from our store.

Retrieving remote data

So far we have been working with local data and hard-coding our information to create a store of records. But in real world applications we have our data in a database or maybe we get the information using web services.

Ext JS uses proxies to send and retrieve the data to the source. We can use one of the available proxies to configure our store or model.

A proxy uses a reader to decode the received data and a writer to encode the data to the correct format and send it to the source. We have three available readers to encode and decode our data: the Array, JSON, and XML readers. But we have only two writers available, only for JSON and XML.

There are seven types of proxies at our disposal. If we want to change our source of data, we should only change the type of proxy and everything should be fine. For example, we may define an Ajax proxy for our store or model and then we can change it for a local storage proxy.

Ajax proxy

In order to use this proxy we need to set up a web server to make the Ajax requests correctly. If we don't have a web server to test our code, we can use the WAMP server. If we are in Windows (http://www.wampserver.com/), WAMP installs an Apache 2 web server, a MySQL database, and PHP. If we are on Mac, we can enable the **Web Sharing** service in the **System Preferences** section or we can also install XAMP (http://www.apachefriends.org/es/xampp.html). Using a web server is required so we can make Ajax request correctly.

When we have everything ready, we can modify our previous example, where we created the `Invoices` class to add the required proxy.

```
Ext.define('MyApp.store.Invoices',{
extend  : 'Ext.data.Store',
model   : 'MyApp.model.Invoice',

proxy  : {
    type    : 'ajax',
    url     : 'serverside/data.json'
    }
});
```

The previous code adds a new property to the store called `proxy`. We are setting a configuration object containing only two properties.

The `type` property defines the type of proxy that we're going to use. In this case we specified `ajax`, but we can use any of the available proxies. We can find a list of proxies at `http://docs.sencha.com/ext-js/4-1/#!/api/Ext.data.proxy.Proxy`.

The `url` property defines the resource that we will request using Ajax. It's important to mention that the URL must be in the same domain so we won't get any errors when making the Ajax request.

At this point we can load the data from our web server using Ajax. In order to test our code let's create an HTML file importing the Ext library, our model, and our store.

```
var store = Ext.create("MyApp.store.Invoices");   //Step 1

store.load(function(){ //Step 2

store.each(function(record){   //Step 3
console.log(record.get("name"));
        });

});
```

The steps are explained as follows:

- **Step 1**: We create the store as usual and save the reference in a variable.
- **Step 2**: We execute the `load` method. This method internally executes the read operation, makes the Ajax call to the server, and then loads the data into the store. The function that we give to the `load` method as a parameter is a callback that will be executed after the records are loaded into the store. We are doing it in this way because Ajax is asynchronous and we don't know for sure when the server is going to respond.
- **Step 3**: The last step iterates through the records of the store and prints the name for each invoice in the JavaScript console.

Before we execute our example we should create the `serverside/invoices.json` file. We're going to use JSON to encode the data as follows:

```
{
  "success"  : true,
  "data"     : [{
    "idInvoice"  : 1,
    "taxId"     : "12345",
    "date"      : "2012-05-13 15:25:32",
    "name"      : "Software & Design Solutions Inc",
```

```
        "address"   : "123th ST, St. Luis Mo."
    },{
        "idInvoice"   : 2,
        "taxId"       : "43221",
        "date"        : "2012-05-13 15:25:32",
        "name"        : "Text and Code Inc",
        "address"   : "123th ST, San Antonio TX."
    },{
        "idInvoice"   : 3,
        "taxId"       : "432743",
        "date"        : "2012-05-13 15:25:32",
        "name"        : "Developers Rlz Inc",
        "address"   : "123th ST, San Francisco CA."
    }]
}
```

We have an object that contains an array of objects that holds our information, each object contains the same properties as that of our `Invoice` model.

Now if we execute the test, we won't see anything in the console, just an empty space. If we execute the `count` method in our store, we will see that it only contains one element, but it should contain three instead.

This is happening because the proxy is missing a reader. When configuring a reader we define the type of data that the proxy will receive and a few other things in order to interpret correctly the sever response.

JSON reader

JSON is the most popular format in the Ext community to send and receive data from the server. We can configure our reader so we will be able to understand the response and to fill the store with models containing the correct information.

Let's modify our `Invoices` store to add the JSON reader to the proxy.

```
Ext.define('MyApp.store.Invoices',{
extend   : 'Ext.data.Store',
model    : 'MyApp.model.Invoice',

proxy    : {
    type   : 'ajax',
    url    : 'serverside/invoices.json',
    reader   : {
      type   : 'json',
      root   : 'data'
    }
  }
});
```

We are defining a new property called reader, which accepts an object configuration; we can also pass an instance of the Ext.data.reader.Json class.

The configuration object requires at least two properties. There are a few other configurations we can set, but these two are required in order to work properly.

The type property defines how our information is decoded. In this case we are assigning the json type to the property, but we can also use the xml type if needed.

The root property allows us to define the name of the property in the server response, where all objects containing the information for our models are located. This property should be an array in our JSON response. In this case we set data because our JSON response uses that name, but it could be anything. If we have nested objects, we can use a dot (.) to go as deep as we need, for example, let's suppose we get the following response:

```
{
   "success"  : true,
   "total"    : 300,
   "output"    : {
     "data"  : [{

       //... our data

     }]
   }
}
```

The previous response contains the array of information inside of an object output; we need to configure our reader so it should be able to read this response correctly. We need to change the root property as follows:

```
Ext.define('MyApp.store.Invoices',{
extend  : 'Ext.data.Store',
model   : 'MyApp.model.Invoice',

proxy   : {
    type  : 'ajax',
    url     : 'serverside/invoices.json',
    reader  : {
      type  : 'json',
      root  : 'output.data'
    }
    }
});
```

We have only modified the root property using a dot to get one level deeper. We can go as deep as we need. It doesn't matter how many levels we have to go, but we need to make sure that we are setting correctly this configuration, pointing to the array of data, where our models will be filled.

Let's test our code again by refreshing the browser, now we'll see the three names in our JavaScript console as shown in the following screenshot:

XML reader

If we would like to use XML instead of JSON, we should only change the type or the reader to our proxy. We can set an instance of the Ext.data.reader.Xml class or set the right type to our configuration object as follows:

```
proxy   : {
  type    : 'ajax',
  url    : 'serverside/invoices.xml',
  reader: {
    type   : 'xml',
    root   : 'data',
    record: 'invoice'
  }
}
```

We have only changed the url property to our reader to point to an XML file that contains our information instead of the JSON file. We also change the type property to xml. This way our reader will be able to read the server response correctly. Lastly, we added a new property to our reader called record. This property allows us to define the tag where the information will be in the XML response, in this case we use invoice.

Now let's create the XML file that holds our information. This file should be called serverside/invoices.xml and will contain the following code:

```
<?xml version="1.0" encoding="UTF-8"?>
<data success="true">
  <invoice>
```

```
      <idInvoice>1</idInvoice>
      <taxId>12345</taxId>
      <dateIssued>2012-05-13 15:25:32</dateIssued>
      <name><![CDATA[Software & Design Solutions Inc]]></name>
      <address>123th ST, St. Luis Mo.</address>
    </invoice>
    <invoice>
      <idInvoice>2</idInvoice>
      <taxId>43221</taxId>
      <dateIssued>2012-05-13 15:25:32</dateIssued>
      <name><![CDATA[Text and Code Inc]]></name>
      <address>123th ST, San Antonio TX</address>
    </invoice>
    <invoice>
      <idInvoice>3</idInvoice>
      <taxId>432743</taxId>
      <dateIssued>2012-05-13 15:25:32</dateIssued>
      <name><![CDATA[Developers Rlz Inc]]></name>
      <address>123th ST, San Francisco CA</address>
    </invoice>
  </data>
```

First we have defined the root node that contains the invoices information. This root node is called `data`. If we change the name of this node, we should also change the `root` property in our reader to match this node.

The `invoice` node contains the data for our models. We have defined a new `record` property in our reader configuration to set the name of the node, where the information should be in our XML response.

Now let's test our changes by refreshing our browser. If everything goes fine, we will see three names in our JavaScript console as shown in the following screenshot:

The result is exactly the same when we use the JSON reader, however if we go to the **Network** tab in the developers tools, we can see that in this case the server is responding with XML:

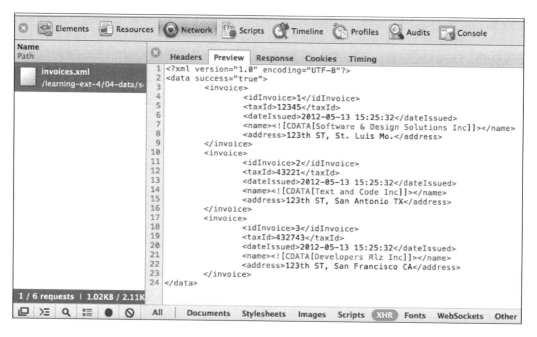

By using readers we can switch easily from using JSON or XML as our source of data. We don't have to change anything else in our code, just configure each reader correctly.

Mappings

If we look at the XML response again, we will notice that in each `invoice` node we have all the information for our models. In this case the name of each tag matches the name of the properties in our models. This is why the data gets into the right field, however, if for some reason the names of the tags in this XML file don't match the name of the fields in our model, we can configure our model to map each field with the right node.

Let's change the XML response with different names in the tags that contain the final information.

```
<?xml version="1.0" encoding="UTF-8"?>
<data success="true">
  <invoice id="1">
    <taxId>12345</taxId>
    <date>2012-05-13 15:25:32</date>
```

```
    <client><![CDATA[Software & Design Solutions Inc]]></client>
    <addr>123th ST, St. Luis Mo.</addr>
  </invoice>
  <invoice id="2">
    <taxId>43221</taxId>
    <date>2012-05-13 15:25:32</date>
    <client><![CDATA[Text and Code Inc]]></client>
    <addr>123th ST, San Antonio TX</addr>
  </invoice>
  <invoice id="3">
    <taxId>432743</taxId>
    <date>2012-05-13 15:25:32</date>
    <client><![CDATA[Developers Rlz Inc]]></client>
    <addr>123th ST, San Francisco CA</addr>
  </invoice>
</data>
```

Now, if we execute our previous example again, we should see three blank spaces in our JavaScript console. This is because the name of the fields in our model don't match with the nodes in our XML file.

In order to fix the problem we can add a new configuration to our field's definition in our model. Let's go back to our `Invoice` class and add the `mapping` property to each field as follows:

```
Ext.define('MyApp.model.Invoice',{
extend  : 'Ext.data.Model',

idProperty  : 'idInvoice',
fields  : [
    {name:'idInvoice',mapping:'@id'},
    {name:'taxId'},
    {name:'dateIssued',type:'date',dateFormat:'Y-m-d
h:i:s',mapping:'date'},
    {name:'name',mapping:'client'},
    {name:'address',type:'string',mapping:'addr'},
    {name:'creditCard'}
    ],

    //...

});
```

The mapping property allows us to define from where each field will be filled. By default it searches for a node with the same name as the property, but if we defined a `mapping` property, the reader will look for what we defined in here.

The previous code shows how we use the `mapping` property. In this case we set the `idInvoice` property to take its value from `@id`. This means that the reader will not look for a tag or node in our XML, it will look for the attribute `id` in the invoice node to take its value.

The `dateIssued` property will take its value from the `date` node. The `name` field will get its value from the `client` node and finally the `address` field will be filled from the `addr` node.

If we refresh our browser again, we will see the three names in our JavaScript console displayed correctly, this is because we set the correct mapping to each field:

The mapping property works exactly the same in the JSON reader. By default the reader looks for a property in our response with the same name as the field, but if we define a `mapping` property in our field definition then the reader will use this property instead to fill the field.

Sending data

Once we have added, modified, or even deleted our original data we should send our changes to our server. The Ext allows us to do that by using a writer to encode our data to the right format. We have two types of writers available, for JSON and XML format.

Let's modify our `store` class and define a JSON writer to our proxy:

```
Ext.define('MyApp.store.Invoices',{
extend  : 'Ext.data.Store',
model   : 'MyApp.model.Invoice',

    //Ajax proxy with JSON reader and writer
proxy   : {
    type : 'ajax',
    url     : 'serverside/invoices.json',
    reader  : {
      type : 'json',
```

```
    root    : 'data'
  },
  writer  : {
    type    : 'json',
    allowSingle  : false
  }
  }
});
```

By setting a `writer` property we can define the type of format to encode our data. In this case we are setting `json` in the `type` property. Also we have defined the `allowSingle` property to `false`. This means that even if we modify only one model, it will be sent wrapped in an array. This way we will always receive an array of elements in our server containing our information.

Now let's create an HTML file to test our changes. Import the Ext library, our model, and our store class too, then we add the following code:

```
var store = Ext.create("MyApp.store.Invoices");

store.load({
callback    : function(){
var model1 = Ext.create("MyApp.model.Invoice",{
taxId   : "3E72KO",
name    : "Carl Jr",
address : "789 ST, TX USA",
creditCard  : "1234567890123456"
        });
var model2 = Ext.create("MyApp.model.Invoice",{
taxId   : "897HG56",
name    : "Hazel Doe",
address : "987 ST, CA USA",
creditCard  : "1234567890123456"
        });
store.add([model1,model2]);

store.removeAt(0);

store.sync();
    }
});
```

First we create an instance of our `Invoices` class and save the reference in the `store` variable.

Then we perform a `load` call to make an Ajax request to the server and fill the store with the initial information.

After the server responds and the store is filled with the initial information, we create two new instances of our `Invoice` model and add them to the store. We also remove the record that is in the position zero.

Once we have modified our data we should synchronize our changes with the server. We do this by calling the `sync` method in our store. Executing this method will create two Ajax calls to our server. The first one to add the new records and the second one to send the information to delete just one record. If we look at the **Network** tab in the Chrome Developer Tools, we will see the two calls that are being made:

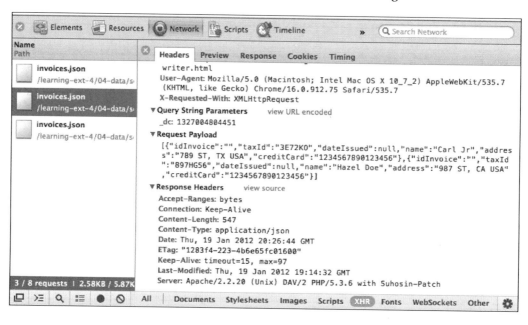

We will also notice that all the requests are being made to the same URL. At this point we don't have a way to differentiate if the records sent are going to be deleted or added.

In order to fix this we need to send each request to a different URL so the server can perform the right task with our data. Let's modify our `store` class to set the right URL for each action:

```
Ext.define('MyApp.store.Invoices',{
extend  : 'Ext.data.Store',
model   : 'MyApp.model.Invoice',

    //Ajax proxy with JSON reader and writer
```

```
proxy   : {
    type   : 'ajax',
    //url     : 'serverside/invoices.json',
    api     : {
      create  : 'serverside/save',
      read    : 'serverside/invoices.json',
      update  : 'serverside/update',
      destroy  : 'serverside/remove'
    },
    reader  : {
      type  : 'json',
      root  : 'data'
    },
    writer      : {
      type  : 'json',
      allowSingle  : false
    }
    }
});
```

Using the `api` property in our proxy we can set a different URL for each CRUD operation. This property accepts four operations to create, read, update, and delete. We can set different URLs for each operation.

Before we test our example again we need to create the files we defined in the `api` property, otherwise we'll get a 404 error and the synchronization process will fail. Once we have our files in place let's refresh our browser and see the request in the **Network** tab as shown in the following screenshot:

Name Path	Method	Status Text	Type	Initiator	Size Content	Time Latency	Tim
invoices.json /learning-ext-4/04-data/serverside	GET	200 OK	applicatio...	ext-all-dev.js:27958 Script	879B 547B	2ms 2ms	
save /learning-ext-4/04-data/serverside	POST	200 OK	text/plain	ext-all-dev.js:27958 Script	371B 47B	1ms 1ms	
remove /learning-ext-4/04-data/serverside	POST	200 OK	text/plain	ext-all-dev.js:27958 Script	373B 49B	2ms 2ms	

Now we can see how the proxy is calling the right URL in the server to perform the right operation. If we inspect the request, we will see the parameters that are sent. All we need to do in our server is to take those parameters and perform the required task.

Summary

In this chapter we have been working with data, we learned how to create models with fields, mappings, validations, and relationships. We also worked with a collection of models using the `store` class, pulling, and sending data to the server using proxies, readers, and writers.

It's important to mention that every widget in Ext JS that displays data uses a store and models to manage all the data. When we modify a model in our store, the widget will automatically refresh its view. For example, if we have a grid and we want to delete a record, we only use the `remove` method from the store. By doing this the grid automatically will update the rows and the deleted row won't appear anymore.

In the next chapter we are going to learn about events and how we can respond to the user interaction. So far we haven't used events, but events are one of the most important parts of the JavaScript development world.

5
Buttons and Toolbars

When dealing with buttons we will definitely need a way to arrange them whether we use them in a window or panel. Using a toolbar is a great way to add our buttons to the top or bottom of our panel; we can also use groups or menus. The Ext provides us with a lot of flexibility to create beautiful interfaces.

Once we have our UI ready we can add actions to our widgets using callbacks and events to process the user interaction. In this chapter we are going to learn about the observable pattern used by the Ext components and widgets. We'll also learn how to define buttons and handlers to execute actions when the user clicks on them.

We need to understand how events are defined in Ext JS so we can take advantage of them when creating custom components.

Event driven development

Before we start talking about the components we need to understand how the events and listeners work behind the scenes. The first thing we need to learn is the observable pattern.

Basically the observable pattern is designed to allow entities or objects to communicate between each other using events. When a certain action occurs inside an object or component, this object should broadcast an event to whoever is listening.

For example, when a button is clicked, the button fires the `click` event, when a row of a grid is clicked the grid fires the `itemclick` event. All components have defined events that are fired when an action occurs.

The component that is firing the event doesn't know who will listen to its messages, but its responsibility is to let the others know that something happened and maybe other components will do something about it or nothing at all.

The `Ext.util.Observable` base class allows us to add, fire, and listen to events from a specific object or component and do actions when that event is executed. All widgets included in the Ext JS library extend from the `Ext.util.Observable` class, (as a mixing) and they all fire events that we can listen to perform actions and bring our widgets to life.

As mentioned before we can define and fire new events on our custom components using the same `Ext.util.Observable` class.

Let's create an HTML page and import the Ext JS library, then let's create another JS file to define a new class; we're going to name this class as `Employee`.

```
Ext.define('MyApp.users.Employee',{
extend       : 'Ext.util.Observable',
attempts   : 0
});
```

The previous code shows how we can add support for custom events to our classes. In this example we are extending from the `Ext.util.Observable` class, but we can add this class as a mixin too.

Once we have the support for events in our classes, we can define new events using the `addEvents` method as follows:

```
Ext.define('MyApp.users.Employee',{
extend       : 'Ext.util.Observable',
attempts: 0,

constructor: function(){

        this.addEvents('success','fail');

this.callParent();
    }
});
```

We are defining a `constructor` method and inside of this method we define two new events. In this case we are defining the `success` and `fail` events, but we can define as much as we need.

The `callParent` method is important because it calls the constructor of the superclass. Every time we overwrite a method on the subclass we should call the original method on the superclass.

We are going to create a fake login method and fire the event according to the result of the validation.

```
Ext.define('MyApp.users.Employee',{
  //...

  login: function(usr,pwd){
  var me = this;

  Ext.Msg.wait('Please wait','Loading...',{
  interval: 300
  });
  //faking the server response
  setTimeout(function(){
  Ext.Msg.hide();
  me.attempts++;
  if(usr === 'john' &&pwd === '123'){
  me.fireEvent("success",me);
  }else{
  me.fireEvent("fail",me.attempts);
  }
  },3000);
      }
  });
```

In the previous code we are faking a login method. We first show a `wait` message, then a timeout will be executed three seconds later. Lastly, we fire the `success` or `fail` event depending on the `usr` and `pwd` parameters.

We use the `fireEvent` method to broadcast a message to all the listeners. Our `employee` class doesn't know who is listening for that event, but it just fires the event with the corresponding parameters.

 The previous code is just an example of a login for educational purposes only. We should never validate the username/password on the client side.

Now we are able to listen to the event from the outside. Let's create an HTML file, import the Ext library and our `employee` class, and then we'll create an instance of our `employee` class as follows:

```
<!DOCTYPE html>
<html>
<head>
<meta http-equiv="Content-Type" content="text/html; charset=utf-8">
<title>Observable pattern</title>

<!-- Importing the Ext JS library -->
<script type="text/javascript" src="../ext-4.1.1a-gpl/ext-all-dev.
js"></script>
<linkrel="stylesheet" href="../ext-4.1.1a-gpl/resources/css/ext-all.
css" />

<script type="text/javascript" src="js/MyApp/users/Employee.js"></
script>

<script type="text/javascript">
Ext.onReady(function(){

var employee = Ext.create("MyApp.users.Employee");

});
</script>
</head>
<body>
</body>
</html>
```

We're using the `onReady` method to execute our code when the DOM is ready to be used. Once everything is ready we can create our `employee` instance and then listen for the `success` or `fail` event using the `on` method as in the following code:

```
employee.on("success",function(user){
Ext.Msg.alert("Success","Welcome to our application");
});

employee.addListener("fail",function(attempts){
Ext.Msg.alert("Error","Wrong credentials! "+attempts+" attempts");
});
```

The on method is the shorthand version of the `addListener` method. We can use any of them to listen to events. These methods are defined in the `Observable` class that we are extending.

The first parameter is the event name that we want to listen to. In this case `success` and `fail`. The second parameter is the function that we want to execute when the event is fired. In this case we are using an anonymous function, but we can pass a reference to a function too such as the following example:

```
employee.on("success",callback);

functionclallback(user){
Ext.Msg.alert("Success","Welcome to our application");
}
```

In the previous code we are using only two parameters on the on method, but there are two more parameters that we can pass. The third parameter is the scope of the function that will be executed and the last parameter is an object with options (commonly known in Ext JS as a `config` object) such as delay, buffer, and many others.

At this point we have defined our events and listeners. Now is time to execute the `login` method and wait for the fake response.

```
Ext.onReady(function(){
var employee = Ext.create("MyApp.users.Employee");

employee.on("success",function(user){
Ext.Msg.alert("Success","Welcome to our application");
});

employee.addListener("fail",function(attempts){
Ext.Msg.alert("Error","Wrong credentials! "+attempts+" attempts");
});

employee.login('john','123');

});
```

In the previous code we are using wrong credentials. This means that the `fail` event will be fired; if we refresh our browser we'll see something like the following screenshot:

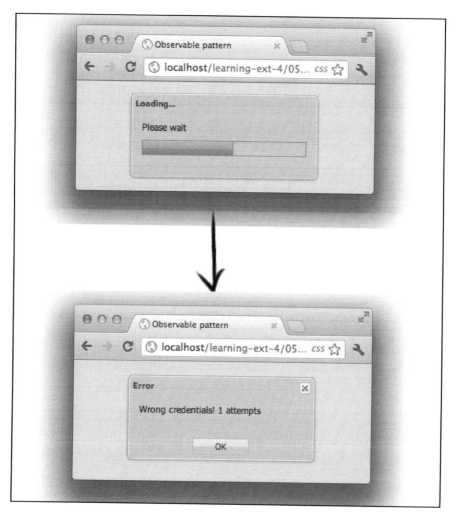

As we can see the `fail` event is executed. Now, if we execute our example with the right credentials then the `success` event will be fired and we'll see the welcome message.

Events are the way we can execute actions when something is happening; as we can see in the previous example the `Employee` class is responsible only for broadcasting the result of the validation. The class itself doesn't care about who may be listening, but on the outside an object is listening and reacts according to the messages received.

This is a very powerful feature in Ext JS, the ability to add, fire, and listen to custom events.

A simple button

Once we know how the `Ext.util.Observable` base class works and the methods that we can use, it's time to dig into the widgets. We're going to start with the buttons. In order to create a button we need to instantiate the `Ext.button.Button` class. This class manages all the ins and outs of a single button.

Let's create an HTML file and import the Ext library and instantiate the `Button` class as follows:

```html
<!DOCTYPE html>
<html>
<head>
<meta http-equiv="Content-Type" content="text/html; charset=utf-8">
<title>Button</title>

<!-- Importing the Ext JS library -->
<script type="text/javascript" src="../ext-4.1.1a-gpl/ext-all-dev.js"></script>
<linkrel="stylesheet" href="../ext-4.1.1a-gpl/resources/css/ext-all.css" />


<script type="text/javascript">
Ext.onReady(function(){

varbtn1 = Ext.create("Ext.button.Button",{
text: "Remove",
renderTo: Ext.getBody()
});

});
</script>
<style type="text/css">
body{padding:50px;}
</style>
</head>
<body>
</body>
</html>
```

In the previous example we are creating an instance as usual and passing an object with only two configurations. There are many more configurations, but for now these two are enough.

The text property allows us to define the text that will be shown when the button will be rendered on the DOM.

The renderTo property allows us to define the place where we want to render our button. In this case we are rendering the button on the body of the document, but we can also add the button to any other container using the ID of the DOM element.

If we refresh our browser, we'll see a button in the document's body as shown in the following screenshot:

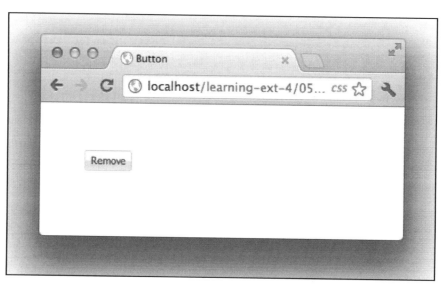

By default the button is small, but we can change the size to medium and large. There's a scale property that we can use to set the size of the button.

```
varbtn1 = Ext.create("Ext.button.Button",{
text: "Remove",
scale: 'small',
renderTo: Ext.getBody()
});

varbtn2 = Ext.create("Ext.button.Button",{
text: "Remove",
scale: 'medium',
renderTo: Ext.getBody()
});
```

```
varbtn3 = Ext.create("Ext.button.Button",{
text: "Remove",
scale: 'large',
renderTo: Ext.getBody()
});
```

The previous code creates three buttons using the three different sizes available. We can also set a custom size using the width and height properties. This is possible because the Button class extends from Component class:

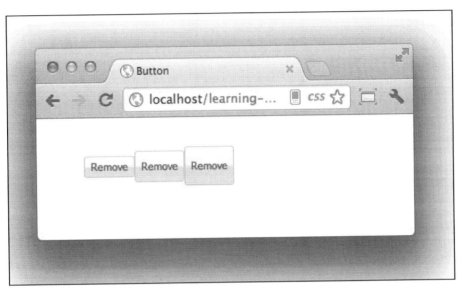

It's very common in any application to use icons to differentiate buttons. We can use the iconCls property to set a CSS class that adds an image as a background. For the small buttons we use a 16 x 16 icon, for the medium buttons we use a 24 x 24 icon, and for the large buttons we can use a 32 x 32 icon.

First we need to create the CSS class as follows:

```
.remove-icon16{
background:transparenturl('images/delete16.png') center 0 no-repeat
!important;
}
.remove-icon24{
background:transparenturl('images/delete24.png') center 0 no-repeat
!important;
}
.remove-icon32{
background:transparenturl('images/delete32.png') center 0 no-repeat
!important;
}
```

We have defined three CSS classes for each available size. Please note that you have to use your very own icons. The previous code assumes that we have a folder called `images` with three different images inside. In order to make our example work we need to include those images in that folder. Feel free to use your own images for this example.

Once we have our CSS in place we need to set one of them to each of our buttons.

```
varbtn1 = Ext.create("Ext.button.Button",{
text: "Remove",
//scale: 'small',// By default is small
iconCls: "remove-icon16",
renderTo: Ext.getBody()
});

varbtn2 = Ext.create("Ext.button.Button",{
text: "Remove",
iconCls: "remove-icon24",
scale: 'medium',
renderTo: Ext.getBody()
});

varbtn3 = Ext.create("Ext.button.Button",{
text: "Remove",
iconCls: "remove-icon32",
scale: 'large',
renderTo: Ext.getBody()
});
```

Using the `iconCls` property we can relate any CSS class to the button. If we refresh our browser we can see that each button has an icon as shown in the following screenshot:

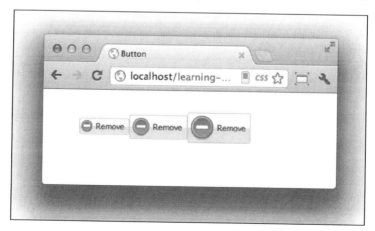

By default the icon is aligned to the left-hand side, but we can set the position to the top, bottom, and right-hand side too. We do this by using the `iconAlign` property.

```
varbtn1 = Ext.create("Ext.button.Button",{
text: "Remove",
scale: 'small',
iconCls: "remove-icon16",
iconAlign: 'top',
renderTo: Ext.getBody()
});

varbtn2 = Ext.create("Ext.button.Button",{
text: "Remove",
iconCls: "remove-icon24",
iconAlign: 'right',
scale: 'medium',
renderTo: Ext.getBody()
});

varbtn3 = Ext.create("Ext.button.Button",{
text: "Remove",
iconCls: "remove-icon32",
iconAlign: 'bottom',
scale: 'large',
renderTo: Ext.getBody()
});
```

The previous code sets the alignment of the icon. If we refresh our browser we can see how every button has the icon in a different position as shown in the following screenshot:

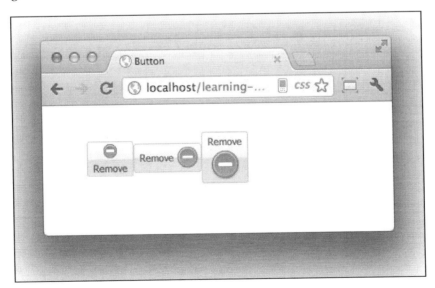

Once we have our buttons in place it is very likely that we want to add some actions when they are clicked. In the coming chapters we will see how to listen to events using the MVC pattern. For now we will listen to events directly on the buttons.

The `Button` class extends from the `Observable` class by using a mixin; therefore, we can listen to events using the `addListener` method.

Every component has many predefined events that we can use. If we go through the documentation, we can see all the available events with a description of when the event is fired and what parameters are received by the listeners (`http://docs.sencha.com/ext-js/4-1/#!/api/Ext.button.Button`). In this case the `Button` class contains the `click` event that is fired when the button is clicked by the user; we can listen to this event by using the `on` (a shorthand method for the `addListener` method) method.

```
btn1.on('click',function(){
Ext.Msg.confirm('Confirm','Are you sure you do this?');
});
```

In the previous code we used the `on` method to listen to the `click` event. When this event is fired, it will show a confirmation message. If we refresh our browser and click in the first button, we should see the message as follows:

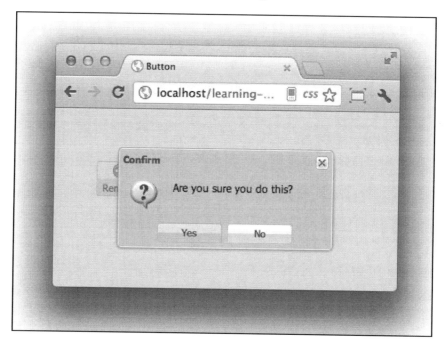

We can do whatever we want inside the callback function. In this case we are only showing a confirmation message, but we could also load a store to pull some data from our server. We could show a window component or create a panel with a form inside.

There are many more events that we can listen to, for example the show, hide, enable, disable, and many more events. We can define any number of listeners to the same event and when the event is fired all the listeners will be executed.

Adding menus

There are times when we need to create a menu to allow the user to choose from the available options. We can achieve this by setting the menu property of the buttons. This will create a floating menu for the selected button that will be shown when the user clicks the button.

Let's create a button that contains a menu of options. For the following example we need to create an HTML page, import the Ext JS library, and listen for the DOM ready event. Inside the callback we should write the following code that creates our button with three options:

```
varbtn1 = Ext.create("Ext.button.Button",{
text: 'Payment',
scale: 'large',
iconCls: 'card-icon32',
renderTo: Ext.getBody(),
menu: [{
text: 'Master Card'
},{
text: 'Visa'
},{
text: 'American Express'
}]
});
```

As we can see in the previous code the menu property receives an array of objects. This array will be used to create an instance of the Ext.menu.Menu class; this class is responsible for managing and displaying the floating menu.

It is also important to say that each object inside of the array uses the `menu` item as the default `xtype`. As a result we should see something like the following screenshot when opening our HTML file in our browser:

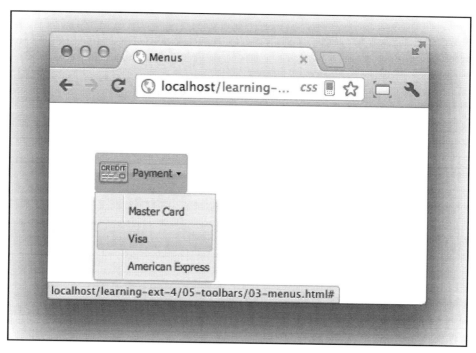

In the previous code we use literals to create our menu. If we want to use the constructors instead of the literals, we should create an instance of the `Ext.menu.Menu` and `Ext.menu.Item` classes as follows:

```
//Step 1
var menu = Ext.create('Ext.menu.Menu',{
items : [
//Step 2
Ext.create('Ext.menu.Item',{text:'Master card'}),
Ext.create('Ext.menu.Item',{text:'Visa'}),
Ext.create('Ext.menu.Item',{text:'American Express'})
]
});

varbtn2 = Ext.create("Ext.button.Button",{
text: 'Payment',
scale: 'large',
iconCls: 'card-icon32',
renderTo: Ext.getBody(),
menu: menu //Step 3
});
```

In step one, we create an instance of the Menu class and add three instances of the Item class in step two.

Once we have our menu created we add our instance to the menu property of the button. When the button is created, it detects that the menu property is not an array and it's an instance of the Menu class.

As a result we have two buttons with a menu containing the same options as shown in the following screenshot:

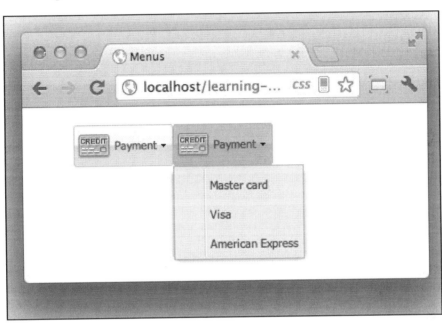

Adding a menu was really easy, now if we want to add some functionality to those options, we need to set a listener to each item in the menu. If we go to the documentation, we'll find out that the Ext.menu.Item class contains a click event. This is the event that we need to listen to perform some actions when it is fired.

So far we have used the on method to set a listener to our components, but in order to use this method we need to have a reference to the item in the menu. By using the constructor instead of the literals we can use a variable to hold our reference, but there are times when we don't have this reference and for these cases we can define our listeners in a literal way too.

```
varbtn1 = Ext.create("Ext.button.Button", {
text: 'Payment',
scale: 'large',
iconCls: 'card-icon32',
```

```
renderTo: Ext.getBody(),
menu: [{
text: 'Master Card',
listeners : {
click : function(){
document.location = 'http://google.com';
}
}
},{
text: 'Visa',
listeners : {
click : function(){
document.location = 'http://google.com';
}
}
},{
text: 'American Express',
listeners : {
click : function(){
document.location = 'http://google.com';
}
}
}]
});
```

By using the `listeners` property in each item we can set all the listeners we need for our new components. These listeners will be assigned just when the component is created.

In the previous code the `listeners` property receives an object. This object defines the event that we want to listen to, in this case the `click` event. Every event receives a function to be executed when the event is fired.

In this case all of the items will redirect the user to google.com when clicked, but in here we can do anything we need inside the callback functions.

We can also add a second level menu. We only need to define the `menu` property in one of the items in our original menu; this will create a second menu inside the given option.

```
varbtn1 = Ext.create("Ext.button.Button",{
text: 'Payment',
scale: 'large',
iconCls: 'card-icon32',
renderTo: Ext.getBody(),
menu: [{
text: 'Master Card',
```

```
menu: [{
text: 'Submenu 1'
},{
text      : 'Submenu 2'
}],
listeners : {
click : function(){
document.location = 'http://google.com';
}
}
},
.

.

.
});
```

We can add as many levels of submenus as we need, however I wouldn't recommend cascading your menus too deeply because the user experience will be affected:

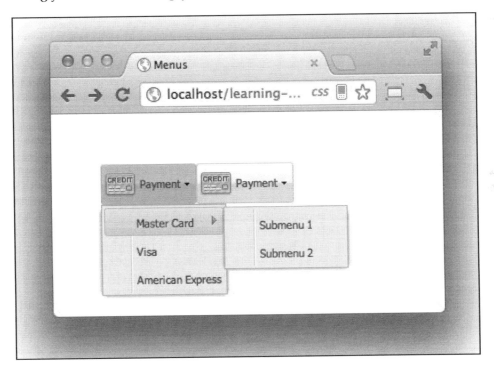

Toolbars

Now we know how to create buttons and menus, so let's keep moving to the next component in our journey of learning Ext JS. It is very common in applications to have many buttons in the same module. In these cases the toolbar component is very handy because we can arrange our buttons the way we need. We can also set the position of our toolbar inside of a panel, window, or any other component that extends from the panel.

In Ext 4 the toolbar component has been redesigned completely. Now it's possible to define a toolbar in any of the four sides of our containers. We can also add more than one toolbar to each side.

Let's start by creating a simple toolbar in the top of a panel. First we need to create an HTML file, import the Ext library, and in the DOM ready callback we're going to write the following code:

```
<!DOCTYPE html>
<html>
<head>
<meta http-equiv="Content-Type" content="text/html; charset=utf-8">
<title>Toolbar</title>

<!-- Importing the Ext JS library -->
<script type="text/javascript" src="../ext-4.1.1a-gpl/ext-all-dev.
js"></script>
<linkrel="stylesheet" href="../ext-4.1.1a-gpl/resources/css/ext-all.
css" />


<script type="text/javascript">
Ext.onReady(function(){

Ext.create('Ext.panel.Panel',{
title: 'My first toolbar',
width: 300,
height: 200,
dockedItems : [{ //Step 1
xtype : 'toolbar',
docked: 'top', //Step 2
items : [{text:'Save'}]
}],
renderTo: Ext.getBody()
});

});
</script>
```

```
<style type="text/css">
body{padding:50px;}
</style>
</head>
<body>
</body>
</html>
```

Using the `dockedItems` property we can define an array of components. Any component can be placed on any of the four sides of the panel. In this case we are using a toolbar and as shown in step two we used the `docked` property to set the side of where we would like to place our toolbar. We can also set the component to the `left`, `right`, and `bottom`. By default it is placed to the `top`.

We usually define toolbars as docked items, but in fact we can define a grid, form, or any other component:

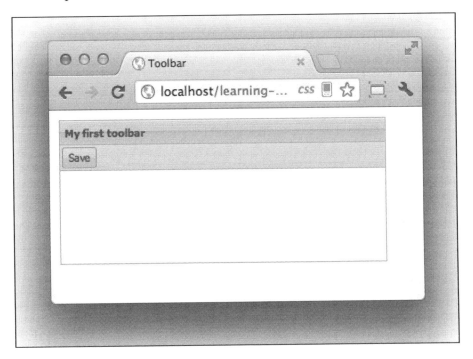

One more thing to highlight from the previous code is that by default the components on the `items` array of the toolbar are `buttons`. That's why we didn't set explicitly an `xtype`. We can also add any other component to the toolbar, such as a `textfield`, `combo`, and `radiobuttons`.

Let's add a few more buttons with beautiful icons as shown in the following code:

```
Ext.create('Ext.panel.Panel',{
.

.

.

dockedItems : [{
xtype : 'toolbar',
docked: 'top',
items : [
{text:'New',iconCls:'new-icon16'},
{text:'Save',iconCls:'save-icon16'},
{text:'Remove',iconCls:'remove-icon16'},
{text:'Export',iconCls:'export-icon16'},
{text:'Print',iconCls:'print-icon16'}
]
}],
.

.

.

});
```

Once we have our buttons configured correctly we need to create the CSS classes that will set an image as a background. Let's add the following code to our HTML document inside of a `style` tag:

```
<style type="text/css">
.new-icon16{
background:transparenturl(images/page_add.png) center 0 no-repeat
!important;
}
.save-icon16{
background:transparenturl(images/disk16.png) center 0 no-repeat
!important;
}
.remove-icon16{
background:transparenturl(images/delete16.png) center 0 no-repeat
!important;
}
.export-icon16{
background:transparenturl(images/page_go.png) center 0 no-repeat
!important;
}
.print-icon16{
background:transparenturl(images/printer.png) center 0 no-repeat
!important;
}
</style>
```

Again, you need to find your own images and set the correct path to each CSS rule:

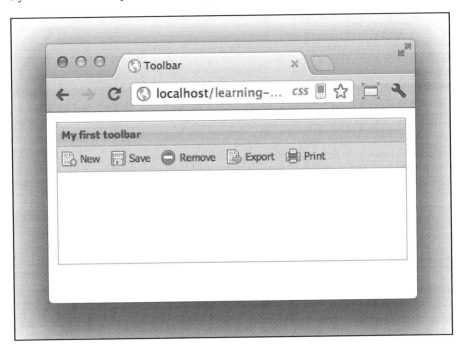

The previous screenshot shows the new buttons with an icon. By default the icons are horizontally aligned, but we can arrange them in groups. For example, we can create a group for the new, save, and remove buttons and another group for the export and print buttons.

```
Ext.create('Ext.panel.Panel',{
    .
      .
        .
dockedItems : [{
xtype : 'toolbar',
docked: 'top',
items : [{
xtype : 'buttongroup',
title : 'Actions',
items : [
{text:'New',iconCls:'new-icon16'},
{text:'Save',iconCls:'save-icon16'},
{text:'Remove',iconCls:'remove-icon16'}
]
},{
```

```
xtype : 'buttongroup',
title : 'Print & Export',
items : [
{text:'Export',iconCls:'export-icon16'},
{text:'Print',iconCls:'print-icon16'}
]
}
]
}],
renderTo: Ext.getBody()
});
```

Instead of adding the buttons directly to the toolbar, we added two `buttongroup` components; using a group of buttons we can define a title and the buttons that will be in each group. The following screenshot shows the result of the previous code:

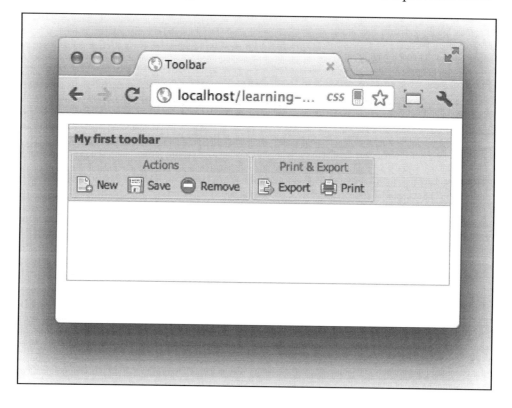

It's important to mention that the xtype `buttongroup` represents the
`Ext.container.ButtonGroup` class. If we take a look in the documentation
(`http://docs.sencha.com/ext-js/4-1/#!/api/Ext.container.ButtonGroup`)
for this class, we can see that we can set columns of buttons.

```
Ext.create('Ext.panel.Panel',{
  .
    .
      .
dockedItems : [{
      .
        .
items : [{
xtype : 'buttongroup',
title : 'Actions',
columns: 2,
items : [
{text:'New',iconCls:'new-icon32',scale:'large',rowspan:2,iconAlign:'t
op',width:50},
{text:'Save',iconCls:'save-icon16'},
{text:'Remove',iconCls:'remove-icon16'}
]
},{
xtype : 'buttongroup',
title : 'Print & Export',
defaults:{iconAlign:'top',scale:'large',width:50},
items : [
{text:'Export',iconCls:'export-icon32'},
{text:'Print',iconCls:'print-icon32'}
]
}
]
}],
renderTo: Ext.getBody()
});
```

In the previous code we have set the `columns` property to 2. This means that all the
buttons that we create should be rendered in only two columns. One important thing
to observe closely is the `rowspan` property from the `save` button. This property is set
to 2, which means that the `save` button will use two rows. We have also modified the
size of the button to `large` and we have updated the icon with a 32 x 32 image.

```
.new-icon32{
background:transparenturl(images/page_add32.png) center 0 no-repeat
!important;
}
```

With these few changes in place we'll have a better layout and organized buttons, giving the final user interface a very elegant look and feel as shown in the following screenshot:

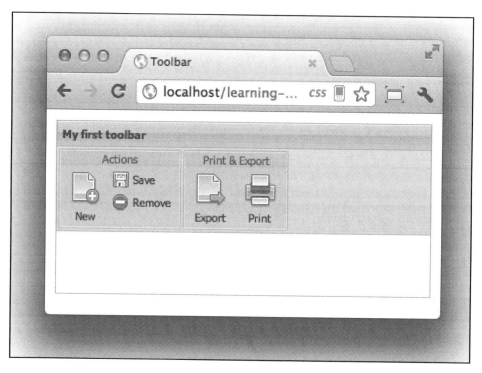

We can use as many columns as we want and as we did in our previous example we can mix button sizes too.

The main menu for our application

At this point we are in a position to create the main menu for our final application. If you remember in *Chapter 1*, *The Basics*, we defined several wireframes for our final application. We haven't worked so much in this application yet, mainly because we have been learning the basics about the Ext framework, but from now on we can focus more on our final product.

The following screenshot shows how we need to do the main menu for our invoice management application:

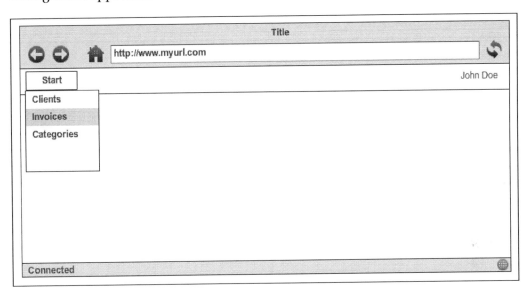

As we can see from the screenshot, we need to create a toolbar docked to the top, then we need to add a button with a menu, we already know how to achieve this. However, we need a component to take all the available space in the browser. So far we have been using panels as containers, but this time we are going to use a Viewport.

The Ext.container.Viewport component takes all the available space and is always listening to the resize event of the window's browser to recalculate the new dimensions every time the user resizes the browser.

Let's start by creating a class that extends from the Viewport class. Just remember that we need to create the file inside the view folder in the application directory.

```
Ext.define('MyApp.view.Viewport',{
extend       : 'Ext.container.Viewport',

layout       : 'fit',
initComponent   : function(){

this.callParent();
    }
});
```

The `Viewport` class extends from the `container` component, which means that we can use any of the available layouts. In this case we are going to use a `fit` layout because we want to expand the children of the viewport.

As mentioned before if we want to dock a component to any of the four sides, we need to use a panel. The following code adds an empty panel to the viewport as a child:

```
Ext.define('MyApp.view.Viewport',{
extend        : 'Ext.container.Viewport',

layout: 'fit',

initComponent    : function(){
var me = this;

me.items = [{
xtype : 'panel'
         }];

me.callParent();
     }
});
```

We are using the `fit` layout to expand the panel to fit all the viewport, now we can set the `docked` items for this empty panel and dock a toolbar to the top.

```
Ext.define('MyApp.view.Viewport',{
extend        : 'Ext.container.Viewport',

layout: 'fit',

initComponent    : function(){
var me = this;

me.items = [{
xtype : 'panel',
dockedItems : [{
xtype : 'toolbar',
docked: 'top',
items : [{
text : 'Start',
iconCls : 'home-icon16'
}]
}]
```

```
        }];
    me.callParent();
    }
});
```

As a result, we have our toolbar with a button in it. Let's make sure we define the CSS class to an addan icon. If we want to test our application we need to create an HTML file, import the Ext library, and our `viewport` class as follows:

```
<!DOCTYPE html>
<html>
<head>
<meta http-equiv="Content-Type" content="text/html; charset=utf-8">
<title>Invoice app</title>

<!-- Importing the Ext JS library -->
<script type="text/javascript" src="../ext-4.1.1a-gpl/ext-all-dev.
js"></script>
<linkrel="stylesheet" href="../ext-4.1.1a-gpl/resources/css/ext-all.
css" />

<script type="text/javascript" src="js/MyApp/view/Viewport.js"></
script>

<script type="text/javascript">
Ext.onReady(function(){

Ext.create("MyApp.view.Viewport");


});
</script>
<style type="text/css">
.home-icon16{
background:transparenturl(images/house.png) center 0 no-repeat
!important;
}
</style>
</head>
<body>
</body>
</html>
```

For now we are just creating an instance of our `viewport` class when the DOM is ready, but as we keep moving forward we're going to change this:

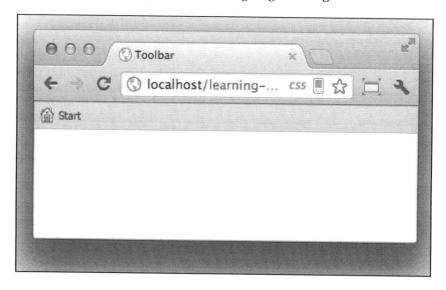

Once we have our `start` button in place we need to define the menu, we already know how to do this. We just need to set the `menu` property with the needed options.

```
Ext.define('MyApp.view.Viewport',{

    .

    .

    .

initComponent    : function(){
var me = this;

me.items = [{
xtype : 'panel',
dockedItems : [{

    .

        .

        .

items : [{
text : 'Start',
iconCls : 'home-icon16',
menu: [
{text:'Clients',iconCls:'clients-icon16'},
{text:'Invoices',iconCls:'invoices-icon16'},
{text:'Categories',iconCls:'categories-icon16'}
]
```

```
        }]
        }]
            }];

    me.callParent();
        }
    });
```

For now we are setting three options in our main menu. Each option should open the corresponding module. We're going to work on the modules as we learn about the needed components; so far our application is looking like the following screenshot:

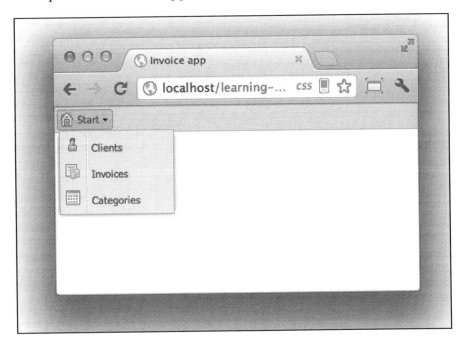

Please make sure you have the needed icons for this example, you can use your own images by changing the path of the CSS definitions.

The last requirement in our wireframes is to add the name of the logged user in the right-hand side of the toolbar. Just for now we are going to hard-code the name of the user, but later we should get the name from the server using Ajax.

```
Ext.define('MyApp.view.Viewport',{
    extend      : 'Ext.container.Viewport',

    layout: 'fit',
```

```
initComponent   : function(){
var me = this;

me.items = [{
xtype : 'panel',
dockedItems : [{
xtype : 'toolbar',
docked: 'top',
items : [{
text : 'Start',
.

    .
    .

},{
xtype: 'tbfill'
},{
text : 'John Doe',
icon : 'images/user_suit.png'
}]
}]
        }];

me.callParent();
    }
});
```

The previous code shows two important concepts. First we are using a tbfill xtype, which is an alias for the Ext.toolbar.Fill class. We are using this class to fill the space between the two buttons, allowing us to align to the right-hand side the button for the user name. It's important to understand that this class will *push* all the components to the right-hand side. In this case we have only one button, but we can have any number of components and all of them will be aligned to the right-hand side. Even if we resize the toolbar, the space will be resized accordingly.

We can also use an arrow (->) to create an instance of the Fill class. The -> symbol is basically a shorthand version of the Fill class. The following code is the same as our previous code:

```
Ext.define('MyApp.view.Viewport',{
    .

    .
    .

initComponent   : function(){
var me = this;

me.items = [{
    .

        .
        .
```

```
dockedItems : [{
xtype : 'toolbar',
docked: 'top',
items : [{
text : 'Start',
  .

              .
              .
},
            '->',
            {
text : 'John Doe',
icon : 'images/user_suit.png'
}]
}]
        }];

me.callParent();
    }
});
```

 Using the arrow(->) symbol is a very common practice in the Ext community, but it's worth knowing the real class that is doing the job of filling the available space.

If we refresh our browser we can see the same result in both examples:

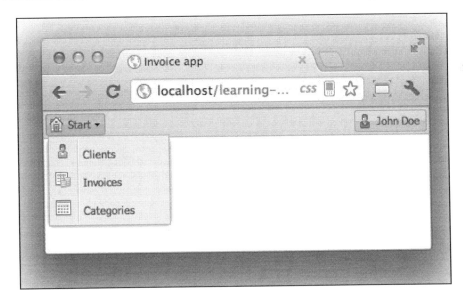

If you noticed in the previous examples, we are using the `icon` property inside a button definition. In this case we are not using a CSS class, instead we are using a path to the image. This is a common way when we need to add dynamic images to buttons. In this example the image should be the user's avatar, this is a perfect example of when we should use the `iconCls` or `icon` properties.

The following code shows the complete `Viewport` class that we have been writing in the previous steps, but it is provided here in case you would like to copy and paste it:

```
Ext.define('MyApp.view.Viewport',{
extend        : 'Ext.container.Viewport',

layout: 'fit',

initComponent    : function(){
var me = this;

me.items = [{
xtype : 'panel',
dockedItems : [{
xtype : 'toolbar',
docked: 'top',
items : [{
text : 'Start',
iconCls : 'home-icon16',
menu: [
{text:'Clients',iconCls:'clients-icon16'},
{text:'Invoices',iconCls:'invoices-icon16'},
{text:'Categories',iconCls:'categories-icon16'}
]
},{
xtype: 'tbfill'
},{
text : 'John Doe',
icon : 'images/user_suit.png'
}]
}]
        }];

me.callParent();
    }
});
```

The complete HTML code to test our `Viewport` class looks as follows:

```
<!DOCTYPE html>
<html>
<head>
<meta http-equiv="Content-Type" content="text/html; charset=utf-8">
<title>Invoice app</title>

<!-- Importing the Ext JS library -->
<script type="text/javascript" src="../ext-4.1.1a-gpl/ext-all-dev.
js"></script>
<linkrel="stylesheet" href="../ext-4.1.1a-gpl/resources/css/ext-all.
css" />

<script type="text/javascript" src="js/MyApp/view/Viewport.js"></
script>

<script type="text/javascript">
Ext.onReady(function(){

Ext.create("MyApp.view.Viewport");


});
</script>
<style type="text/css">
body{padding:10px;}
.home-icon16{
background:transparenturl(images/house.png) center 0 no-repeat
!important;
}
.clients-icon16{
background:transparenturl(images/user_green.png) center 0 no-repeat
!important;
}
.invoices-icon16{
background:transparenturl(images/table_money.png) center 0 no-repeat
!important;
}
.categories-icon16{
background:transparenturl(images/application_view_icons.png) center 0
no-repeat !important;
}
</style>
</head>
<body>
</body>
</html>
```

Summary

In this chapter we learned about events and how we can add, fire, and listen to events. We also learned about buttons, menus, and toolbars. At the end we worked in the main layout of our application, but we didn't listen to our events. At this point we could use the `addListener` or `on` methods to add some actions when the buttons and options are clicked, but in the next chapters we are going to learn about how to listen for events in a more convenient way.

6
Doing it with Forms

Ext JS comes with powerful widgets to collect and edit data; we have the form component and many types of input widgets. These include textfields, textarea, radios, checkbox, combos, sliders, and many more.

In this chapter we are going to learn about the components we can use to collect data from our users. Also we are going to be working on our final application as well as creating the required forms in the wireframes we defined in *Chapter 1, The Basics*.

We are going to cover the following topics in this chapter:

- The form component
- The available field types
- Field container
- Submitting the data

The form component

In order to collect and handle data Ext comes with the Ext.form.Panel class. This class extends from the panel so we can place the form in any other container. We also have all the functionality the panel offers, such as adding a title and using layouts.

If we look at the wireframes, we can see that we need to have the functionality of creating, editing, and deleting clients from our database:

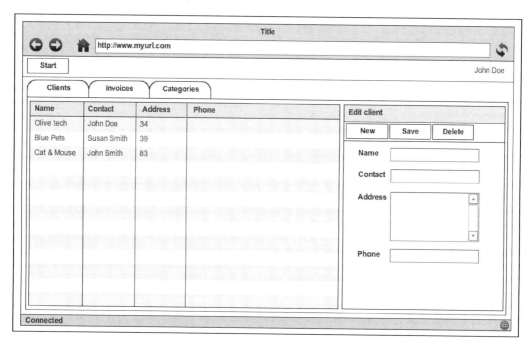

We are going to work on this form. As seen in the previous screenshot the form contains a title, a toolbar with some buttons, and a few fields.

> One important thing to keep in mind when working with Ext JS is that we should create our components isolated from the other components as much as we can. This way we can reuse them in other modules or even extend them to add new functionality.

First we need to extend from the Form class, so let's create a JavaScript file with the following code:

```
Ext.define('MyApp.view.clients.Form', {
    extend      : 'Ext.form.Panel',
    alias       : 'widget.clientform',

    title       : 'Client form',
```

```
initComponent    : function(){
var me = this;

me.callParent();
  }
});
```

Please keep in mind the conventions defined in *Chapter 2, The Core Concepts*, when creating classes. We need to create the file in the following path:

```
MyApp/view/clients/Form.js
```

The previous code doesn't do much, it's only extending from the form panel, defining an alias and a title. The initComponent method is empty, but we're going to create some components for it.

Now let's create an HTML file, where we can test our new class. We need to import the Ext JS library, our JS file, where our new class is, and wait for the DOM ready event to create an instance of our class:

```html
<!DOCTYPE html>
<html>
<head>
<meta http-equiv="Content-Type" content="text/html; charset=utf-8">
<title>Texfield</title>

<!-- Importing the Ext JS library -->
<script type="text/javascript" src="../ext-4.1.1a-gpl/ext-all-dev.
js"></script>
<linkrel="stylesheet" href="../ext-4.1.1a-gpl/resources/css/ext-all.
css" />

<script type="text/javascript" src="MyApp/view/clients/Form.js"></
script>

  <script type="text/javascript">
Ext.onReady(function(){

  Ext.create('MyApp.view.clients.Form',{
    width : 300,
    height      : 200,
    renderTo: Ext.getBody()
  });
```

```
});
   </script>
   <style type="text/css">
   body{padding:10px;}
   </style>
</head>
<body>
</body>
</html>
```

We are creating an instance of the `Client` form as usual. We have set the width, height, and the place where the form is going to be rendered, in this case the body of our document. As a result we have our form created as shown in the following screenshot:

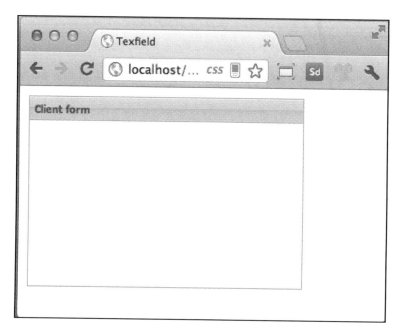

So far we have an empty form. We can add any of the available components and widgets, let's start with the `textfield` property:

```
Ext.define('MyApp.view.clients.Form',{
extend       : 'Ext.form.Panel',
alias        : 'widget.clientform',

title     : 'Client form',
bodyPadding  : 5,
defaultType  : 'textfield', //Step 1
```

```
initComponent    : function(){
var me = this;

me.items = me.buildItems(); //Step 2

me.callParent();
    },

buildItems        : function(){ //Step 3
return [{
fieldLabel    : 'Name',
name          : 'name'
        },{
fieldLabel    : 'Contact',
name          : 'contact'
        }];
    }
});
```

The steps are explained as follows:

- **Step 1**: We have defined the default type of component we are going to use. This way we don't have to define the `xtype` property every time we want to create `textfield`.

- **Step 2**: We use the `items` property to add components to our form. We are calling a function that should return an array of components.

- **Step 3**: We are defining two textfields. First we set the value of the label for each textfield and then we set `name`. It's important to use name if we want to send or retrieve data to our server. Setting the `name` property will allow us to set and retrieve data to our fields in an easy way.

 Using a function to define the items array is a great way to write our code for readability. Also if we would like to extend this class, we can override this method and add more components to our form in the subclass.

With the previous lines of code we have added two textfields to our form as shown in the following screenshot:

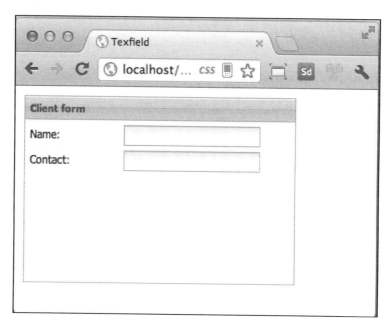

Now let's add the `Address` field to our form using a `textarea` property. In order to do that we need to override the default `xtype` property as follows:

```
Ext.define('MyApp.view.clients.Form',{
    //...



buildItems    : function(){
return [
            //...
,{
        xtype    : 'textarea',
        fieldLabel   : 'Address',
        name    : 'address'
}
];
}
});
```

If we want to define new components we can override the `xtype` property with the component we need. In this case we are using a `textarea` xtype, but we can use any of the available components.

The last field in our wireframe is a textfield to collect the phone number. We already defined the default xtype as textfield so we only need to define the name and the label of our new textfield as follows:

```
Ext.define('MyApp.view.clients.Form',{
    //...

buildItems    : function(){
return [
//...
,{
fieldLabel   : 'Phone',
name         : 'phone'
            }
];
        }
});
```

As a result we have all the required fields in our form. Now if we refresh our browser, we should see something like the following screenshot:

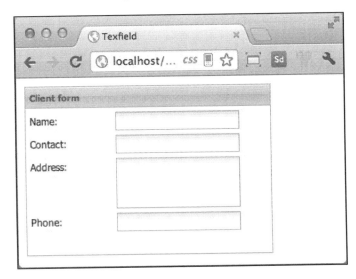

We have our form ready, but if we see our wireframe we can realize that something is missing. We need to add three buttons to the top of the panel.

We already know how to create toolbars and buttons; the following code should be familiar for us:

```
Ext.define('MyApp.view.clients.Form',{

    //...

initComponent    : function(){
var me = this;

me.items = me.buildItems();

me.dockedItems = me.buildToolbars(); //Step 1

me.callParent();
    },

buildItems        : function(){
        //...
    },

buildToolbars     : function(){ //Step 2
return [{
xtype    : 'toolbar',
docked   : 'top',
items    : [{
text     : 'New',
iconCls : 'new-icon'
            },{
text     : 'Save',
iconCls : 'save-icon'
            },{
text     : 'Delete',
iconCls : 'delete-icon'
            }]
        }];
    }
});
```

In the previous code, we are defining the dockedItems property; we are using the same pattern of defining a function that returns the array of items in the first step.

In the second step we define a function that returns an array of components to be docked. In this case we are only returning a toolbar docked to the top; this toolbar contains three buttons. The first button is for a new client, the second one is to save the current client, and the third button is to delete the current client in the form.

As mentioned in *Chapter 5, Buttons and Toolbars*, we need to use CSS classes to add an icon to the buttons. The previous code is using three different classes so we need to create them:

```
<style type="text/css">
.new-icon{background:transparent url(images/page_add.png) 0 0 no-
repeat !important;}
.save-icon{background:transparent url(images/disk.png) 0 0 no-repeat
!important;}
.delete-icon{background:transparent url(images/delete.png) 0 0 no-
repeat !important;}
</style>
```

Once we have defined our CSS classes let's refresh our browser and see our latest changes in action:

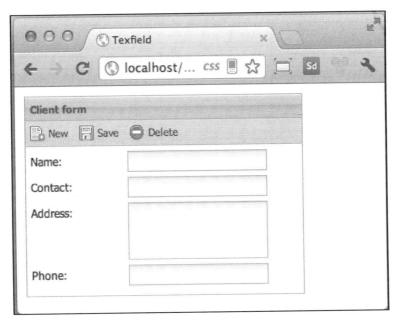

We have finished our wireframe, but the form is not doing anything yet. We will add the functionality in the next chapters when we integrate everything using the MVC pattern. For now let's just move forward and see what other components we have available.

Anatomy of the fields

Ext JS provides many components to give the user a great experience when using their applications. The following fields are components we can use in a form or outside of the form, for example, we can add a textfield or a combobox to a toolbar, where we place some filters or search options.

Every input field extends from the Ext.Component class; this means that every field has its own lifecycle, events, and also can be placed on any container.

There's also a class called Ext.form.field.Base that defines common properties, methods, and events across all form fields. This base class also extends from the Ext.form.Labelable and Ext.form.field.Field classes (using mixins).

The Labelable class gives the field the ability to display a label and errors in every subclass such as textfields, combos, and so on.

The Field class gives the fields the ability to manage their value, because it adds a few important methods, such as the getValue and setValue methods to set and retrieve the current value of the field; also this class introduces an important concept, the **raw value**.

A great example of the raw value is when we pull data from our server and we get a date value in string format, the raw value is in plain text, but the value of the date field should be in a native Date object so that we can work easily with dates and time. We can always use the raw value, but it's recommended to use the value instead, which in this example is a Date object.

Available fields

Ext JS provides many widgets that we can use to collect and edit data in our forms. We are going to learn about the most useful widget and configurations that we can use to create beautiful forms.

For the following examples we are going to create a class that extends from the Form class and hold the fields that we are going to explain in detail later on:

```
Ext.define('MyApp.view.AvailableFields',{
extend      : 'Ext.form.Panel',
alias       : 'widget.availablefields',

title : 'Available fields',
  width : 280,
  bodyPadding : 5,
```

```
initComponent    : function(){
  var me = this;

  me.items = me.buildItems();

  me.callParent();
},

buildItems : function(){
    //We are going to create the fields here
  return []
  }
});
```

In the `buildItem` form we are going to instantiate the required classes.

The Textfield class

We have already used this class to create our wireframe and we used the `xtype` property to create it. We can always create the instance using the `Ext.create` method and the class that we should instantiate is `Ext.form.field.Text`.

This class extends from the base class and is intended to manage text as a string value. This class defines some important events such as `keydown`, `keypress`, and `keyup`. These events are very useful to catch the keys the user is entering into a textfield.

It's important to keep in mind that if we want to use these events, we need to set the `enableKeyEvents` property as `true`.

```
Ext.define('MyApp.view.AvailableFields',{
extend       : 'Ext.form.Panel',

  //...

  buildItems : function(){
    //Step 1
var txt = Ext.create('Ext.form.field.Text',{
    fieldLabel : 'First name',
    name       : 'firstname',
    enableKeyEvents : true
  });
```

```
      //Step 2
    txt.on('keyup',function(field,event,options){
      if(event.getCharCode() === event.ENTER){
        Ext.Msg.alert('Alert','Welcome: '+field.getValue());
      }
    });

    return [txt];
  }
});
```

In the first step we create a textfield component. We define some properties, such as the name and the label of the field and enable the key events.

In the second step we are setting a listener to the `keyup` event. Every time the user releases a key on his keyboard the callback function will be executed. In the previous example we are waiting for the *Enter* key and whenever it is pressed we show an alert message with the value entered into the textfield.

 Ext JS provides a wrapper for the native event object. This wrapper defines many constants such as the *Enter* key. We can see all the available constants on the documentation at `http://docs.sencha.com/ext-js/4-1/#!/api/Ext.EventObject`.

Let's test our code in a new HTML page as follows:

```
<!DOCTYPE html>
<html>
<head>
<meta http-equiv="Content-Type" content="text/html; charset=utf-8">
<title>Texfield</title>

<!-- Importing the Ext JS library -->
<script type="text/javascript" src="../extjs-4.1.1a-glp/ext-all-dev.
js"></script>
<linkrel="stylesheet" href="../extjs-4.1.1a-glp/resources/css/ext-all.
css" />

<!-- Importing our custom class -->
<script type="text/javascript" src="MyApp/view/AvailableFields"></
script>

<script type="text/javascript">
Ext.onReady(function(){
```

```
Ext.create('MyApp.view.AvailableFields',{
    renderTo : Ext.getBody()
  });
});
  </script>
  <style type="text/css">
  body{padding:10px;}
  </style>
</head>
<body>
</body>
</html>
```

The following screenshot shows how our **Textfield** is working with the listener attached:

As we can see in the previous example all the fields extend from the Observable class, therefore we are able to add events and listeners to all form fields.

We should take a look at the documentation to see all the available events that we can use to our advantage.

The number field

When dealing with numbers we can use the number field that only accepts numbers as a value. This way we can assure that the user will not be able to introduce any invalid characters.

Let's add the following code to the `buildItems` method to see how the number field works:

```
Ext.define('MyApp.view.AvailableFields',{
extend        : 'Ext.form.Panel',

  //...

  buildItems : function(){

    //...

    //Step 1
    var num = Ext.create('Ext.form.field.Number',{
      fieldLabel  : 'Price',
      name        : 'price'
    });

    return [txt,num]; //Step 2
  }
});
```

In the first step we create the instance. We are only assigning the label and the name of our field. There are many more options, but for now we are only using these two.

In the second step the field is added to the returning array that will be added to the items of the form.

As a result we will have something as shown in the following screenshot:

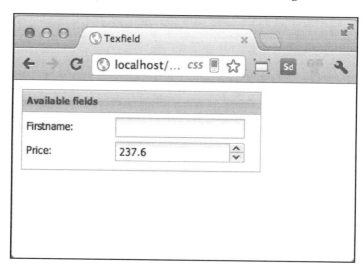

As we can see in the previous screenshot the number field contains two arrows or spinners. If the user clicks on them, the value will increase or decrease accordingly.

By default the value is incremented or decremented by one, but we can control that by setting the `step` configuration as follows:

```
//...

var num = Ext.create('Ext.form.field.Number',{
  fieldLabel  : 'Price',
  name     : 'price',
  step     : 10
});

//...
```

Now if we click on the spinners, we will see how they are increased by ten. Another useful configuration is to set the maximal or minimal value that this field will accept; we can achieve this by setting the `minValue` and `maxValue` configurations as follows:

```
//...

var num = Ext.create('Ext.form.field.Number',{
  fieldLabel  : 'Price',
  name     : 'price',
  step     : 10,
minValue   : 30,
  maxValue: 100
});

//...
```

Finally, if we don't want to show the spinners, we can hide them by using the `hideTrigger` configuration as follows:

```
//...

var num = Ext.create('Ext.form.field.Number',{
  fieldLabel   : 'Price',
  name     : 'price',
  step     : 10,
minValue   : 30,
  maxValue   : 100,
hideTrigger : true
  });

//...
```

This way the spinners will not be shown and we will have a textfield with the ability to accept only numbers.

There are many more configurations for this field, such as the ability to change the decimal separator so only numbers without decimals will be allowed and many more options that we can use to our advantage.

 Even if we accept only numbers in our textfield, we should always run the validations in the server side, never rely only on the client side.

The combobox field

The combobox is one of the most useful widgets to display a list of options. This is a very flexible component that we can customize to our needs.

Let's start with the basics! First we need to rely on the data package that we have already learned earlier in this book. We are going to use the `Store` class with a local data to fill our combobox.

```
Ext.define('MyApp.view.AvailableFields',{
extend      : 'Ext.form.Panel',

//...

buildItems : function(){

  //...

  //Step 1
  var store = Ext.create('Ext.data.Store',{
    fields  : ['key','label'],
    data      : [
      {key:'xs',label:'Extra Small'},
      {key:'s',label:'Small'},
      {key:'m',label:'Medium'},
      {key:'l',label:'Large'},
      {key:'xl',label:'Extra Large'}
    ]
  });
```

```
    //Step 2
varcombobox = Ext.create('Ext.form.ComboBox',{
    fieldLabel  : 'Size',
    name        : 'size',
    store       : store,
    queryMode   : 'local',
    displayField: 'label',
    valueField  : 'key'
    });

    return [txt,num,combobox]; //Step 3
   }
});
```

In the first step we are creating a store with a static data. By defining the `fields` property the store internally creates the model to be used with this store.

In the second step we create our combobox. We are defining the name and the label as any other fields, but there are some specific configurations that are required for the combobox in order to work properly. First we set the store that the combobox will use to display the data. Then we need to set the `queryMode` property to `local`, by doing this the combobox will not try to load the data of the store remotely when the list of options is displayed. After that we need to define which of the properties in the store will be used for displaying the label in the list of options and which will be used as a value; we use the `displayField` and `valueField` properties to specify this.

The last step is to append our combobox to the returning array of fields that will be added to our form.

The following screenshot shows the result of our code:

Since we are using a store to hold the displayed data we can use an Ajax proxy to get the content of the store from our server.

Let's modify our previous example to get all the available sizes from our server side. First we need to create the service that will return the data; in this case we are going to use a static data, but this data can be stored in a database or somewhere else.

```
{
  "success" : true,
  "data"    : [
    {"key":"xs","label":"Extra Small"},
    {"key":"s","label":"Small"},
    {"key":"m","label":"Medium"},
    {"key":"l","label":"Large"},
    {"key":"xl","label":"Extra Large"}
  ]
}
```

The previous code should be located in a new file at `serverside/size.json` or anywhere else where you can make an Ajax request.

Once we have defined the source of data we need to perform some changes in our code as follows:

```
Ext.define('MyApp.view.AvailableFields',{
extend        : 'Ext.form.Panel',

//...

  buildItems : function(){

      //...

    var store = Ext.create('Ext.data.Store',{
        fields    : ['key','label'],
        autoLoad: true,
        proxy     : {
          type : 'ajax',
          url  : 'serverside/sizes.json',
          reader : {
            type : 'json',
                        root    : 'data'
                  }
              }
          });

      //...
    }
});
```

As you can see we have changed the proxy of the store only. We defined an Ajax proxy and a JSON reader, now if we refresh our browser, we can see that the data is loading remotely.

This is one of the greatest advantages of Ext JS. We can change things very easily because Ext is built with small classes that can be switched at any time. We have seen how to read data locally and remotely.

At this point the user can type into the combobox and the list that will be displayed will contain only those records that matche with the current text entered. This is a very handy feature, but in most cases we want the user to select only one of the available options and not enter some invalid text. We can use the `forceSelection` property to force the user to select only one option even if he/she starts typing text into the field:

```
Ext.define('MyApp.view.AvailableFields',{
    extend      : 'Ext.form.Panel',

    //...

    buildItems : function(){

        //...

      varcombobox = Ext.create('Ext.form.ComboBox',{
        fieldLabel  : 'Size',
        name        : 'size',
        store       : store,
        queryMode   : 'local',
        displayField: 'label',
        valueField  : 'key',
        forceSelection : true
      });
      return [txt,num,combobox];
    }
});
```

Now we can be sure that the user is going to select only one of the available options in the list:

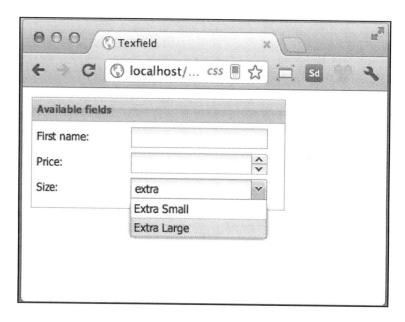

It's very common that we need to do something when an option of the list is selected, for example load another combo or hide/show some other fields. We can listen to the `select` event and perform the required actions:

```
combobox.on('select',function(combo,records){
    Ext.Msg.alert('Alert',records[0].get('label'));
});
```

The previous code is listening to the `select` event, and only shows an alert message with the label of the record selected. Here we can do whatever we need, such as loading the data of another combobox depending on the selection of the first.

The callback receives the array of records selected; it's an array because we can also configure our combobox to allow the user to select more than one option.

We can use any of the available events to perform some actions but one of the most important events for this widget is the select event.

The date field

Ext provides an easy way to collect dates; we have at our disposal a date picker that will handle the selection of a date using a fancy calendar or by allowing the user to type the date in the format we define.

The most basic usage is by only setting the name and the label of the field such as the following code:

```
Ext.define('MyApp.view.AvailableFields',{
extend       : 'Ext.form.Panel',

  //...

  buildItems : function(){

    //...

    vardatefield =              Ext.create('Ext.form.field.Date',{
      fieldLabel  : 'Date',
      name      : 'date'
    });

    return [txt,num,combobox,datefield];
  }
});
```

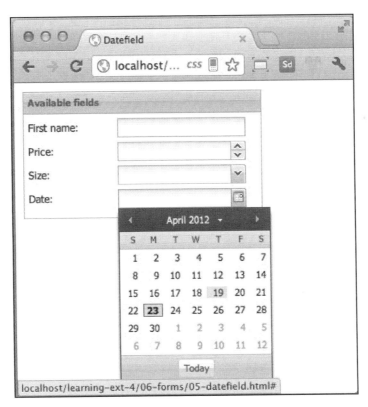

We are defining our date field in a very simple way, but there are many more configurations we can use. Let's dig a little bit more to customize these fields to meet our requirements.

By default the format used to display the date is m/d/Y (05/22/2012); this is a common format used in the U.S., but not in other countries. To define a custom format for a different region or country we need to use the format property as follows:

```
vardatefield = Ext.create('Ext.form.field.Date',{
    fieldLabel   : 'Date',
    name        : 'date',
    format       : 'd/m/Y',
    submitFormat: 'Y-m-dH:m:s'
});
```

We can use any format to display the date and also we can set the format that we want the field to be sent, when we submit the form, or retrieved, when we get the values. Defining the submitFormat property is very important because it's this format that we will be using under the hood; in this example we are using a common format in databases.

The m/d/Y format refers to the commonly mm/dd/yyyy format. This may be confusing, but we should take a look at the Ext.Date object documentation to see all the supported formats that we can use at http://docs.sencha.com/ext-js/4-1/#!/api/Ext.Date.

Right now the user is able to type into the field to enter the date in the correct format, however using slashes may slow down the user. We can allow alternative formats to make things easier for the user, for example we could define d m Y as a valid format and as many formats as needed:

```
vardatefield = Ext.create('Ext.form.field.Date',{
    fieldLabel   : 'Date',
    name        : 'date',
    format       : 'd/m/Y',
    submitFormat: 'Y-m-d H:m:s',
    altFormats   : 'd-m-Y|d m Y|d.m.Y'
});
```

Using the altFormats property we can define all the formats we want. We only need to separate each format by a pipe character (|) and those formats will be used to parse the text to a date object. We should not use the pipe inside any of the format because there is no way to escape this character. A format like m|d|Y will not work.

We have many more properties available, such as `minValue` and `maxValue`, the ability to disable some specific dates such as weekends or holidays:

```
vardatefield = Ext.create('Ext.form.field.Date',{
  fieldLabel  : 'Date',
  name        : 'date',
  format      : 'd/m/Y',
  submitFormat: 'Y-m-d H:m:s',
  altFormats  : 'd-m-Y|d m Y|d.m.Y',
  minValue    : new Date(),
  disabledDates: ['30/04/2012','15/05/2012']
});
```

If we want to disable a range of days, we can use regular expressions to match the dates that we want to disable. Some examples are as follows:

```
//disable everyday in march 2012
disabledDates: ['../03/2012']

//disable everyday in march for every year
disabledDates: ['../03/..']

//disable the 05 and 21 of march for every year
disabledDates: ['05/03','21/03']
```

We can also use the `select` event that is fired when the user selects a date. We can do whatever we need inside the callback function as we did in the combobox.

The checkbox

We can use a single checkbox to set a record in our database as active or inactive, or maybe we can have a group of options that we need to display and allow the user to select a few of them:

```
Ext.define('MyApp.view.AvailableFields',{
extend      : 'Ext.form.Panel',

  //...

  buildItems : function(){

    //...

    //Step 1
varchkbox = Ext.create('Ext.form.field.Checkbox',{
      fieldLabel  : ' ',
      labelSeparator : '',
      boxLabel   : 'Active',
      name     : 'active'
  });

    return [
txt,
num,
combobox,
datefield,
chkbox //Step 2
];
  }
});
```

In the first step we are creating our checkbox. We are using the `boxLabel` property to set the label of our checkbox; it's important to know that we are setting the `fieldLabel` and `labelSeparator` properties as an empty space. This way the checkbox will be aligned correctly.

In the last step we just add our new component to the returned array. The following screenshot shows our latest changes to the code:

Now we have our checkbox in place. Having a single checkbox is great, but there are times when we need to define a few more options. We can use a group of checkboxes to arrange the components horizontally, vertically, or in columns:

```
Ext.define('MyApp.view.AvailableFields',{
extend       : 'Ext.form.Panel',

    //...

    buildItems : function(){

        //...

        //Step 1
        var group = Ext.create('Ext.form.CheckboxGroup',{
            fieldLabel   : 'Languages',
            columns      : 2,
            items        : [
                {name:'lan',boxLabel:'JavaScript',inputValue:'js'},
                {name:'lan',boxLabel:'C/C++',inputValue:'c/cpp'},
                {name:'lan',boxLabel:'Java',inputValue:'java'},
                {name:'lan',boxLabel:'PHP',inputValue:'php'},
                {name:'lan',boxLabel:'SQL',inputValue:'sql'},
```

```
        {name:'lan',boxLabel:'Python',inputValue:'py'},
        {name:'lan',boxLabel:'Ruby',inputValue:'rb'}
     ]
   });


   return [txt,num,combobox,datefield,chkbox,group];
  }
});
```

In the first step we are creating an instance of the CheckboxGroup class. We defined the label of the group and gave each item a checkbox with its label and value. We are arranging the items in two columns.

In the last step we added the group to the returning array so it appears in our form:

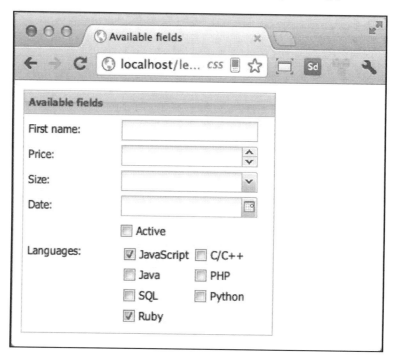

The radio button

Radio buttons are useful when we want to force the user to select one item from a small group of choices. If we want to present more choices, a combobox is an easier widget to code and to use.

The radio button is very similar to the checkbox. In fact the radio button extends from the Checkbox class. This means the radio buttons also have the same properties and methods as the checkbox.

```
Ext.define('MyApp.view.AvailableFields',{
extend        : 'Ext.form.Panel',

    //...

    buildItems : function(){

      //...

        var yes = Ext.create('Ext.form.field.Radio',{
          name    : 'option',
          fieldLabel   : 'Are you a developer?',
          labelSeparator : '',
          boxLabel: 'Yes',
          inputValue   : true
        }),
        no = Ext.create('Ext.form.field.Radio',{
          name        : 'option',
          fieldLabel   : ' ',
          labelSeparator : '',
          boxLabel: 'No',
          inputValue   : false
        });

        return [txt,num,combobox,datefield,chkbox,group,yes,no];
    }
});
```

We are creating two instances of the Radio class exactly the same as we created the Checkbox class. In the creation of the Checkbox class we added two radio buttons to the returning array.

The following screenshot shows how the two radios were created:

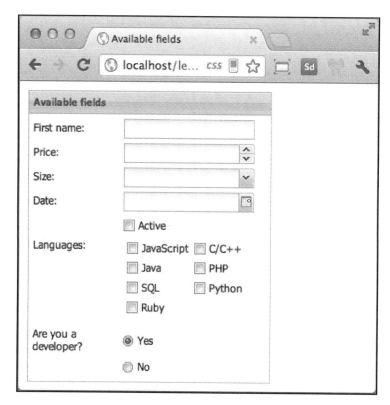

It is important to assign the same name to the radio buttons so that only one option can be selected among the available ones.

As we can see in the previous screenshot the radios are arranged one over the other, but what if we want to align them horizontally? We can use a `radiogroup` component and set the number of columns as two. That way we will have our two radio buttons in the same line:

```
Ext.define('MyApp.view.AvailableFields',{
extend     : 'Ext.form.Panel',

//...

buildItems : function(){

    //...
```

```
var radiogroup = {
    xtype   : 'radiogroup',
    columns : 2,
    fieldLabel: 'Are you a developer?',
    items   : [yes,no]
};

    return [txt,num,combobox,datefield,chkbox,group,radiogroup];
}
});
```

This is very similar to what we did with the checkbox group. We can define as many radio buttons as we need, and all of them will be arranged in two columns as shown in the following screenshot:

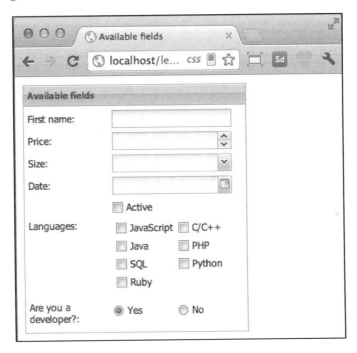

The field container

There are times when we need to group textfields or any other components other than checkbox and radio buttons. We can use the field container to group any type of field.

One of the advantages of using a field container is the ability to use a layout; we can use any of the available layouts in the framework. We have learned about the layouts in the previous chapters.

The following code shows how we can group a textfield and a combobox to show these fields in the same line. We need to edit our previous code to add a few configurations to the price and size fields:

```
Ext.define('MyApp.view.AvailableFields',{
extend      : 'Ext.form.Panel',

  //...

  buildItems : function(){

    //...

    //Step 1
    var num = Ext.create('Ext.form.field.Number',{
      emptyText   : 'Price',
      name      : 'price',
      step      : 10,
      minValue  : 30,
      maxValue  : 100,
      flex      : 1,
      margins     : '0 5 0 0'
      //hideTrigger : true
    });

    //...

    //Step 1
    varcombobox = Ext.create('Ext.form.ComboBox',{
      emptyText   : 'Size',
      name      : 'size',
      store     : store,
      queryMode   : 'local',
      displayField: 'label',
      valueField  : 'key',
      forceSelection : true,
      flex      : 1
    });

    //...

    //Step 2
    varpricesize = {
      xtype     : 'fieldcontainer',
```

```
        fieldLabel   : 'Price/Size',
        layout       : 'hbox',
        items : [num,combobox]
    };

    return [txt, pricesize //Step 3
  ,datefield,chkbox,group,container];
    }
});
```

In the first step we have removed the fieldLabel property and instead we defined the emptyText property, this way the label will be shown only when the field is empty. Also we have defined the flex property to make it flexible.

In the second step we created the field container with an hbox layout. This way the two fields will be flexible and grouped horizontally.

Finally, in the third step we removed the price and the size from the array and added the group. The following screenshot shows the changes in our code:

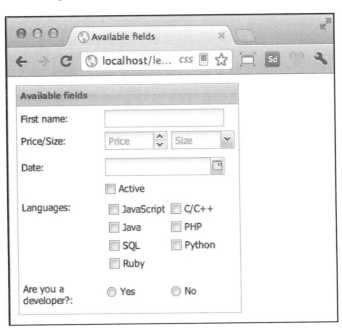

This is how we can arrange the fields in any way we want; using the field container is a great way to accomplish this task.

We can add as many components as we need, we can use any of the available layouts, the possibilities are endless.

Submitting the data

So far we have learned how to create and configure the components to collect data using the available widgets, but we need to do something with it. Ext JS provides different ways to submit the captured data to our server.

The `Ext.form.Panel` class contains an instance of the `Ext.form.Basic` class. This class is used to manage the data within the form, such as validations, settings and retrieving data to the fields, submitting and loading data from the server, and so on.

In order to send the data to the server we can use the `submit` method from the basic form. Let's add a button to our form and then submit the entered data to our server:

```
Ext.define('MyApp.view.AvailableFields',{
extend        : 'Ext.form.Panel',

  //...

  initComponent    : function(){
    var me = this;

    me.items = me.buildItems();
     //Step 1
    me.tbar = [{text:'Save',handler:me.saveData,scope:me}];

    me.callParent();
  },

  buildItems : function(){

     //...

  },

  //Step 2
  saveData   : function(){
    var me = this;

    me.getForm().submit({
      url     : 'serverside/save.do',
      success : function(form,action){
        Ext.Msg.alert('Success','Successfully saved');
      },
      failure : function(form,action){
        Ext.Msg.alert('Failure','Something is wrong');
      }
    });
  }
});
```

In the first step we defined a top toolbar with one button on it. When the button is clicked, the `saveData` function is executed.

In the second step we defined the `saveData` function. In this function we get the basic form and then execute the `submit` method. This method receives an object with the URL, where the Ajax request will be made, and the success/failure callback:

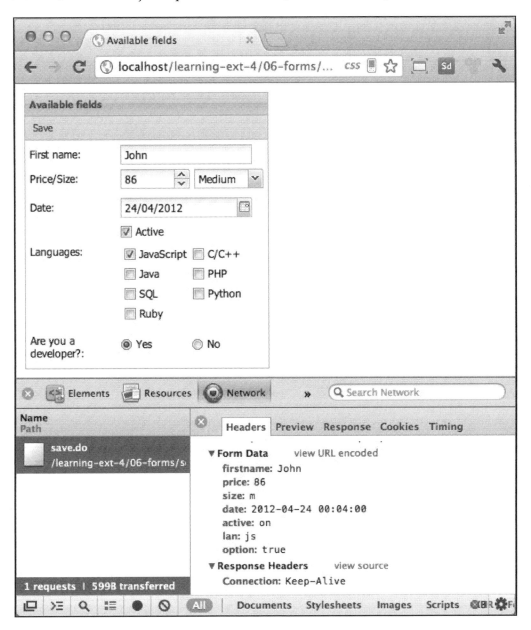

As shown in the previous screenshot the `submit` method executes an Ajax request using the POST method and sends all the entered data by the user. The way we get these parameters on the server side depends on the technology that we are using; for example if we are using PHP, we can do something like the following code:

```php
<?php

$firstname = $_POST['firstname'];
$price = $_POST['price'];
```

If we are using Java, we probably would do something like the following code:

```java
String firstname = request.getParameter("firstname");
String size = request.getParameter("size");
```

This depends on the framework, language, or technology that we use in the server side; the important thing is that Ext submits the data using the POST method and each parameter is sent using the name of the field.

The server code provided here is just an example and is not complete. The implementation of that is out of the scope of this book. However, based on the received data you can take that information and do whatever you need to do with it.

Summary

In this chapter we have learned about the forms and fields that we can use to collect and edit data. We have many options and configurations available that we can use to customize our forms.

The field container is one of the new components added to Version 4 of the Ext JS framework. This allows us to arrange the fields using any of the available layouts in the framework giving us a powerful layout system.

In the following chapter we are going to learn about the grid component. This is one of the most powerful widgets in the framework because it's very flexible with lots of plugins and configurations.

7
Give me the Grid

The grid component is the most popular and used component in the Ext JS library. It allows us to display, sort, group, and edit data very easily, or at least in a very common format. Grids are excellent for showing large amounts of tabular data.

In Ext JS 4 the grid panel was completely rewritten. The purpose was to enhance performance and change the way the component renders data. The result was a set of classes that boost the application performance.

In this chapter we are going to learn how the grid panel works and what are the configurations needed to get the best of this component.

The topics we are going to cover in this chapter are as follows:

- The data connection (models and stores)
- A basic grid panel
- Columns
- Renderers
- Selection models
- Grid listeners
- Features
- Plugins

The data connection (models and stores)

The grid panel is the component used to display data, but where does the data come from? In *Chapter 4, It's all about Data*, we talked about the data package that comes in Ext JS 4 and we mentioned the use of models and stores. Like other components, the grid component uses a store to contain the data it displays. This happens because the library splits the responsibilities; on one hand the grid panel is only responsible for displaying data, while the store is responsible for fetching and updating that data. So let's start by defining the model and the store for our grid panel.

Defining a model for the store of the grid

We are going to define a client model that has the following properties:

- Client ID
- Name
- Last name
- Age
- E-mail
- Country
- Pay date

Now that we have defined the properties of our model, let's write the code to define it in the grid view definition as shown in the following code:

```
//The definition of the client model
Ext.define('Client', {
extend:'Ext.data.Model',
fields:[
        'name', 'lastname' , 'email', 'country',
        {name:'client', type:'int'},
        {name:'age', type:'int' },
        {name:'active', type:'boolean' },
        {name:'amount', type:'float' },
        'paydate'
        ]
});
```

In the preceding code we have created a `Client` model that extends from `Ext.data.Model` and has all the properties of our client.

Defining a store for the grid

Once we have defined our model, we need to define the store for our clients in the grid view definition as shown in the following code:

```
//defining the client`s store
Ext.create('Ext.data.Store', {
model:'Client',
data:[
{
 client:1,
 name:'David',
 lastname:'Lee', age:24,
 email:'david@email.com',
 country:'China',
 paydate:'08/08/2012',
 amount:120.5,
 active:true
},{
 client:2,
 name:'Lisa',
 lastname:'Brown',
 age:25,
 email:'lisa@email.com',
 country:'Australia',
 paydate:'08/08/2012',
 amount:120.5, active:false
},{
 client:3,
 name:'Armando',
 lastname:'Gonzalez',
 age:30,
 email:'armando@email.com',
 country:'Mexico',
 paydate:'08/28/2012',
 amount:120.5,
 active:true
},{
```

```
    client:4,
    name:'Mike',
    lastname:'Chang',
    age:27,
    email:'mike@email.com',
    country:'Japan',
    paydate:'08/08/2012',
    amount:120.5,
    active:false
},{
    client:5,
    name:'Kevin',
    lastname:'Smith',
    age:28,
    email:'kevin@email.com',
    country:'Usa',
    paydate:'08/08/2012',
    amount:120.5, active:true
}]
});
```

In the previous code, we have the definition of the store we are going to use to show the data on our grid. We have defined an inline set of data to simplify our example, but in a real application you should get the data from the server with the help of store proxies.

A basic grid panel

Once we have our model and store, we are ready to define the grid that will show our clients information as shown in the following code:

```
/**
 * @classMyApp.view.BasicGridPanel
 * @extendsExt.grid.Panel
 * @author Armando Gonzalez <iam@armando.mx>
 * This the basic grid panel definition.
 */
Ext.define('MyApp.view.BasicGridPanel', {
    extend: 'Ext.grid.Panel',

    width:700,
    height:180,
    title:'Clients',
```

```
initComponent: function() {
  var me = this;
  me.createModel();
  me.columns = me.buildColumns();
  me.store =  me.buildStore();

  this.callParent(arguments);
},
createModel:function(){ //The definition of the client model

},
buildStore:function(){  //defining the client`s store

},
buildColumns : function(){
  return [
        {
        text:'Name',
        width:100,
        dataIndex:'name'
        },{
        text:'Last Name',
        width:100,
        dataIndex:'lastname'
        },{
        text:'Age',
        width:50,
        dataIndex:'age'
        },{
        text:'Email Address',
        width:150,
        dataIndex:'email'
        },{
        text:'Country',
        width:80,
        dataIndex:'country'
        },{
        text:'Pay Date',
        flex:1,
        dataIndex:'paydate'
        },{
        text:'Total',
        flex:1,
```

```
                        dataIndex:'amount'
                        },{
                        text:'Active?',
                        flex:1,
                        dataIndex:'active'
                        }];
        }
    });
```

In the preceding code we have created a grid panel that renders itself in the body of our page. In the store property we have assigned the client store so the grid gets the data from it to display. We have defined a columns property that is an array of objects. These objects define the columns of our grid.

We need to create an HTML page to import the Ext library and then wrap our code on the Ext.onReady function. The result will be as shown in the following screenshot:

Clients							
Name	Last Name	Age	Email Address	Country	Pay Date	Total	Active?
David	Lee	24	david@email.com	China	08/08/2012	120.5	true
Lisa	Brown	25	lisa@email.com	Australia	08/08/2012	120.5	false
Armando	Gonzalez	30	armando@email.com	Mexico	08/28/2012	120.5	true
Mike	Chang	27	mike@email.com	Japan	08/08/2012	120.5	false
Kevin	Smith	28	kevin@email.com	Usa	08/08/2012	120.5	true

The model fields' names have to match with the column's data index so that the grid renders the data properly.

Columns

The columns property in the grid panel matches the model fields with the columns of the grid. By default, the columns are sortable and will toggle the sorting direction between ascending and descending when you click on the column header. Each column header has a menu that shows up when you click on the right-hand side of the header. In that menu you can sort data, or show and hide columns of the grid panel as shown in the following screenshot:

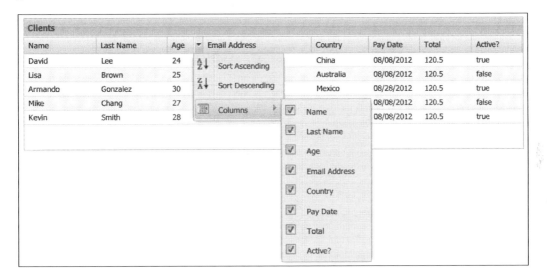

The Ext JS 4 offers six kinds of column classes and all are located under the `Ext.grid.column` namespace. We are going to explain how each of these column classes work by adding an extra configuration to our columns in the grid as shown in the following code:

```
columns:[{
    xtype:'rownumberer' //step 1
    },{
    text:'Name',
    xtype:'templatecolumn', //step 2
    flex:1,
    dataIndex:'name',
    tpl:'<b>{name} {lastname} </b> (age: {age})</br>{email}'
    //step 3
    },{
```

```
text:'Country',
width:80,
dataIndex:'country'
},{
text:'Pay Date',
xtype:'datecolumn', //step 4
width:80,
dataIndex:'paydate',
format:'m-d-Y'
},{
text:'Total',
xtype:'numbercolumn', //step 5
width:80,
dataIndex:'amount'
},{
text:'Active?',
xtype:'booleancolumn', //step6
width:80,
dataIndex:'active',
trueText:'YES',
falseText:'NO'
},{
xtype:'actioncolumn', //step 7
width:40,
items:[{
        icon:'pencil.png',//step 8
        handler:function () {
        alert('edit');
        }
        },{
        icon:'cross.png',//step9
        handler:function () {
        alert('delete');
        }
        }]
}]
```

The previous column configuration outputs the grid shown in the following screenshot:

The steps are explained as follows:

- **Step 1**: We declared the `Ext.grid.RowNumberer` column by its `xtype`. This is the first column of our grid and automatically adds numbers to our grid rows.

- **Step 2**: We are using the `Ext.grid.column.Template` type column. This type of column renders HTML on our column with the help of the library templates.

- **Step 3**: We are displaying the value of three fields of our model on a single column of our grid. This is achieved by the `tpl` property of step three.

- **Step 4**: The fourth column has an `Ext.grid.column.Date` type defined. This column class renders a date according to the default locale, or a preconfigured format property defined in `format`.

- **Step 5**: We have an `Ext.grid.column.Number` type defined for rendering our total column. This type of column renders numeric data according to a format string.

- **Step 6**: The `Ext.grid.column.Boolean` type that is used to display boolean data fields. With the `trueText` and `falseText` properties we can define the text to display in each case. In our example we are setting `YES` and `NO` respectively.

- **Step 7**: We defined an `Ext.grid.column.Action` type. This type of column is very useful, because on older versions of the framework we have to make some tweaks to accomplish this kind of behavior. Now we only have to set the icon or a series of icons in a grid cell as items of the column and add the respective handlers for each icon, so we can process icons by clicking on them individually. In our example we are adding a pencil icon on step eight and a cross icon on step nine that will perform editing and deleting rows from our grid respectively.

- **Step 8**: We added a pencil icon that will edit rows from our grid.

- **Step 9**: We added a cross icon for deleting rows from our grids.

Now that we have described the grid columns behavior we are ready to learn how column renderers work.

Columns renderers

The column renderers are a great feature to customize behavior and rendering of the cells in the grid panel. A renderer is tied to a particular column, where we can customize the behavior or the styles of a cell. The renderers are methods that are called for each cell of the column with the following arguments:

- **Value**: The data value for the current cell.

- **Metadata**: A collection of metadata of the current cell, typically used to modify the styles of the cell or row.

- **Record**: The record of the current row.

- **Row index**: The index of the current row.

- **Column index**: The index of the current column.

- **Store**: The store of our grid.

- **View**: The current grid view, so we can modify it or refresh it.

Some of the most common renderers are included in `Ext.util.Format`, like `Ext.util.Format.dateRenderer` or `Ext.util.Format.usMoney`. We can write our own renderers too, so let's add some renderers to our grid as follows:

```
columns:[{
      text:'Country',
      width:60,
      dataIndex:'country',
      renderer:function (v) { //step 1
            return '<imgsrc="' + v.toLowerCase() + '.png">';
```

```
        }
    },{
        text:'Total',
        xtype:'numbercolumn',
        width:80,
        dataIndex:'amount',
        renderer: Ext.util.Format.usMoney //step 2
    },{
        text:'Active?',
        //xtype:'booleancolumn',//step 3
        width:80,
        dataIndex:'active',
        trueText:'YES',
        falseText:'NO',
        renderer:function(v,m){ //step 4
        var color = v ? 'red' : 'green',
        v = v ? 'YES' : 'NO';
            m.style = 'color:' + color;
            return v;
        }
    }]
```

In the preceding code we have applied renderers to three columns of our grid, let's describe each one of them:

- **Step 1**: We added a renderer to display the flag of the country instead of the text. We have added the icons to the chapter source files.

- **Step 2**: The renderer `Ext.util.Format.usMoney` that was added on step two takes the number value of the column and renders it in U.S. money format.

- **Step 3**: We commented the `xtype` property of the column, so we can apply to it a custom renderer and give format to the YES and NO text.

- **Step 4**: We did some logic to render a green YES text or a red NO text.

The previous configuration outputs the result shown in the following screenshot:

	Name	Country	Pay Date	Total	Active?	
Clients						
1	**David Lee** (age: 24) david@email.com		08-08-2012	120.50	YES	✏️✖️
2	**Lisa Brown** (age: 25) lisa@email.com		08-08-2012	120.50	NO	✏️✖️
3	**Armando Gonzalez** (age: 30) armando@email.com		08-28-2012	120.00	YES	✏️✖️
4	**Mike Chang** (age: 27) mike@email.com		08-08-2012	12.55	NO	✏️✖️
5	**Kevin Smith** (age: 28) kevin@email.com		08-08-2012	54.50	YES	✏️✖️

Selection models

Once we have defined the way we want to display our data, we need the tools to interact with it. That's where the selection models are needed. The grid panels use selection models for selecting some part of the grid's data. There are two main selection models on the framework, the `Ext.selection.RowModel` model, where an entire row of the grid is selected, or the `Ext.selection.CellModel` model, where individuals cells are selected.

By default, the grid panel uses the row selection model that selects all the rows of our grid. In our example we are going to use the `RowSelectionModel` class to get the record we are going to edit or delete.

```
{
        xtype:'actioncolumn',
        width:40,
        items:[{
                icon:'pencil.png',
                handler:function (grid, rowIndex, colIndex) {

                        varselectionModel= grid.getSelectionModel(),
                          record;
                        selectionModel.select(rowIndex);
                        record = selectionModel.getSelection()[0];
                        alert('You are going to edit ' +
                          record.get('name'));
                }
        },{
```

```
            icon:'cross.png',
    handler:function (grid, rowIndex, colIndex) {
    var selectionModel= grid.getSelectionModel(), record;
    selectionModel.select(rowIndex);
    record = selectionModel.getSelection()[0];
    alert('You are going to delete ' + record.get('name'));
                        }
                    }
            ]
    }
```

In the previous code we have modified the actioncolumn xtype. First we get the selection model of the grid (by default it is row selection), then we select the row, where the icon was clicked with the select method, then we used the getSelection method to get the selected records, and finally we use a JavaScript alert function to display a message for editing or deleting the selected record.

The CellSelectionModel class behaves differently from the RowSelectionModel class. Now when you click on a cell only the cell you clicked on is selected and the key navigation will move focus from cell to cell. Let's accomplish the same functionality of the previous example but now with a CellSelectionModel class.

First we have to set the selection type to our grid as shown in the following code:

```
    store:clientStore,
    width:600,
    selType: 'cellmodel',
    height:210,
    title:'Clients',
```

Next, we have to change the following line of the code:

```
    selectionModel.select(rowIndex);
```

We will replace it with the following code snippet:

```
    selectionModel.setCurrentPosition({
            row: rowIndex,
            column: colIndex
    });
```

The following screenshot is the output of our selection model example:

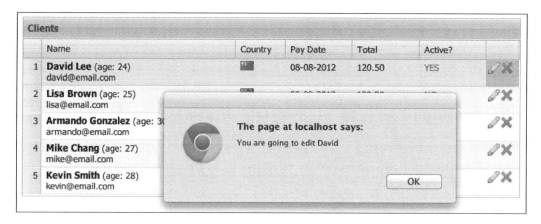

Grid listeners

The event listener is a core feature in components of the Ext JS library. The grid panel is not an exception. Because of its nature this panel has a very well designed set of listeners that will allow us to process all kind of events.

Let's write some code to update our grid information; to achieve this task we are going to use a form panel.

We have to define the form panel used for editing the grid data as shown in the following code:

```
/**
 * @classMyApp.view.Form
 * @extendsExt.form.Panel
 * @author Armando Gonzalez <iam@armando.mx>
 * This the form for the grid listeners example.
 */
Ext.define('MyApp.view.Form', {
        extend:'Ext.form.Panel',
        layout:'anchor',
        title:'client',
        flex:1.5,
        frame:true,
        defaultType:'textfield',
        defaults:{
                allowBlank:false,
                anchor:'100%'
        },
```

```
items:[{
        fieldLabel:'Name',
        name:'name'
        },{
        fieldLabel:'Last Name',
        name:'lastname'
        },{
        fieldLabel:'Age',
        xtype:'numberfield',
        name:'age'
        },{
        fieldLabel:'Email',
        name:'email',
        vtype:'email'
        },{
        fieldLabel:'Country',
        name:'country',
        xtype:'combobox',
        displayField:'name',
        store:Ext.create('Ext.data.Store', {
        fields:['name'],
        data:[
        {"name":"China"},
        {"name":"Australia"},
        {"name":"Mexico"},
        {"name":"Japan"},
        {"name":"Usa"}
                ]
            })
},
        {
fieldLabel:'Pay Date',
xtype:'datefield',
name:'paydate'
},
        {
fieldLabel:'Total',
xtype:'numberfield',
name:'amount',
allowDecimals:true
},{
```

```
fieldLabel:'Active?',
xtype:'checkbox',
name:'active'
        }
    ]
});
```

Then we need to create the form and grid panel, this code goes in the
`Ext.onReady` method:

```
var grid = Ext.create('MyApp.view.Grid',{
    listeners:{ //step 1
    itemclick:function (view, record, htmlItem, index,
    eventObject, opts) {
    form.loadRecord(record);
        }
      },
    }),
    form = Ext.create('MyApp.view.Form',{
    buttons:[
            {
    text:'Reset',
    handler:function () {
    this.up('form').getForm().reset();
            }
          },
          {
    text:'Save',
    formBind:true,
    disabled:true,
    scope:this,
    handler:function () {
    varselectionModel = grid.getSelectionModel(), record;
    record = selectionModel.getSelection()[0];
    record.set(form.getValues());//step 2
    grid.getView().refresh();//step 3
        }
      }
    ]
    });
```

The steps are explained as follows:

- **Step 1**: We added the listener to the grid, the `itemclick` listener. It handles the event when an item of the grid has been clicked. In our example we are listening to that event and loading a record to the form panel.

- **Step 2**: We set the edited values of the form to the grid panel.

- **Step 3**: We refresh the grid view to see the updated data.

Once we have our form and grid defined we are putting them in a `Ext.container.Viewport` property so we can display them properly as shown in the following code:

```
Ext.create('Ext.container.Viewport', {
        layout:{
                type:'hbox',
                align:'stretch'
        },
        items:[grid, form]
});
```

In the previous code, we add our grid and form to the viewport; the result is the output shown in the following screenshot:

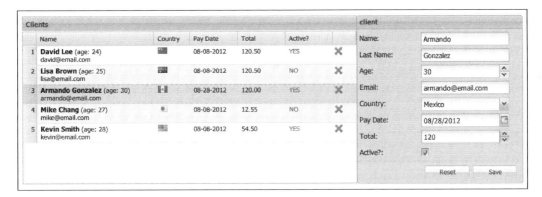

Features

The `Ext.grid.Feature` class is a new class included in Ext JS 4 designed for creating optional grid features. In older versions of the framework plugins were one way of adding custom functionality to grids, but the Sencha team have created a more organized way of doing this. With this class we can inject additional functionality in certain points of the grid's creation cycle.

In Ext JS 4 we have four main classes that extend from `Ext.grid.Feature`.

Ext.grid.feature.Grouping

This feature displays the grid rows in groups; the configuration has to be done in the grid with the feature property and has to be done on the grid store as well.

First we have to change our store a little bit as shown in the following code:

```
Ext.create('Ext.data.Store', {
        model:'Client',
        groupField:'country',
        data:[{
                client:1,
                name:'David',
                lastname:'Lee', age:24,
                email:'david@email.com',
                country:'China',
                paydate:'08/08/2012',
                amount:120.5,
                active:true
                },{
                client:2,
                name:'Lisa',
                lastname:'Brown',
                age:25,
                email:'lisa@email.com',
                country:'Japan',
                paydate:'08/08/2012',
                amount:120.5, active:false
                },{
                client:3,
                name:'Armando',
                lastname:'Gonzalez',
                age:30,
                email:'armando@email.com',
                country:'Mexico',
                paydate:'08/28/2012',
                amount:120,
                active:true
                },{
                client:4,
                name:'Mike',
                lastname:'Chang',
                age:27,
                email:'mike@email.com',
                country:'Japan',
                paydate:'08/08/2012',
                amount:12.5456,
                active:false
                },{
```

```
                    client:5,
                    name:'Kevin',
                    lastname:'Smith',
                    age:28,
                    email:'kevin@email.com',
                    country:'Mexico',
                    paydate:'08/08/2012',
                    amount:54.5,
                    active:true
                    }]
    });
```

Now we create the grid with the grouping feature as shown in the following code:

```
/**
 * @classMyApp.view.GroupingFeature
 * @extendsExt.grid.Panel
 * @author Armando Gonzalez <iam@armando.mx>
 * This the grouping feature example.
 */
Ext.define('MyApp.view.GroupingFeature', {
        extend: 'Ext.grid.Panel',
        flex:1,
        title:'Clients',
        features:[Ext.create('Ext.grid.feature.Grouping', {
groupHeaderTpl:'Group: {name} ({rows.length})'
        })],
    initComponent: function() {
        var me = this;
        me.createModel();
        me.columns = me.buildColumns();
        me.store =  me.buildStore();
        this.callParent(arguments);
    },
    createModel:function(){ //The definition of the client model
....},
    buildStore:function(){  //defining the client`s store
      ....
    },
    buildColumns : function(){
        return [{
```

```
            xtype:'rownumberer'
            },{
            text:'Name',
            xtype:'templatecolumn',
            flex:1,
            dataIndex:'name',
            tpl:'<b>{name} {lastname} </b> (age: {age})</br>{email}</br>'
            },{
            text:'Country',
            width:60,
            dataIndex:'country'
            },{
            text:'Pay Date',
            xtype:'datecolumn',
            width:80,
            dataIndex:'paydate',
            format:'m-d-Y'
            },{
            text:'Total',
            xtype:'numbercolumn',
            width:80,
            dataIndex:'amount',
            renderer:Ext.util.Format.usMoney
            },{
            text:'Active?',
            width:80,
            dataIndex:'active',
            trueText:'YES',
            falseText:'NO',
            renderer:function (v) { //step 4
                    var color = v ? 'red' : 'green',
        v = v ? 'YES' : 'NO';
                    m.style = 'color:' + color;
                    return v;
                }
            }
    ];
    }
});
```

The previous code outputs the grid shown in the following screenshot:

Ext.grid.feature.GroupingSummary

This feature adds an aggregate summary row at the bottom of each group that is defined by the `Ext.grid.feature.Grouping` feature.

Let's add a grouping summary feature to our grid as shown in the following code:

```
/**
 * @classMyApp.view.GroupingSummaryFeature
 * @extendsExt.grid.Panel
 * @author Armando Gonzalez <iam@armando.mx>
 * This the grouping summary example.
 */
Ext.define('MyApp.view.GroupingSummaryFeature', {
        extend: 'Ext.grid.Panel',
        flex:1,
        title:'Clients',
        features:[ //step 1
        {
                ftype:'groupingsummary',
                groupHeaderTpl:'Group: {name} ({rows.length})'
        }],
```

```
initComponent: function() {
        var me = this;
        me.createModel();
        me.columns = me.buildColumns();
        me.store =  me.buildStore();
        this.callParent(arguments);
},
    createModel:function(){ //The definition of the client model
    ...
    },
    buildStore:function(){  //defining the client`s store
      ...
    },
    buildColumns : function(){
      return [{
              xtype:'rownumberer'
              },{
              text:'Name',
              xtype:'templatecolumn',
              flex:1,
              dataIndex:'name',
              tpl:'<b>{name} {lastname} </b> (age: {age})</br>
              {email}</br>',
              summaryType:'count',
              summaryRenderer:function (value) { //step 2
                  return value + ' client' + (value === 1 ? '' : 's');
              }
              },{
                  text:'Country',
                  width:60,
                  dataIndex:'country'
              },{
                  text:'Pay Date',
                  xtype:'datecolumn',
                  width:80,
                  dataIndex:'paydate',
                  format:'m-d-Y'
              },{
                  text:'Total',
                  xtype:'numbercolumn',
                  width:80,
                  dataIndex:'amount',
                  renderer:Ext.util.Format.usMoney,
```

```
summaryType:'sum',//step 3
summaryRenderer:Ext.util.Format.usMoney
},{
text:'Active?',
xtype:'booleancolumn',
width:80,
dataIndex:'active',
trueText:'YES',
falseText:'NO'
}];
}
});
```

In the previous example we are using the same store we used on the `Ext.grid.feature.Grouping` example. The steps are explained as follows:

- **Step 1**: We defined our `Ext.grid.feature.groupingSummary` feature by its `ftype` property and assigned a `groupHeaderTpl` property.
- **Step 2**: We are counting how many users are there in each group.
- **Step 3**: We are summarizing the total column for each group.

The output of our grouping summary example is shown in the following screenshot:

Clients					
Name		Country ▲	Pay Date	Total	Active?
☐ Group: China (1)					
1	**David Lee** (age: 24) david@email.com	China	08-08-2012	120.50	YES
	1 client			$120.50	
☐ Group: Japan (2)					
2	**Lisa Brown** (age: 25) lisa@email.com	Japan	08-08-2012	120.50	NO
3	**Mike Chang** (age: 27) mike@email.com	Japan	08-08-2012	12.55	NO
	2 clients			$133.05	
☐ Group: Mexico (2)					
4	**Armando Gonzalez** (age: 30) armando@email.com	Mexico	08-28-2012	120.00	YES
5	**Kevin Smith** (age: 28) kevin@email.com	Mexico	08-08-2012	54.50	YES
	2 clients			$174.50	

Ext.grid.feature.RowBody

This feature adds a body section for each grid row that can contain any markup. This grid feature is useful to associate additional data of a particular record. It will also expose additional events to the grid view like `rowbodyclick`, `rowbodydbclick`, and `rowbodycontextmenu`.

Now let's add the row body feature to our grid as shown in the following code:

```
/**
 * @classMyApp.view.RowBodyFeature
 * @extendsExt.grid.Panel
 * @author Armando Gonzalez <iam@armando.mx>
 * This the grouping summary feature example.
 */
Ext.define('MyApp.view.RowBodyFeature', {
        extend: 'Ext.grid.Panel',
        flex:1,
        title:'Clients',
        features:[{
                ftype:'rowbody', //step 1
                getAdditionalData:function (data, index, record, orig)
                  {//step 2
                    return{
                    rowBody:'<span style="padding-left: 10px">' +
                      Ext.util.Format.usMoney(data.amount) + '</span>'
                    }
                  }
        }],
initComponent: function() {
        var me = this;
        me.createModel();
        me.columns = me.buildColumns();
        me.store =  me.buildStore();
        this.callParent(arguments);
},
   createModel:function(){ //The definition of the client model
      ...
   },
   buildStore:function(){  //defining the client`s store
      ...
   },
buildColumns : function(){
        return [{
                text:'Name',
```

```
        xtype:'templatecolumn',
        flex:1,
        dataIndex:'name',
        tpl:'<b>{name} {lastname} </b> (age: {age})</br>{email}</br>'
        }];
    }
});
        ]
});
```

The steps are explained as follows:

- **Step 1**: We have defined the `rowbody` feature.
- **Step 2**: In the `getAdditionalData` method we are rendering the total data of our client in the `rowBody` property.

With this configuration we have the output as shown in the following screenshot:

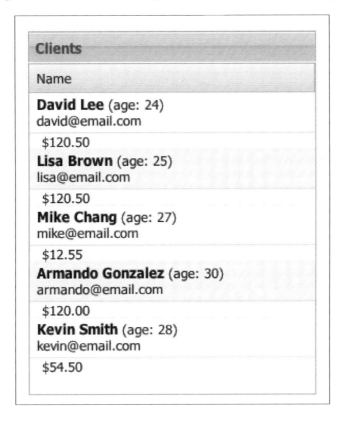

Ext.grid.feature.Summary

This is the last grid feature we are going to explain; this feature adds a summary row at the bottom of all the grid rows with aggregate totals for a column.

The code for this grid feature is as follows:

```
/**
 * @classMyApp.view.SummaryFeature
 * @extendsExt.grid.Panel
 * @author Armando Gonzalez <iam@armando.mx>
 * This the summary feature example.
 */
Ext.define('MyApp.view.SummaryFeature', {
        extend: 'Ext.grid.Panel',
        flex:1,
        title:'Clients',
        features:[{
                ftype:'summary'
}],
initComponent: function() {
        var me = this;
        me.createModel();
        me.columns = me.buildColumns();
        me.store =  me.buildStore();
        this.callParent(arguments);
},
   createModel:function(){ //The definition of the client model
      ...
   },
   buildStore:function(){  //defining the client`s store
      ...
   },
buildColumns : function(){
        return [{
                text:'Name',
                xtype:'templatecolumn',
                flex:1,
                dataIndex:'name',
                tpl:'<b>{name} {lastname} </b> (age: {age})
                  </br>{email}</br>',
```

```
            summaryType:'count',
            summaryRenderer:function (value) {
            return value + ' client' + (value === 1 ? '' : 's');
            }
        }];
        }
    });
```

We have highlighted the simple configuration that our grid needs to have, so we can see our `Ext.grid.feature.Summary` feature working. When we execute our previous code the result is shown in the following screenshot:

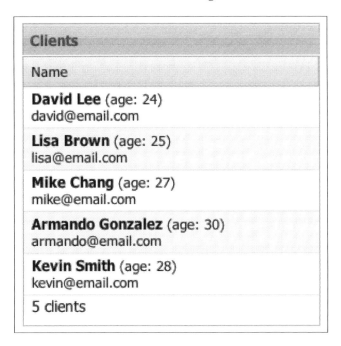

Plugins

In Ext JS 4 plugins provide custom functionality for the components. A plugin is an Ext JS class that usually doesn't need to extend another Ext JS class. A plugin must always have an `init` method that the Ext JS plugin system calls to initialize the plugin.

The `init` method will take the component, which has the plugin as a parameter. This method will configure all custom events, if any, and will also set up the methods to listen to those events.

For the grid panel we have a set of five plugins already implemented in the Ext JS library. They are the `Ext.grid.plugin.Editing`, `Ext.grid.plugin.CellEditing`, `Ext.grid.plugin.RowEditing`, `Ext.grid.plugin.DragDrop`, and `Ext.grid.plugin.HeaderResizer` plugins.

Ext.grid.plugin.Editing

This is an abstract class that provides grid editing on the selected columns. The editable columns are specified in the column configuration of the grid. This class should not be used directly; instead we should use the `Ext.grid.plugin.CellEditing` and `Ext.grid.plugin.RowEditing` classes that are subclasses of this abstract class.

Ext.grid.plugin.CellEditing

This plugin makes editing a single cell of our grid possible. We can only edit a single cell at a time. The editor is defined in the `editor` property of our columns configuration. If we don't define an editor in a column, it will be skipped by the `editor` plugin.

We should always choose an appropriate field type to match our data, so if we were using a number type it would be useful to use an `Ext.form.field.Number` class.

```
/**
 * @classMyApp.view.GridCellEditingPlugin
 * @extendsExt.grid.Panel
 * @author Armando Gonzalez <iam@armando.mx>
 * This is the cell editing plugin example.
 */
Ext.define('MyApp.view.GridCellEditingPlugin', {
        extend: 'Ext.grid.Panel',
        flex:1,
        title:'Clients',
        plugins:[{
                ptype:'cellediting', //step 1
                clicksToEdit:1
        }],
initComponent: function() {
        var me = this;
        me.createModel();
        me.columns = me.buildColumns();
        me.store =  me.buildStore();
        this.callParent(arguments);
},
```

```
   createModel:function(){ //The definition of the client model
      ...
   },
   buildStore:function(){  //defining the client`s store
      ...
   },
   buildColumns : function(){
return [{
        text:'Name',
        xtype:'templatecolumn',
        flex:1,
        dataIndex:'name',
        tpl:'<b>{name} {lastname} </b> (age: {age})</br>{email}</br>'
        },{
        text:'Country',
        dataIndex:'country',
        editor:{ //step 2
                xtype:'combo',
                allowBlank:false,
                displayField:'name',
                store:Ext.create('Ext.data.Store', {
                fields:['name'],
                data:[
                {"name":"China"},
                {"name":"Australia"},
                {"name":"Mexico"},
                {"name":"Japan"},
                {"name":"Usa"}
                        ]
                })
                }
            },
            {
text:'Pay Date',
dataIndex:'paydate',
xtype:'datecolumn',
format:'m/d/Y',
editor:{ //step 3
xtype:'datefield',
allowBlank:false
                }
            }
        ];
   }
});
```

In our previous code we have added a cell editor. The steps are explained as follows:

- **Step 1**: We added our editing plugin so our grid becomes editable when the user clicks on the cell.
- **Step 2**: We added a `combo` field as an editor for our **country** column.
- **Step 3**: We added a `date field` xtype so we can edit our clients' pay date.

Our previous code outputs the grid shown in the following screenshot:

Ext.grid.plugin.RowEditing

This plugin adds full row editing capabilities to the grid panel. When the editing begins each editable column will show the field for editing, a **Save** button, and a **Cancel** button will be display in the dialog for editing.

```
/**
 * @classMyApp.view.GridRowEditingPlugin
 * @extendsExt.grid.Panel
 * @author Armando Gonzalez <iam@armando.mx>
 * This the grid row editing example.
 */
Ext.define('MyApp.view.GridRowEditingPlugin', {
```

```
extend: 'Ext.grid.Panel',
flex:1,
title:'Clients',
plugins:[{
ptype:'rowediting', //step 1
clicksToEdit:1
     }],
initComponent: function() {
  var me = this;
    me.createModel();
      me.columns = me.buildColumns();
      me.store =  me.buildStore();
    this.callParent(arguments);
  },
  createModel:function(){ //The definition of the client model
     ...
  },
  buildStore:function(){  //defining the client`s store
    ...
  },
  buildColumns : function(){
return [{
text:'Name',
xtype:'templatecolumn',
flex:1,
dataIndex:'name',
tpl:'<b>{name} {lastname} </b> (age: {age})</br>{email}</br>'
},{
text:'Country',
dataIndex:'country',
editor:{ //step 2
xtype:'combo',
allowBlank:false,
displayField:'name',
store:Ext.create('Ext.data.Store', {
fields:['name'],
data:[
{"name":"China"},
{"name":"Australia"},
{"name":"Mexico"},
```

```
                              {"name":"Japan"},
                              {"name":"Usa"}
                    ]
           })
        }
   },
   {
text:'Pay Date',
dataIndex:'paydate',
xtype:'datecolumn',
format:'m/d/Y',
editor:{ //step 3
xtype:'datefield',
allowBlank:false
           }
        }
     ];
   }
});
```

The preceding code creates a grid panel with a row editing plugin. The steps are explained as follows:

- **Step 1**: We defined our row editing plugin.
- **Step 2** and **step 3**: We declared our column editors.

This configuration outputs the grid shown in the following screenshot:

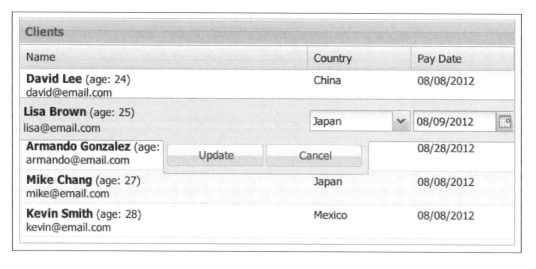

Grid paging

The grid panel supports paging through a large set of data via a `PagingToolBar` item. To accomplish this we have to do some modifications to our store and add a `PagingToolBar` item to our grid.

First we need to create our store as shown in the following code:

```
Ext.create('Ext.data.Store', {
  autoLoad:true,
  model:'Client',
  pageSize:10,
    proxy:{
    type:'ajax',
    url:'clients.php,
    reader:{
    type:'json',
    root:'data',
    totalProperty:'num'
  }
  }
});
```

In the definition of our store we declared a `pageSize` property of 10, and defined a proxy so we can get the data from the server, so we can be able to paginate our data.

Then we define our grid and the `PagingToolbar` item our grid will have:

```
/**
 * @classMyApp.view.GridPaging
 * @extendsExt.grid.Panel
 * @author Armando Gonzalez <iam@armando.mx>
 * This the grid paging example.
 */
Ext.define('MyApp.view.GridPaging', {
  extend: 'Ext.grid.Panel',
    flex:1,
    title:'Clients',
initComponent: function() {
    var me = this;
    me.createModel();
      me.columns = me.buildColumns();
      me.store =  me.buildStore();
      me.dockedItems= me.buildDockedItems();
    this.callParent(arguments);
  },
```

```
buildDockedItems : function(){
  return [{
    xtype:'pagingtoolbar',
    dock:'bottom',
    store:this.store,
    displayInfo:true
  }];
  },
  createModel:function(){ //The definition of the client model
    ...
  },
  buildStore:function(){  //defining the client`s store
    ...
  },
buildColumns : function(){
  return [{
    xtype:'rownumberer'
        },{
    text:'Name',
    xtype:'templatecolumn',
    flex:1,
    dataIndex:'name',
    tpl:'Clent : {name} {lastname}'
  }];
  }
});
```

In the previous code we declared a pagingToolbar item on the dockedItems property of our grid; here we assigned the same store of our grid so the pagingToolbar item references the same store.

The previous code generates the output shown in the following screenshot:

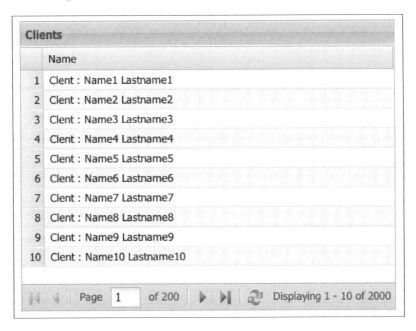

Infinite scrolling

If we don't like the pagingToolbar item, Ext JS 4 introduces a new type of grid, the **infinite scrolling** grid. This grid can render thousands of records without needing the pagingToolbar item. The grid should be bound to a store with a pageSize property that will load data dynamically according to the pageSize property.

Let's see an infinite scrolling example. First we need to add some configuration to our store:

```
Ext.create('Ext.data.Store', {
  autoLoad:true,
  model:'Client',
  pageSize:100, //step 1
  purgePageCount:0, //step 2
  proxy:{
type:'ajax',
url:'clients.json',
reader:{
type:'json',
root:'data'
          }
      }
    });
```

In our previous store configuration, we declared a `pageSize` property of `100` and set the `purgePageCount` property to `0`. Setting the `purgePageCount` property indicates that there is no need to purge data. This option is only relevant when the buffered option is set to true. The buffered option allows the store to prefetch pages of records.

Now let's see the definition of our grid as shown in the following code:

```
/**
 * @classMyApp.view.InfiniteScrolling
 * @extendsExt.grid.Panel
 * @author Armando Gonzalez <iam@armando.mx>
 * This the infinite grid scrolling example.
 */
Ext.define('MyApp.view.InfiniteScrolling', {
    extend: 'Ext.grid.Panel',
    title:'Clients (Infinite scrolling)',
  flex:1,
  verticalScrollerType:'paginggridscroller', //step 1
    invalidateScrollerOnRefresh:false, //step 2
    disableSelection:true, //step 3
initComponent: function() {
        var me = this;
    me.createModel();
        me.columns = me.buildColumns();
        me.store =  me.buildStore();
    this.callParent(arguments);
},
  createModel:function(){ //The definition of the client model
      ...
    },
    buildStore:function(){  //defining the client`s store
      ...
    },
buildColumns : function(){
    return [{
      text:'Name',
      xtype:'templatecolumn',
      flex:1,
      dataIndex:'name',
      tpl:'Clent : {name} {lastname}'
            }
        ];
    }
});
```

The steps are explained as follows:

- **Step 1**: We have declared a `paginggridscroller` property. This will set our infinite scrolling feature.
- **Step 2**: We set the `invalidateScrollerOnRefresh` property to `false` so when we refresh the grid view our grid scroll does not reset.
- **Step 3**: We are disabling selection on our grid because infinite scrolling does not support selection.

With these configurations been made we have the output as shown in the following screenshot:

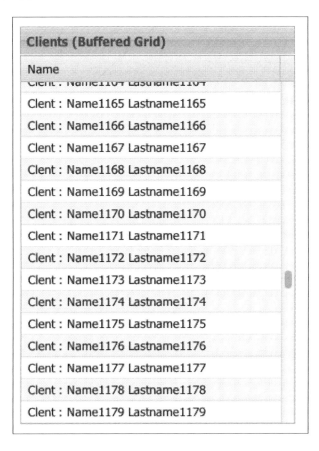

Summary

In this chapter we have learned how to configure our grid panels so we can get the best of grid panels when developing our applications. It is important to know what are the grid panel capabilities and how can we add custom functionality using column renderers, grid features, or grid plugins.

You probably don't need to know all possible grid configurations, but if you forget anyone you can always go and take a look to the Ext JS 4 documentation.

In the next chapter we are taking a look at the MVC application pattern. This pattern is the way we should be doing applications in Ext JS 4.

8
Architecture

Before Ext 4 came out, we had to define our own architecture for every project; this was a big problem because it's really easy to write bad code with JavaScript. Many projects don't even have a defined architecture or standards to code.

There are many issues caused by not having a good architecture. One of the main problems is when our application starts growing up and our code is not reusable and maintainable. Therefore, it's really important to understand how we can create a good architecture to work with big applications.

One of the main goals of the latest version of Ext JS is to define a common architecture for all our Ext JS projects. It should be easy to follow and understand. This way when a new developer joins the team it should be easier to explain and understand the way everything works.

In this chapter we are going to learn about how we can tie everything together using the MVC pattern, how to observe the events of the controller, and also we are going to keep working on our final application example. The topics covered in this chapter are as follows:

- The MVC pattern
- File system structure
- Creating views to represent our data
- Adding user interaction with controllers

The MVC pattern
One of the greatest things about using the MVC pattern is that many developers are familiar with it. We probably use this pattern on our server side. This allows new JavaScript developers to easily understand how to build the architecture of their own applications.

In case you don't know anything about the MVC pattern I suggest you read about it. It's important to understand this before we continue. In a few words the **Model-View-Controller (MVC)** pattern allows us to define three layers, where we define specific responsibility for each layer.

The **model layer**, as previously mentioned in *Chapter 4, It's All About the Data*, is intended to define our domain objects with the required data structure. Ext comes with a powerful data package, where we can handle all our data easily.

The **view layer** allows us to display the data that we already have in memory to the end user. Ext contains many components, layouts, and widgets that we can use in order to show our data. We have already seen forms and grids in the previous chapters.

The **controller layer** will serve as an observer; we can listen for events in our views to perform some actions. We will define the logic of our application in this layer, such as showing and hiding some component depending on certain rules and user's input and sending data to the server.

By having these three layers we can write better code, which is easier to maintain and easier to expand when our application grows.

It's important to mention that Sencha is introducing this feature as a recommendation. We can always use the architecture we want, but by using these recommendations it's going to be easier to share code with others, easier to understand other people's code, and easier to integrate a new developer to our project.

Creating our first application

Ext 4 introduces the `Ext.app.Application` class. The main purpose of this class is to define the namespace, where our application will reside, and the point of entry. This code will be executed at the beginning and will be used to start our application.

We can create an instance of the `application` class manually or even extend it to add any modification or behavior that we need; however Ext defines a method that creates the `application` instance for us:

```
Ext.application = function(config) {
    Ext.require('Ext.app.Application');

    Ext.onReady(function() {
        new Ext.app.Application(config);
    });
};
```

The previous code has been extracted from the Ext JS library. The `application` method requires the `Ext.app.Application` class; we don't have to worry about setting the Ext path to the loader because it's set automatically by the library when importing the `ext-dev.js` file.

Let's start by creating a simple application using the `application` method. We need to create a file called `app.js` and write the following code:

```
Ext.application({
    name          : 'MyApp',
    appFolder     : 'app',
    controllers   : [],
    launch        : function(){
        console.log('Ready!');
    }
});
```

First we define the `name` configuration of our application; in this case we are using `MyApp` as the name, but we can use any name. It's important to note that we should use `MyApp` as the root namespace for all the classes that we create. This will allow us to wrap our code in the `MyApp` object and avoid collisions with the third-party code.

The `appFolder` configuration allows us to set the path to the loader for the `MyApp` object. By default, a folder called `app` will be used, but we can define any other folder, for example something like `js/MyApp` or `js/app`.

The `controllers` configuration is an empty array for now, but in here we can define all the controllers that we need to load and instantiate at the very beginning when launching our application. At the moment we don't have anything in here, but we'll come back and add our main controller later in this chapter.

Finally, the `launch` method will be executed when everything is ready. In here we can execute anything we want, some people use this function to create the main viewport of the application.

In order to execute our application in the browser we need to create the HTML file and import the Ext library and the `app.js` file that we have just created.

```
<!DOCTYPE html>
<html>
<head>
<meta charset="UTF-8" />
<title>Application</title>
```

```
<!-- Importing the Ext JS library -->
<script type="text/javascript" src="../extjs-4.1.0/ext-dev.js"></
script>
<link rel="stylesheet" href="../extjs-4.1.0/resources/css/ext-all.css"
/>

<script type="text/javascript" src="app.js"></script>

</head>
<body>
</body>
</html>
```

Now we are ready to test our code. Using our favorite browser let's navigate to the HTML file. For now we will only see a message in the JavaScript console and nothing else. This is because at the moment we have only created an empty application.

 We need to run our code using a web server; this is required because we are going to perform some Ajax calls later in this chapter.

Once we have our application definition in place we need to start creating the content. First we need to define the folder structure as shown in the following screenshot:

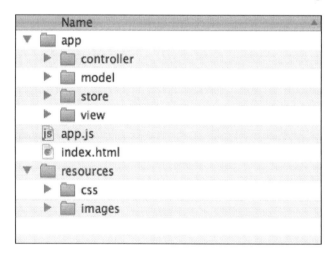

We create the **app** folder because that's the path we defined in our application (using the `appFolder` configuration). We can use any name we want, but the convention name is `app`.

The main folder for our application contains four folders within it: **controller**, **model**, **store**, and **view**. Each of these folders will contain our JavaScript classes.

In the `controller` folder we will create classes that will listen for events in the views and make Ajax requests to the server in order to send and receive data. Basically all the logic for our application will be in this folder.

In the `model` folder we will create our model classes with all the properties, relationships, and all the information that we need to handle.

The `store` folder will contain classes that extend from the `Ext.data.Store` class and will serve as a collection for the defined models. We have created this folder because it's a convention. If we use the Sencha Architect, we will see this folder when saving the project.

In the `view` folder we will create all the required components to show our data, components such as grids, forms, trees, buttons, and so on.

Also we have defined a **resources** folder, where we will add our CSS stylesheets and the images that we are going to use for our application.

This is a typical folder structure for a project; this is the recommendation and convention that Sencha is introducing in this new version of the Ext JS library. It's important to note that we can change this structure and make our own if we want. This structure is just a recommendation.

In real world applications we usually add the third-party code, extensions, plugins, or reusable components developed by other people. It's a good idea to have the **app** folder inside of a **js** folder, where we can also create more folders to add other people's code, something as shown in the following screenshot:

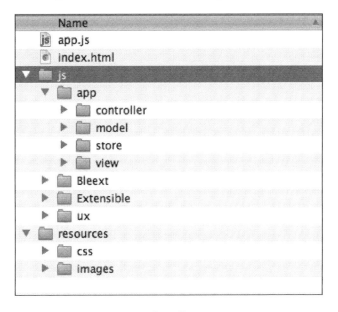

This way we can group all the JavaScript code that we are going to use, even components from the third-party companies. For now we are going to keep working with the previous structure, but if you want to continue with the second option, just make sure to change the `appFolder` property in the application definition accordingly.

The views

As mentioned before we use views to define our user interface with the available components and widgets of the library. We will start by creating the main viewport.

We can create the viewport manually using the `Ext.create` method inside of the `launch` callback, but the `Application` class is able to create the viewport automatically using a convention of defining a `Viewport` class in our `views` folder.

At the end of *Chapter 5, Buttons and Toolbars*, we created the main menu of our final application. We used a viewport to take all the available space in the browser, now we are going to use that same code. Let's create a `Viewport.js` file under the `app/view` folder and paste the code that we already have:

```
Ext.define('MyApp.view.Viewport',{
    extend      : 'Ext.container.Viewport',

    layout      : 'fit',

    initComponent    : function(){
        var me = this;

        me.items = [{
        xtype : 'panel',
        dockedItems : [{
            xtype : 'toolbar',
            docked: 'top',
            itemId: 'mainmenu',
            items : [{
                text : 'Start',
                iconCls : 'home-icon16',
                itemId    : 'startbutton',
                menu    : [
                    {text:'Clients',iconCls:'clients-icon16'},
                    {text:'Invoices',iconCls:'invoices-icon16'},
                    {text:'Categories',iconCls:'categories-icon16'}
                ]
            },{
```

```
        xtype: 'tbfill'
    },{
        text : 'John Doe',
        icon : 'resources/images/user_suit.png'
    }]
  }]
    }];

    me.callParent();
  }
});
```

The only changes we have made here were the definition of the itemId property for the toolbar and for the start button, also we have modified the icon path to fit our folder structure. The rest of the code is the same.

> An itemId property can be used as an alternative way to get a reference to a component when no object reference is available. It is an identification that we assign to components and we can search for a component by its itemId property at any time. We don't need to worry about collisions; the itemId property should be unique only for the siblings of the component but not globally.

Also we need to modify two more files. First we need to create the viewport automatically, to do this let's modify our app.js file as follows:

```
Ext.application({
    name        : 'MyApp',
    appFolder   : 'app',
    controllers    : [],
    autoCreateViewport  : true
});
```

We have added the autoCreateViewport property to our definition. By doing this the Application class will look for a class called MyApp.view.Viewport. It will include the JavaScript file in the document using the loader and it will create the instance of this class. Keep in mind that the file of this class should be in the app/view/Viewport.js file. We have also removed the launch callback because we are not going to use it.

The previous code uses some icons, we need to define the styles for them. Let's create a `style.css` file under `resources/css` and paste the code that we already have from *Chapter 5, Buttons and Toolbars*:

```css
.home-icon16{
  background:transparent url(../images/house.png) center 0 no-repeat
!important;
}
.clients-icon16{
  background:transparent url(../images/user_green.png) center 0 no-
repeat !important;
}
.invoices-icon16{
  background:transparent url(../images/table_money.png) center 0 no-
repeat !important;
}
.categories-icon16{
  background:transparent url(../images/application_view_icons.png)
center 0 no-repeat !important;
}
```

Also we need to copy all the required images to the `resources/images` folder. Finally, we need to modify our `index.html` file to include the CSS file:

```html
<!DOCTYPE html>
<html>
<head>
<meta charset="UTF-8" />
<title>Application</title>

<!-- Importing the Ext JS library -->
<script type="text/javascript" src="../extjs-4.1.0/ext-dev.js"></
script>
<link rel="stylesheet" href="../extjs-4.1.0/resources/css/ext-all.css"
/>
<link rel="stylesheet" href="resources/css/style.css" />

<script type="text/javascript" src="app.js"></script>

</head>
<body>
</body>
</html>
```

Once we have all the new changes, let's try our application in our favorite browser. We will see a viewport that contains a toolbar at the top with the **Start** menu and some options on it as shown in the following screenshot:

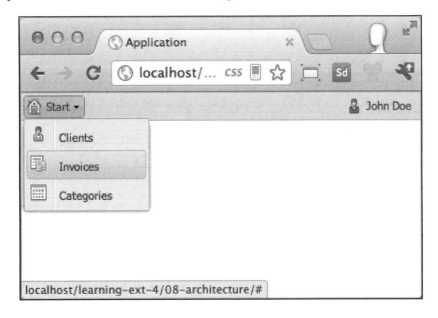

It's important to mention that when we use the `ext.js`, `ext-debug.js`, or `ext-dev.js` files the loader is enabled by default so we don't have to worry about it.

The controller

We have our main view in place, but it doesn't do anything. In order to add some functionality we need to create a controller that listens to events on the menu and shows the corresponding module.

Let's start by creating a new JavaScript file called `app/controller/main/Main.js`, where we are going to write our `Controller` class. We are also creating a `main` folder for our module.

 It's a good idea to create folders to group controllers, views, models, or stores that belong to the same module. This way is going to be easier to locate each class when our application starts growing.

Once we have our empty file let's write the following code in it:

```
Ext.define('MyApp.controller.main.Main',{
    extend        : 'Ext.app.Controller', //Step 1

    init    : function(){ //Step 2
        var me = this;

        console.log('Initializing the controller');
    }
});
```

We are creating a class using the `Ext.define` method as usual. It's important to note that the name of the class corresponds to the folder structure and the filename. This is a convention so the loader can work properly. It is explained in detail in *Chapter 2, The Core Concepts*.

In the first step we extend from the `Ext.app.Controller` class. This class contains several methods that will help us listen to events and save references; basically we are going to add our logic in here.

In the second step we have defined a method called `init`. This method will be executed when our controller is created. This method is like a constructor for our class, it will be the first code executed in our controller; in here we usually create the listeners.

Now we have an empty controller that only shows a message on the JavaScript console. We need to add this controller to our application definition. Let's modify the `app.js` file as follows:

```
Ext.application({
    name          : 'MyApp',
    appFolder     : 'app',
    controllers   : [
        'MyApp.controller.main.Main'
    ],
    autoCreateViewport  : true
});
```

By adding our new class to the `controllers` array we are indicating to our application to load and execute our main controller at the very beginning. We can even define as many controllers as required in the array and all of them will be loaded and executed in the order we have declared them.

If we execute our application, we will only see the message on the JavaScript console. This means our main controller is working!

Listening events

Once we have our controller in place let's add some actions to our view. We need to open a new module when the user clicks on any option of the menu. All we need to do is to add a listener to the `click` event of each option. We do that by using the `control` method that is defined in the `Controller` class that we are extending.

```
Ext.define('MyApp.controller.main.Main',{
    extend      : 'Ext.app.Controller',

    init    : function(){
      var me = this;

        //Step 1
      me.control({
          'toolbar[itemId=mainmenu] button[itemId=startbutton] menuitem: {
            click : me.openModule
          }
        });
    },

    //Step 2
    openModule : function(menuoption){
        console.log('Open the module now!');
      }
});
```

In the first step we are calling the `control` method. This method receives an object containing a selector to find the menu items, then we add the listener to the `click` event. Each event receives a function to be executed when the event gets fired. In here, we can define as many selectors and events as required. To keep things simple we are only defining one listener. Later in this chapter we will see an example with more listeners.

In the second step we are defining the function that will be executed when the event is fired. For now we are only sending a message to the console, but in here we are going to do a lot of things later on.

Before we move forward, let's understand in detail how the selectors work and the classes involved in this process.

Ext 4 introduces this concept to the library. We can search for components using selectors. It is similar to performing DOM search using CSS selectors. In this case we've used the following selector:

```
toolbar[itemId=mainmenu] button[itemId=startbutton] menuitem
```

We can read the previous selector as follows:

Find a `toolbar` component whose `itemId` property should be equal to `mainmenu`. Then search for a `button` component inside of the previous toolbar, whose `itemId` property is equal to `startbutton`, then find all the `menuitems` that are children to the `startbutton`.

When we create components they usually are inside of a container. In this specific case the `toolbar` component is the main container, and we are using the `itemId` property in case we have more toolbars. By using the `itemId` property we make sure we are referring to the right component. The `toolbar` component contains buttons; we have two buttons here, the start menu button and the button where the name of the user is shown. Finally, inside of the start button there's a menu that contains three `menuitem` components.

The following screenshot shows the tree of components that are created. In this screenshot we can see in a better way how our previous selector was constructed:

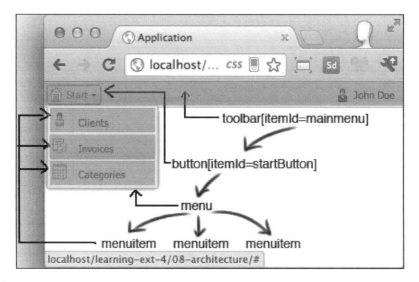

It's important to mention that we are using `xtype` of each component to create our selectors. The syntax of the selectors is very similar to the CSS selectors that we already know; we use brackets when we want to refer to the property of a component. In this case we've been using the `itemid` property, but we can use any of the available properties on the API or even define our own custom properties.

We can also use the numerical symbol (#) to refer to the `id` or `itemId` property. With this in mind we can define our previous selector as follows:

```
#mainmenu #startbutton menuitem
```

Instead of using `xtype` and then the `itemId` property we can only use the numerical symbol with the identification we already defined for each component.

 It's very important to create our selectors as specific as possible because if we define them very generic, the selector will probably match components that we don't want.

Under the hood the `control` method uses a bus of events (`Ext.app.EventBus`) that manages all the events in our application. We can find all our selectors in here.

The bus of events uses a class called `Ext.ComponentQuery`. This class is responsible for performing a search in the tree of components that are created when we start using containers.

The component query class is one of the most useful classes in the framework. There are some methods defined in every container component that we can use to perform a search. For example, we can search for children of a certain component calling the `down` method. We can also search the parents of a component using the `up` method. There's a method called `is` that we can use to see if a component matches a selector.

We are going to be working with selectors over the next chapters. For now let's just keep in mind that the component query class allows us to search for instances of components.

Opening modules

Once we have our listeners in place, we need to open a tab when the user clicks on one of the options of the main menu. In order to do this, we need to create a tab panel, which is a container of tabs. Then we need to import the classes to the document, which were involved in the selected module and finally, create and show the views of the module.

Let's start by modifying our viewport (`app/view/Viewport.js`) to add the tab panel:

```
Ext.define('MyApp.view.Viewport', {
    extend      : 'Ext.container.Viewport',
    requires    : [              //Step 1
    'Ext.tab.Panel',
    'Ext.window.MessageBox'
    ],

    layout      : 'fit',

    initComponent   : function(){
        var me = this;
```

```
            me.items = [{
        xtype : 'panel',
        layout: 'fit',
        dockedItems : [{
          xtype : 'toolbar',
          docked: 'top',
          itemId: 'mainmenu',
          items : [{
            text : 'Start',
            iconCls : 'home-icon16',
            itemId  : 'startbutton',
            menu  : [
              //Step 2
               {text:'Clients',iconCls:'clients-
icon16',controller:'MyApp.controller.clients.Clients'},
               {text:'Invoices',iconCls:'invoices-
icon16',controller:'MyApp.controller.invoices.Invoices'},
               {text:'Categories',iconCls:'categories-
icon16',controller:'MyApp.controller.categories.Categories'}
            ]
          },{
            xtype: 'tbfill'
          },{
            text : 'John Doe',
            icon : 'resources/images/user_suit.png'
          }]
        }],
        items : { //Step 3
          xtype : 'tabpanel',
          itemId: 'maintabs',
          border: false,
          hidden: true
        }
        }];

        me.callParent();
    }
});
```

In the first step we add the classes that we are going to use, in this case, we need to require the Ext.tab.Panel class and the Ext.window.MessageBox class.

In the second step we add a new property to each option. The controller property contains the class that we need to load when the user clicks on the option, we will talk about this later on.

 By loading the classes of our module just when the user needs them allows us to start our main application faster.

Finally, in the last step we create our tab panel. We have assigned an itemId property to get the instance of this component easily; we also hide this component at the beginning.

Once we have those changes in our main viewport we need to go back to our main controller (app/controller/main/Main.js) and dynamically include the selected controller (that we haven't created yet) into our document.

```
Ext.define('MyApp.controller.main.Main',{
   extend       : 'Ext.app.Controller',

   init    : function(){
      //...
   },

   openModule : function(menuoption){
     var me = this,
       maintabs = Ext.ComponentQuery.query('#maintabs')[0]; //Step 1

     Ext.Msg.wait('Loading...');
       //Step 2
     Ext.require(menuoption.controller,function(){
       Ext.Msg.hide();

         console.log('Code is included now!');
     });
   }
});
```

In the first step of the previous code we use the component query to get the reference of the tab panel container; we are going to use this reference to add the tab of our new module.

In the second step we require the controller that has been selected by the user. We show a loading message when we start downloading all the dependencies and when everything is loaded we hide the loading message and print a message to the JavaScript console.

Once we have the controller and its dependencies included in our document we need to create the instance of the controller:

```
openModule : function(menuoption){
  var me = this,
    maintabs = Ext.ComponentQuery.query('#maintabs')[0];

  Ext.Msg.wait('Loading...');
  Ext.require(menuoption.controller,function(){
    Ext.Msg.hide();

    //Step 1
    var controller = me.application.controllers.get(menuoption.
controller);

    if(!controller){
      //Step 2
      controller=Ext.create(menuoption.controller),{
        id          : menuoption.controller,
        application : me.application
      });

    }else{
      //Step 3
      if(controller.container.isDestroyed){


      }
    }

    maintabs.show(); //Step 4
  });
}
```

In the first step of the previous code we verify if the controller already exists. Every controller contains an instance of the main application; this application contains a collection of all the controllers that exist.

The second step will be executed only if the controller has not been created before. In here we create the instance of the selected controller by assigning an identification and the reference to our main application. The id property is used in the first step to retrieve the controller if it exists.

The third step will be executed only if the controller already exists. In here we verify that the container view of this controller also exists. Maybe the controller exists, but if the tab has been closed by the user before, we need to create the view again and open the tab one more time.

In the fourth step we show the main tab panel that is hidden by default.

So far we have included all the classes and its dependencies of our module. We have also created the controller and shown the tab panel container. We are close to the final result; we only need to create the tab, and initialize the main view of our new module.

```
openModule : function(menuoption){
  var me = this,
    maintabs = Ext.ComponentQuery.query('#maintabs')[0];

  Ext.Msg.wait('Loading...');
  Ext.require(menuoption.controller,function(){
    Ext.Msg.hide();

    var controller = me.application.controllers.get(menuoption.
controller);

    if(!controller){
      controller = Ext.create(menuoption.controller, {
        id        : menuoption.controller,
        application  : me.application
      });

        //Step 1
      controller.container = me.createContainer(menuoption);

        //Step 2
      maintabs.add(controller.container);
      controller.addContent();

      //Step 3
      me.application.controllers.add(controller);
      controller.init(me.application);
      controller.onLaunch(me.application);
    }else{
      if(controller.container.isDestroyed){
        //Step 4
          controller.container = me.createContainer(menuoption);
        maintabs.add(controller.container);
        controller.addContent();
      }
    }
```

```
        maintabs.show();
      maintabs.setActiveTab(controller.container);//Step 5
      });
    },

    createContainer : function(menuoption){
        return Ext.widget({
          xtype     : 'container',
          title     : menuoption.text,
          iconCls   : menuoption.iconCls,
          closable  : true,
          layout    : 'fit'
        });
    }
```

In the first step we are creating the tab using the createContainer method. This method returns an instance of the container component with the same title and icon that is defined in the main menu; also we allow the user to close this tab and set the layout to fit. It's important to note that we have created a container property inside of the controller for our module; we are going to use this reference later on.

In the second step we finally add our new tab to the main tab panel container, and also execute a method called addContent defined in our controller. The idea of this method is to initialize the views of the new module.

In the third step we add our new controller to the collection of controllers so that we know this module has been created before; also we execute the init and onLaunch methods on our controller.

The fourth step is executed if the controller already exists and if the view of that controller is destroyed. In here we need to create the view again so we are basically repeating steps one and two, we don't need to repeat step number three.

In the fifth step we show our new tab by executing the setActiveTab method from our tab panel. By doing this we give the focus to our new tab.

If we try our code now we will get a 404 error when loading the controller. This error occurs because we haven't created any file or class for any of our modules.

Before we move forward it's worth saying that the code that we just wrote is very important for our application. We can add more features in here, for example we can make an Ajax request to the server asking for permissions of the module that is going to be loaded; we can restrict permissions here depending on the user's privileges or we may load packages instead of each class. This will help us to speed things up in a production environment. We will talk about preparing our code for deployment later in this book and we will come back to these lines again.

> Security should be always handled on the server side, however sometimes it is necessary to hide or show some buttons or options based on the user's permissions. This data should be provided by the server side only for usability purposes but not for real security.

Creating a module

Let's work on the client module. In *Chapter 1, The Basics*, we defined a mockup for this module. Let's take a look at the mockup so we can remember what we need to do:

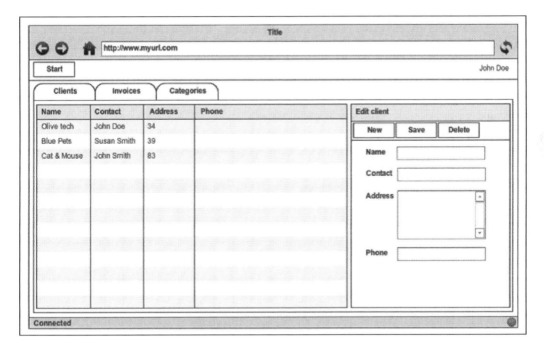

We need a grid to show the existing clients. We should allow users to edit each client by double-clicking on the row. In the left-hand side form we can edit existing records, create new clients, or delete them. To keep things simple we are not going to use a database or any server-side code for this example, we are only going to send and read data from JSON files.

We need to start by creating the controller that is loaded when the user clicks on one of the options of the main menu. Let's create a JavaScript file at app/controller/clients/Client.js and define an empty controller:

```
Ext.define('MyApp.controller.clients.Clients',{
    extend      : 'Ext.app.Controller',

    init    : function(){
      var me = this;

    },

    addContent   : function(){


    }
});
```

Now we have just an empty controller with the init and addContent methods that are executed automatically when this module is opening. We need to make sure that all our controllers that open a new module include a method called addContent, where we can instantiate the main view of this module.

Now if we try our example we can see that an empty tab is opened under the top toolbar, we are not getting the 404 error anymore:

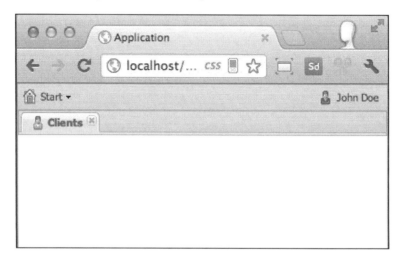

The controller for the client's module is loaded correctly and the container is ready to be filled with the views of the new module. We'll come back to the `controller` class later in this chapter, for now let's keep it empty.

We haven't created any view, so we need to start by creating a border layout to hold the grid and the form for our clients. Let's create a file under `app/views/clients/MainContainer.js`. This class will be the main container for the views of this module:

```
Ext.define('MyApp.view.clients.MainContainer',{
    extend       : 'Ext.container.Container',
    alias        : 'widget.clients.main',
    requires   : [
      'Ext.layout.container.Border',
      'Ext.resizer.BorderSplitterTracker'
    ],

    layout      : 'border',

    initComponent    : function(){
      var me = this;

      me.items = [{
        xtype : 'clients.grid',
        region: 'center'
      },{
        xtype : 'clients.form',
        width : 300,
        region: 'east',
        split : true,
        collapsible : true
      }];

      me.callParent();
    }
});
```

This code should look familiar since we talked about this in previous chapters. We are using a border layout with two regions, one for the grid and one for the form. The most important thing to note here is the way we are defining the `alias` property. We are using a namespace for our `alias` property too; this is a very good practice because we could probably have another main container in our invoice module and in order to avoid collisions we include a namespace.

One more thing to remark from the previous code is that we require two classes in our class definition. These classes are used while creating a grid, and if we don't require them, we are going to get some errors. One class is for the border layout and the other one is for the split configuration.

Our previous code is using two components that we haven't defined yet. We need to create those classes; let's start with the grid by creating a file called `app/views/clients/ClientsGrid.js` and writing the required code for a grid panel:

```
Ext.define('MyApp.view.clients.ClientsGrid',{
   extend        : 'Ext.grid.Panel',
   alias         : 'widget.clients.grid',
   requires  : [
      'Ext.view.TableChunker',
      'Ext.selection.RowModel',
      'Ext.grid.column.Column'
   ],

   border    : false,

   initComponent   : function(){
      var me = this;

      me.store = me.buildStore();
      me.columns = me.buildColumns();

      me.callParent();

      me.store.load();
   },

   buildColumns    : function(){
      return [
         {text:'Name',dataIndex:'name',flex:1},
         {text:'Contact',dataIndex:'contact',flex:1},
         {text:'Address',dataIndex:'address',flex:1},
         {text:'Phone',dataIndex:'phone'}
      ];
   },

   buildStore    : function(){
      return Ext.create('MyApp.store.clients.Clients');
   }
});
```

We've learned about grids in *Chapter 7, Give me the Grid*. The previous code only defines the store and the columns of the grid; we also require some dependencies for this class.

 If we use the `ext-dev.js` file, the library will send warnings to the JavaScript console with those classes that are required to create a component, that's how we know which classes we need to include.

By creating a method to define the columns, we are writing cleaner code. If we extend this class, we can override the `buildColumns` method to add or remove columns easily. The same applies to the `buildStore` method.

Once we have the view for the grid we need to work on our model and store. In our previous code we defined a clients' store; this store will be used to fill our grid with data. In here we will define the proxy and the reader, let's create a file under `app/store/clients/Clients.js` and write the following code:

```
Ext.define('MyApp.store.clients.Clients',{
    extend      : 'Ext.data.Store',
    alias       : 'store.clients',
    model    : 'MyApp.model.clients.Client',

    proxy    : {
      type  : 'ajax',
      url   : 'serverside/clients/list',
      reader  : {
        type  : 'json',
        root  : 'data'
      }
    }
});
```

We are using an Ajax proxy with a JSON reader. The URL, where the data will come, is located at `serverside/clients/list`, so let's create that file and add some dummy data to fill our store:

```
{
  "success" : true,
  "data" : [
    {"id":"1","name":"Tim and Tom Inc", "contact":"John
Doe","address":"123 St San Francisco CA","phone":"(12) 34 56 789"},
    {"id":"2","name":"Monster Inc", "contact":"Susan
Smith","address":"321 St San Antonio TX","phone":"(98) 76 55 321"},
    {"id":"3","name":"Cars and Trucks", "contact":"Jenny
Downy","address":"34th St Kansas City MO","phone":"(81) 32 55 109"}
  ]
}
```

Finally, we need to create our model. This model will define all the fields that we need to fill our grid with. Let's create a JavaScript file at `app/model/clients/Client.js` and write the following code in it:

```
Ext.define('MyApp.model.clients.Client', {
    extend:'Ext.data.Model',

    fields:[
        'id','name','contact','address','phone'
    ]
});
```

The model is a very simple class and now we are ready with the grid. Let's work on the form and create a JavaScript file at `app/view/clients/ClientForm.js` and write the following code:

```
Ext.define('MyApp.view.clients.ClientForm',{
    extend      : 'Ext.form.Panel',
    alias       : 'widget.clients.form',
    requires    : [

    ],

    title    : 'Client form',
    bodyPadding : 5,
    defaults  : {
      xtype  : 'textfield'
    },

    initComponent    : function(){
      var me = this;

      me.items = me.buildItems();
      me.dockedItems = me.buildToolbars();

      me.callParent();
    },

    buildToolbars : function(){
      return [{
        xtype : 'toolbar',
        docked: 'top',
        items : [
          {text:'New',iconCls:'new-icon16',action:'new'},
          {text:'Save',iconCls:'save-icon16',action:'save'},
          {text:'Delete',iconCls:'delete-icon16',action:'delete'}
        ]
      }];
    },
```

```
buildItems : function(){
  return [{
    xtype     : 'hidden',
    name      : 'id'
  },{
    fieldLabel  : 'Name',
    name      : 'name'
  },{
    fieldLabel  : 'Contact',
    name      : 'contact'
  },{
    xtype     : 'textarea',
    fieldLabel  : 'Address',
    name      : 'address'
  },{
    fieldLabel  : 'Phone',
    name      : 'phone'
  }];
  }
});
```

In the previous example we are using all the things we have learned in the previous chapters, things such as toolbars, buttons, fields, forms, and so on. One thing we need to remark is that we are adding a custom property to each of the buttons of the toolbar. The `action` property will allow us to create a selector that matches these specific buttons, we could use any name for this property but `action` is a good name.

One more thing to remark is that we are setting the name of each field the same as the names of the fields in our model; this will allow us to fill our form very easily from the grid.

We also need to add the CSS classes that we are using in the buttons. Let's modify our stylesheet (`resources/css/style.css`) and add the three new rules:

```
.save-icon16{
  background:transparent url(../images/disk16.png) center 0 no-repeat
!important;
}
.new-icon16{
  background:transparent url(../images/page_add16.png) center 0 no-
repeat !important;
}
.delete-icon16{
  background:transparent url(../images/delete16.png) center 0 no-
repeat !important;
}
```

Once we have our models, stores, and views we need to tie everything together. We do this in our client's controller that at this moment is empty. Before we create the instance of our main client's view we need to include all the classes that are involved. To do this we need to specify the dependencies in the client's controller as follows:

```
Ext.define('MyApp.controller.clients.Clients',{
    extend       : 'Ext.app.Controller',
    models    : [                //Step 1
      'clients.Client'
    ],
    stores    : [                //Step 2
      'clients.Clients'
    ],
    views     : [                //Step 3
      'clients.ClientForm',
      'clients.ClientsGrid',
      'clients.MainContainer'
    ],

    init    : function(){
      var me = this;

    },

    addContent   : function(){

    }
});
```

In the first step we have defined an array of models, in here we will add all the models that need to be included in this module. Since the models array implicitly maps to the MyApp.model namespace we can avoid defining it, however we can use it and it will work too, it's exactly the same.

In the second step we required all the stores for the client's module, we only have one but we can add as many as we need.

The third step includes the views. In here we have only three classes, but we can have any number of classes, again, we don't need to define the MyApp.view namespace.

With those changes in place all the dependencies will be included once the controller is included. It is important to mention that if one of the classes is already imported, the loader class will not include the file again.

Once all the classes in our module are loaded we need to create an instance of our main client's view and add it to the empty tab. We have defined an `addContent` method in our controller. At the moment it's empty, but let's modify it as follows:

```
Ext.define('MyApp.controller.clients.Clients',{

  //...

  addContent  : function(){
    this.container.add({
      xtype : 'clients.main',
      itemId: 'clientmain'
    });
  }
});
```

We are accessing the `this.container` property; this property contains a reference to the main tab. We are using the `add` method from the container and passing an object to create the instance of the main view in our client's module. We used the alias, but we can also use the `Ext.create` method.

Finally, we can test our changes! Let's open our favorite browser and navigate to our HTML file. When clicking on the client's option we should see something like the following screenshot:

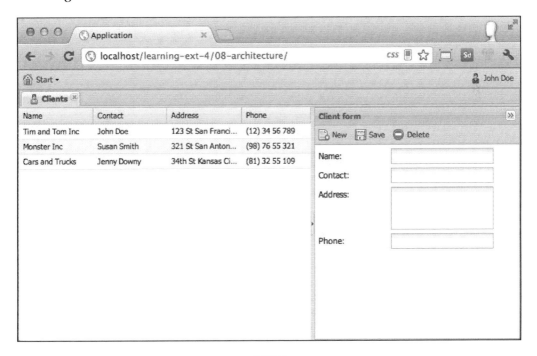

We have everything in place; the classes are loading dynamically when the module is required. In this example we have a few classes, but in the real world this module may have a lot of classes, so it's a good idea to load them just when they are required, otherwise the first time we enter our application we will spend more time loading all the modules and the content.

We also need to prepare our modules for production. We are going to do that in the next chapters; for now we are going to load the classes one by one, which is a lot slower, but it is great for development since we can debug our code easily.

Adding functionality

So far we are only showing data in the grid and an empty form. The buttons don't work, the grid doesn't do anything. We need to add some functionality to our client's module and this is where our controller shines.

We already know how to listen to events using the `control` method. Let's add a listener for the `double click` event on the grid to load the form with the selected data. In our client's controller we need to add the following code:

```
Ext.define('MyApp.controller.clients.Clients',{

    //...

    init    : function(){
      var me = this;

      // step 1
        // Define control method to listen for events
      // Listen for double click in grid
me.control({
        '#maintabs #clientmain grid' : {
          itemdblclick : me.loadForm
        }
      });
    },

    //Step 2
    // Function to load the form with the record in the
      // row that was double clicked.
    loadForm:function(grid,record,item,index,event,ops){
        var form = this.container.down('form'); //Step 3

        form.getForm().loadRecord(record); //Step 4
    },

    //...

});
```

In the first step we define the `control` method to listen for events; our selector is targeting the grid inside the client's container. Then we listen for the `itemdblclick` event that is triggered when the user performs a double-click in any row of the grid.

In the second step we create the `loadForm` function that is going to be called every time the `itemdblclick` event is triggered. In here we are going to load the form with the clicked record. According to the documentation this method receives six parameters. We are going to use only the second parameter that is the record of the row clicked.

In the third step we search for the form. We are using the `down` method from the main container to perform a search in all the descendent components of the container. The selector is targeting the form. We have only one form, that's why our selector is very simple, but in case we have a more complex structure we should modify our selector accordingly.

Once we have the form instance we can assign the record's data. Every form panel contains an instance of the `Ext.form.Basic` class. This class is responsible for handling the data in the form, we can assign, retrieve, validate, load, and so on. To get the basic form we use the `getForm` method from the form panel instance. In this case we load the form from the record using the `loadRecord` method of the basic form.

Let's try our latest changes by double-clicking on one of the rows. We should see something like the following screenshot:

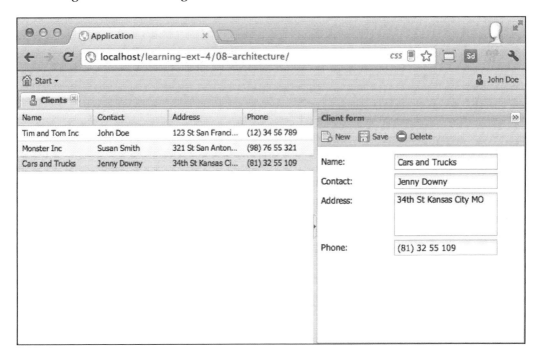

Now we can edit the data, but we can't save it yet. We need to add a listener to the save button and then make an Ajax request to send the data to the server. After that we will show a message to the user with the server response.

Let's modify our client's controller again to add the new listener:

```
Ext.define('MyApp.controller.clients.Clients',{

  //...

  init    : function(){
    var me = this;

    me.control({
      '#maintabs #clientmain grid' : {
        itemdblclick : me.loadForm
      },
      '#maintabs #clientmain form button[action=save]': {//Step 1
        click : me.save
      }
    });
  },

  //Step 2
save      : function(){
    var form = this.container.down('form'); //Step 3

    Ext.Ajax.request({ //Step 4
      url : 'serverside/clients/save',
      params : form.getForm().getValues(),
      success: function(response,options){
          //Step 4
        var data = Ext.decode( response.responseText );

        Ext.Msg.alert('Alert',data.message);
      }
    });
  },

  //...

});
```

In the first step we define a new selector to target the save button; in here we use the `action` property to select the specific button. Also we listen for the `click` event that receives the function to be executed when the event is fired.

In the second step we declare the `save` function, this function contains all the logic to send the form data to the server.

In the third step we search for the form using the `down` method and a simple selector.

In the fourth step we make the Ajax request. In here we collect the data using the `getValues` method from the basic form instance. This method returns an object with the names/value for each field; we are sending these values to the server.

When we perform an Ajax request we need to define a success/failure callback that will be executed when the server responds. In this case we only define the success callback, but we should define the failure too. We expect the server's response to be the following JSON:

```
{
    "success" : true,
    "message" : "The client has been successfully saved"
}
```

Once the JSON response is decoded we can access the `message` property and show an alert to the user as shown in the following screenshot:

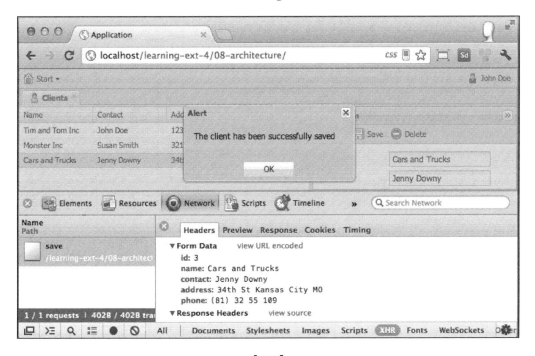

The previous screenshot shows how the `save` request is sending the form fields, which is by default, a POST request. We can receive those parameters on the server side.

In PHP we get those parameters as follows:

```
$name = $_POST['name'];
```

In Java we get those parameters as follows:

```
String name = request.getParameter("name");
```

In Ruby & Rails we get those parameters as follows:

```
name = params['name']
```

We are done with the save action, now it's time to start working on the other two buttons. Let's start with the new button. When the user clicks on the **New** button we should clear the form:

```
Ext.define('MyApp.controller.clients.Clients',{

    //...

    init    : function(){
      var me = this;

      me.control({
        '#maintabs #clientmain grid' : {
          itemdblclick : me.loadForm
        },
        '#maintabs #clientmain form button[action=save]' : {
          click : me.save
        },
        '#maintabs #clientmain form button[action=new]' :{
          click : me.clearForm
        }
      });
    },

    clearForm     : function(){
      var form = this.container.down('form');

      form.getForm().reset();
    },

    //...

});
```

First we define the selector for targeting the new button. This selector is very similar to the other, and the only difference is the value of the action property. Also we are listening for the click event and executing the clearForm method when the event is fired.

Inside the clearForm method we search for the form the same way we did in the other latest examples, then we execute the reset method from the basic form instance to clear the form.

If we try our application, we will see how by clicking on the **New** button the form is cleared and we can start entering data again.

The last feature in our module is the ability to delete a record. In here we need to make an Ajax request to the server sending the ID of the record that we want to delete and if the record is removed correctly in our database, we can remove the record from the grid.

Let's start by modifying the client's controller as follows:

```
Ext.define('MyApp.controller.clients.Clients',{

    //...

    init    : function(){
      var me = this;

      me.control({
        '#maintabs #clientmain grid' : {
          itemdblclick : me.loadForm
        },
        '#maintabs #clientmain form button[action=save]' : {
          click : me.save
        },
        '#maintabs #clientmain form button[action=new]' : {
          click : me.clearForm
        },
        '#maintabs #clientmain form button[action=delete]' : {
          click : me.remove
        }
      });
    },

    remove     : function(){
      var me = this,     //Step 1
        form = me.container.down('form'),
        id = form.getForm().getValues().id;
```

```
        Ext.Msg.confirm('Confirm','Are you sure that you want to delete
this client?',function(btn){ //Step 2
        if(btn === 'yes'){

            Ext.Ajax.request({ //Step 3
              url     : 'serverside/clients/delete',
              params : {id:id},
              success : function(response){
                //Step 4
                var grid = me.container.down('grid'),
                  record = grid.getStore().getById(id);

                grid.getStore().remove(record);
                form.getForm().reset();
              }
            });

        }
    });
  },

  //...

});
```

In the first step we define the selector and the event to listen to. The remove function is where all the magic happens. We get the form reference and the id property of the record to delete.

In the second step we are showing a confirmation from the user to delete the record. If the user clicks on the **Yes** button, we proceed to the next step. If the user clicks on the **No** button, we don't do anything.

In the third step we make the Ajax request and only send the id property of the client to the server, then we wait for the answer.

If everything goes well then the fourth step is executed. In here we search for the grid and get the record by its `id`. Once we have the record we use the `remove` method from the store and clear the form. In this example we are not listening for the failure callback, but it would be a good idea to send a notification to the user if there was an error while deleting the client from the database:

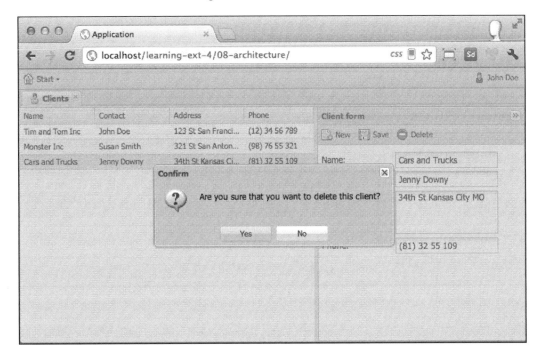

Finally, we are done with our client's module. We have implemented the four CRUD actions using the MVC pattern.

References

Before we move forward we can see one line of code that is the same for all the listeners. We are searching the form over and over again! We should do it only once and then save a reference so we don't have to perform a search every time.

The controller has an easy way to do just this. We can define references using selectors and then we can use them in any of the methods in our controller. Let's modify our client's controller as follows:

```
Ext.define('MyApp.controller.clients.Clients',{

  //...

  views    : [
    'clients.ClientForm',
    'clients.ClientsGrid',
    'clients.MainContainer'
  ],

  refs : [{
    ref      : 'clientForm',
    selector : '#maintabs #clientmain form'
  }],

  init    : function(){
    var me = this;

    //...

  },

  //...

});
```

By using the `refs` array we can define as many references as we want. Each reference should be an object with at least two configurations. First is the `ref` property, which is the name of our reference, and second is the selector for this reference. This selector should match the component that we want to create the reference to.

Once we define our reference we can access it by its name, in this example we can get the reference by the `getClientForm` method. The next step is to replace the following line of code:

```
me.container.down('form');
```

After replacing it, the reference will be as follows:

```
this.getClientForm()
```

Now the search is performed only once and then we only get the reference, this will allow us to speed things up.

Summary

Having a good architecture is a must. If we don't define a scalable and maintainable architecture, our project will be at risk. There are many horror stories by developers who have started a project without a good architecture and believe me when I say that it is a nightmare to work on those projects. By following the guidelines of Sencha we can work happily in a better manner.

Over the pages of this chapter we have learned how to organize our code using classes and following the MVC pattern to assign the right task to each class. Using a controller to write our logic for the views and give life to our components is a great way to keep our code clean and organized.

We also learned how to load new modules on demand with all their dependencies. The method we learned is great for the development phase because it's easy to debug our code. We need to add some changes when deploying our application to production, but that's another story that will be covered in the coming chapters.

In the next chapter we will learn about the `DataView` and `Template` classes. By using a dataview we can create our very own custom components, add an HTML template, and style with CSS.

DataViews and Templates

The dataview component is similar to the grid component but it is lighter. It is used to render an HTML template for each record in the store. For the rendering process, it uses an `Ext.XTemplate` class so that we can give style to each record in the store. This component is very useful when you want to render data and don't need all the power of the grid.

In this chapter, we'll learn how the `Ext.view.View` class (alias dataview) and the `Ext.XTemplate` class work together.

The topics we are going to cover in this chapter are:

- The data connection (models and stores)
- A basic dataview
- Handling events on the dataview
- Templates
- A more complex dataview

The data connection (models and stores)

The dataview component is used to render data of a store like the grid component. In this chapter, we are going to use a user model and a user's store like the ones we defined in *Chapter 8, Architecture* so that we can display our dataview. We will be using the **Model–view–controller** (**MVC**) pattern so we can get used to it, because this is the way we will be writing our ExtJS 4.1 applications from now on.

Defining our User Model

We'll be using the user model we used before. The model code goes as follows:

```
/**
 * @classApp.model.User
 * @extendsExt.data.Model
 * The definition of our user model
 * iam@armando.mx
 * @manduks
 */
Ext.define('App.model.User', {
extend: 'Ext.data.Model',
fields:[
    {name:'id', type:'int'},
    'avatar','firstName', 'twitter_account','lastName',
    {name:'active', type:'boolean' }
  ],
  proxy: {
    type: 'ajax',
    url : 'data/users.json',
    reader:{
      type:'json',
      root:'data'
    }
  }
});
```

In the previous code, we have our user model definition. This code goes in our models definition folder of our application.

In our model definition, we have defined a proxy object. The code is as follows:

```
proxy: {
    type: 'ajax',
    url : 'data/users.json',
    reader:{
      type:'json',
      root:'data'
    }
}
```

This model will get the data through `ajax` calls that is defined in the `type` property of our proxy. The URL will be `'data/users.json'` and the way the reader will fetch the data will be in a `json` format and will get the data from the `root` node of our data response.

Defining the store

With our model defined, we are now going to define our store.

```
/**
 * @classApp.store.Users
 * @extendsExt.data.Store
 * This our users store definition
 * iam@armando.mx
 * @manduks
 */
Ext.define('App.store.Users', {
  extend: 'Ext.data.Store',
  requires:['App.model.User'], //step one

  autoLoad: true,
  model:'App.model.User'
});
```

In the previous code, we have defined our users store definition. We need to require our user model in step one. Remember to put your store code in the `Stores` folder.

A basic dataview

Now, we are going to define the view of our application. We are going to place our `dataview` file in the `views` folder. The purpose of this view is to have a component in our application to activate or cancel users.

```
/**
 * @classApp.view.UsersView
 * @extendsExt.view.View
 * This the definition of our users data view
 */
Ext.define('App.view.UsersView', {
  extend: 'Ext.view.View', //step one
  xtype:'usersview', //step two
  store:'Users', //step three
  emptyText:'No users available', //step four
  tpl:[ //step five
    '<tplfor=".">',
      '<div>{firstName} {lastName}</div>',
    '</tpl>'].join('')
});
```

In the previous code, we have defined our user's dataview.

- In step one, we have extended our class from `Ext.view.view`. That's our base class for all views and our users' view.

- In step two, we have the definition of `xtype` we are using, so we can instantiate our view in a short and easy way.

- Then we add the data source of our view in step three.

- In step four, we have the `emptyText` property, which is a text to display when our view has nothing to show.

- And finally, in step five, we have our `Ext.XTemplate` definition, so we can render our data in a nice way using HTML and CSS.

Getting all our code together

Once we have our model, store, and view defined, we are ready to write the code to see our dataview.

```
/**
 * This is the main code for the application
 */

Ext.Loader.setConfig({
  enabled:true
});
Ext.application({
  name: 'App',

  models: ['User'],
  stores:['Users'],

  requires:['App.view.UsersView'],
  launch: function() {
  Ext.create('Ext.Window',{
      width:200,
      height:200,
      items:[{
        xtype:'usersview'
      }]
    }).show();
    }
});
```

The previous code defines a window that will contain our dataview definition, and this code creates the following window:

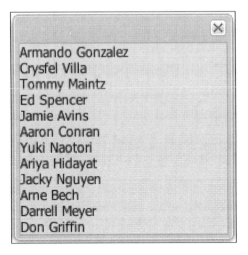

Handling events on the dataview

Once we have our dataview defined, we are going to see some basic events handling for it. To do that, we need to add some new properties in our view definition.

```
/**
 * @classApp.view.UsersView
 * @extendsExt.view.View
 * This the definition of our users data view
 */
Ext.define('App.view.UsersView', {
  extend: 'Ext.view.View',
  xtype:'usersview',
  store:'Users',
    emptyText:'No users available',
    itemSelector: 'div.selector', //step one
    tpl:[
      '<tpl for=".">',
        '<div class ="selector">', //step two
        '{firstName} {lastName}',
        '</div>',
      '</tpl>'].join('')
});
```

- In the previous code, we have added two important lines of code that are required to interact with our dataview.

- In step one, we have the itemSelector property that defines which DOM node item will be used to select each item on our dataview.

- In step two, we have added to our template the DOM node definition, so the itemSelector property will match the node.

Now, we are ready to listen for the itemclick event, which fires whenever a user clicks an item on our dataview.

Adding the listeners to the dataview

Let's add the listener to the dataview:

```
Ext.define('App.view.UsersView', {
  extend: 'Ext.view.View',
    xtype:'usersview',
    store:'Users',
  emptyText:'No users available',
  itemSelector: 'div.selector',
  tpl:[
    '<tpl for=".">',
      '<div class ="selector">',
        '{firstName} {lastName}',
      '</div>',
    '</tpl>'].join(''),
  listeners:{
    itemclick:function(view, rec, item, index, event, opts)
{      Ext.Msg.alert('Ext JS', record.get('firstName')+' '+ record.
get('lastName')+' has been selected.');
    }
  }
});
```

In the previous code, we have added an event listener to our dataview that is executed when we click on one of our dataview items. The following screenshot shows us the result:

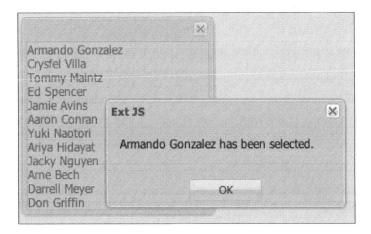

Templates

In the Ext JS 4 library, we have two types of templates – the `Ext.Template` and the `Ext.XTemplate`. Let's see what the main differences between these two classes are.

The `Ext.Template` represents an HTML fragment that will be rendered in the dataview. Let's see an example of this class:

```
<!DOCTYPE HTML>
<html manifest="" lang="en-US">
<head>
<meta charset="UTF-8">
  <linkrel="stylesheet" href="http://cdn.sencha.io/ext-4.1.0-gpl/
resources/css/ext-all.css" />
<title>Ext.Template</title>
  <style type="text/css">
    #container{
      padding:50px;
    }
  </style>
</head>
<body>
  <div id="container"></div>
</body>
</html>
```

```html
<script type="text/javascript" charset="utf-8" src="http://cdn.sencha.
io/ext-4.1.0-gpl/ext-all-debug.js"></script>
<script type="text/javascript">
  //Ext.Template
  var template = new Ext.Template( //step one
    '<div>',
      '<imgsrc="{img}"  height="40" width="120"></br>',
      '<spam>{description}</spam></br></br>',
      '<ahref="{url}">{text}</a>',
      '</div>',
      // a configuration object:
      {
      compiled: true,       // compile for performance
      });
  template.append('container', //step two
    {
      img:'http://www.sencha.com/img/sencha-large.png',
      cls:'awesome',
      text :'Visit sencha!!',
      url :'www.sencha.com',
      description:'Ext JS 4 is the next major advancement in our
JavaScript framework.'
    }
  );
</script>
```

- In step one, we have defined our `Ext.Template` that will show a nice format with an image, some description, and a link to www.sencha.com. We have compiled our template so it renders faster.

- In step two, we are appending our template to the HTML div of our page with the container ID and also are applying some data to our template.

The following screenshot is the result of the previous code:

Ext JS 4 is the next major advancement in our JavaScript framework.

Visit sencha!!

Now, let's talk about the `Ext.XTemplate` class. This class is more complex than the `Ext.Template` class because it supports advanced functionality, such as:

- Auto filling arrays using templates and sub-templates
- Conditional processing with basic comparison operators
- Basic math function support
- Execute arbitrary inline code with special built-in template variables
- Custom member functions

The `Ext.XTemplate` provides the template mechanism for the `Ext.view.View`, so when we use the dataview we have all the `Ext.XTemplate` capabilities. Let's see a basic example of an `Ext.XTemplate` implementation:

In this example, we are going to render information about Sencha:

```html
<!DOCTYPE HTML>
<html manifest="" lang="en-US">
<head>
<meta charset="UTF-8">
  <linkrel="stylesheet" href="http://cdn.sencha.io/ext-4.1.0-gpl/
resources/css/ext-all.css" />
<title>Ext.XTemplate</title>
  <style type="text/css">
    #container{
      padding:50px;
    }
    .product {
      float: left;
      padding: 8px;
      margin: 8px;
    }
    .active{
      opacity:1;
    }
    .inactive{
      opacity:.5;
    }
  </style>
</head>
<body>
  <div id="container"></div>
</body>
</html>
<script type="text/javascript" charset="utf-8" src="http://cdn.sencha.
io/ext-4.1.0-gpl/ext-all-debug.js"></script>
```

```
<script type="text/javascript">
  var data = { // the data definition (step one)
    title:'SenchaInc',
    description:'Sencha equips developers with frameworks, tools and
services to help them build amazing web application experiences using
HTML5 and JavaScript.',
    img:'http://www.sencha.com/img/sencha-large.png',
    products:[
      {
        name:'Ext JS 3',
        description:"JavaScript Framework for Rich Apps in Every
Browser",
        img:'http://www.sencha.com/img/hero-extjs4-alt.png',
        active:0
      },{
        name:'Ext JS 4.1',
        description:"JavaScript Framework for Rich Apps in Every
Browser",
        img:'http://www.sencha.com/img/hero-extjs4-alt.png',
        active:1
      },{
        name:'Sencha Architect 1',
        description:'Build for Mobile and Desktop',
        img:'http://cdn.sencha.io/img/20120417-architect-2-hero-870.
png',
        active:0
      },{
        name:'Sencha Architect 2',
        description:'Build for Mobile and Desktop',
        img:'http://cdn.sencha.io/img/20120417-architect-2-hero-870.
png',
        active:1
      },{
        name:'Sencha Animator',
        description:'Create Mobile Animations with Ease',
        img:'http://www.sencha.com/img/20110930-animator-full-hero.
jpg',
        active:1
      },{
        name:'Sencha.io',
        description:'Sencha.io is a complete cloud platform for
building mobile web apps',
        img:'http://img1.sencha.com/files/misc/sencha-io-deploy60x60.
png',
        active:1
      }
    ]
```

```
    };
  var template = new Ext.XTemplate(
      '<div>',
        '<imgsrc="{img}"  height="40" width="120"></br>',
        '<b>{[values.title.toUpperCase()]}</b></br>', //convert to
uppercase the title (step two)
        '<spam>{description}</spam></br></br>',
        '</div>',
      '<tpl for ="products">',  //loop the products property within
the data (step three)
        '<tpl if="active &gt; 0">', // interrogate if the product is
active (step four)
          '<div class="product active">',
        '<tpl else>',
          '<div class="product inactive">',
        '</tpl>',
          '<div style="float:left;padding:0 5px 0 0;">',
            '<imgsrc="{img}"  height="60" width="60">',
          '</div>',
          '<b>{name}</b></br>',
          '<spam>{description}</spam>',
          '</div>',
      '</tpl>'
    );
  template.overwrite('container', data); //render the template with
data on a DOM node (step five)
</script>
```

- In step one, we define the data that will populate our Ext.XTemplate.

- In step two, we are doing some formatting to the title, so it renders in uppercase.

- In step three, we are looping through the products property of our data and are rendering each product in a nice format.

- In step four, we are using the if operator to provide conditional logic to our template, so we can decide what parts of our template we need to render. In this case, we are adding some CSS styles to our products. When a product is inactive, we change the opacity of our product.

- And finally, in step five, we are rendering our data in our HTML document.

The previous code generates the following output:

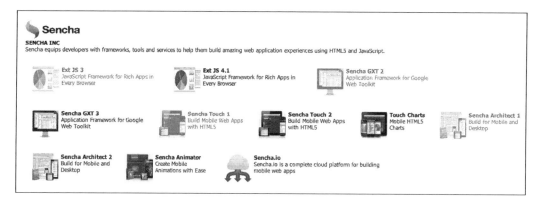

As we can see in the previous screenshot, we are listing some products; the products that are not active and have less opacity than the active ones.

Now that we have learned how the templates work, we are ready to do a more complex example.

A more complex dataview

A dataview component is a great component in the Ext JS library. In the next example, we are going to list the users in the application and we are going to activate or deactivate them with a double-click on the user record.

Let's add to our previous dataview code some lines:

```
/**
 * @classApp.view.UsersView
 * @extendsExt.view.View
 * This the definition of our users data view
 *
 */
Ext.define('App.view.UsersView', {
  extend: 'Ext.view.View',
  xtype:'usersview',
  store:'Users',
  emptyText:'No users available',
  itemSelector: 'div.user',
  tpl:[
    '<tpl for =".">',
      '<tpl if="active &gt; 0">',// interrogate if the user is active
(step one)
```

```
            '<div class="user active">',
        '<tpl else>',
          '<div class="user inactive">',
        '</tpl>',
          '<div class="content">',
            '<imgsrc="resources/images/user48.png"  height="60"
width="60">',
          '</div>',
          '<b>{firstName} {lastName}</b></br>', // render the name of
our users (step two)
          '<spam>{twitter_account}</spam>',
          '</div>',
      '</tpl>'].join(''),
    listeners:{
      itemdblclick:function(view, record, item, index, event, options)
{//listen to the double click (step three)
        if(record.get('active')){ // check if the user is active (step
four)
          Ext.fly(item).removeCls('active');
          Ext.fly(item).addCls('inactive');
        }else{
          Ext.fly(item).removeCls('inactive');
          Ext.fly(item).addCls('active');
        }
        //some server side call
        record.data.active = !record.data.active;
      }
    }
  });
```

The previous code is the new data definition that we will use to activate or deactivate our users, because we are using the MVC pattern. The only code we have to modify is the App.view.UsersView class. We did a few modifications in our dataview code.

- First, in step one, we check if our user is active or not, so we can add some css class if the user is active or not.

- In step two, we are rendering the user data.

- In step three, we are listening to the double-click event, so when the user double-clicks on a dataview item, the user changes status.

- And finally, in step four, we do the logic to add or remove the css class to visually show our activation/deactivation process. We used here the Ext. fly method to get item reference. Remember that this method is used for saving memory.

To complete the dataview styling, we need some `css` class definitions that will go in our `app.css` file:

```css
.user {
  float: left;
  padding: 2px;
  margin: 2px;
  width:200px;
}
.active{
  opacity:1;
  background: #E6FFE6;
}
.inactive{
  opacity:.5;
  background: #F5F5F0;
}
.content{
  float:left;
  padding:0 5px 0 0;
}
```

In the previous code, we had some `css` that will give our dataview items some nice format. Now that we have our code complete, we can see the final result in the following screenshot:

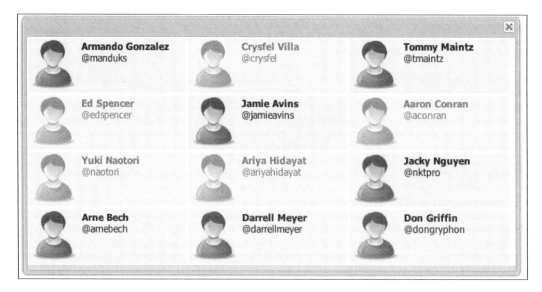

Summary

The dataview is a very flexible component that is useful when we want to render data. It is easy to use and has a powerful API; because of the flexibility of the `Ext.XTemplate` class, we can do a variety of things using these two components.

In this chapter, we have learned how the dataview class works. We have seen how to use stores, models, and views to format the data we want to render. In Ext JS, dataview is used commonly with templates, and the `Ext.XTemplate` class offers a lot of useful configurations to validate and format our data. It is very important to know the `Ext.view.View` capabilities against the `Ext.grid.Panel` features because some times, in terms of performance, it is much better to use a dataview.

In the next chapter, we are going to see another awesome component, `Ext.tree.Panel`; this component is one of the most well-designed and powerful components in the Ext JS library, so keep reading, because we will learn to use one of the most useful components in the library.

10
The Tree Panel

The `Ext.tree.Panel` class is a great component in Ext JS and also a great tool when we want to display hierarchical data; a good example of this is a file directory application.

`Ext.tree.Panel` extends from `Ext.panel.Table`, which is the same class that the `Ext.grid.Panel` extends from. The features like columns, sorting, filtering, renderers, drag-and-drop, the plugins, and extensions are expected to work in `Ext.tree.Panel` as well. The main difference between the `Ext.grid.Panel` and `Ext.tree.Panel` classes is the way they render data.

In this chapter we'll learn how `Ext.tree.Panel` works, its versatility, and ease of use.

The topics we are going to cover in this chapter are as follows:

- A basic tree panel
- The TreeStore
- Tree nodes
- Tree drag-and-drop
- Adding and removing nodes
- The check tree
- The grid tree
- Adding an invoices' categories tree panel

A basic tree panel

In this example we are going to display a file directory using Ext.tree.panel. Remember we are using the MVC pattern so our files need to be placed in the correct folders of our application.

In the following example we are going to display the MVC pattern files' order:

```
/** view/BasicTreePanel
 * @classApp.view.BasicTreePanel
 * @extendsExt.tree.Panel
 * This is a basic Tree Panel example.
 */
Ext.define('App.view.BasicTreePanel', {
  extend: 'Ext.tree.Panel',
    xtype:'basictreepanel',
  title:'MVC pattern',
  root: {//define the data of our tree panel
  text:'Application', //the text the node is going to display
    expanded:true, //when the tree rendersthenode it will be expanded
by default
    children:[ //the children of our Application node
      {
        text:'app',
        children:[ // each node can have their own children
          {
            text:'app.js',
            leaf:true //when we set leaf to true, our node will be
last in the hierarchy and also its icon will change
          },{
            text:'controller'
          },{
            text:'model'
          },{
            text:'store'
          },{
            text:'view',
            children:[
              {
                text:'BasicTreePanel.js',
                leaf:true
              }
            ]
          }
        ]
```

```
        },{
          text:'data'
        },{
          text:'index.html',
          leaf:true
        },{
          text:'resources',
          children:[
            {
              text:'css'
            },{
              text:'resources'
            }
          ]
        }
      ]
    }
});
```

In the preceding code we have the `view` definition of our tree panel. First we have to understand our tree data source format. This data format is different from the store data source format we have used. In this format we need to have a root node. This node will be the main node of our tree from which the rest of the nodes will be drawn

Each node in the `Ext.tree.Panel` component has some properties that will define its behavior, properties like leaf, expanded, text, and others will be discussed later in this chapter.

Now let's see our `Ext.application` code, so we can render the tree panel in our application:

```
/**
 * This is the main code for the application
 */

Ext.Loader.setConfig({
  enabled:true
});
Ext.application({
  name: 'App',

  requires:['App.view.BasicTreePanel'], // we need to require the
BasicTreePanel class sou we can used later.
```

```
launch: function() {
  Ext.create('Ext.Window',{
      width:630,
      height:318,
      title:'ExtTreePanel',
      autoScroll:true,
      frame:false,
      layout:'fit',
      items:[{
          xtype:'basictreepanel' // adding our tree panel definition to
  our window
      }]
  }).show();
  }
});
```

In the preceding code we have our `Ext.application` definition. Here we are creating a new `Ext.Window` that will be the container of our `App.view.BasicTreePanel` definition. When the application launches, the window will be created and shown with the tree panel in it.

The following screenshot shows our final result:

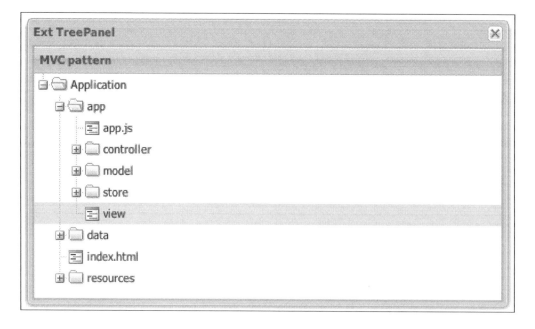

As we have seen in the previous example the configuration and use of an `Ext.tree.Panel` component is very simple, but there are some properties that we need to know so we can understand this component better.

The TreeStore

The TreeStore is a store implementation designed for the `Ext.tree.Panel` component. It provides methods for loading nodes, and it has the ability to use the hierarchical tree structure combined with the store capabilities. The `Ext.data.TreeStore` class is a subclass of the `Ext.data.AbstractStore` class, that's why it behaves very similar to other stores.

When we define our `Ext.data.TreeStore` class we need to specify a model, but if no model is specified, an implicit model will be created. This model will then be the main model for our tree panel. For the tree to read the nested data, we need to apply a set of data in a tree format as shown in the previous example.

Let's see an example of an `Ext.tree.Panel` component with an `Ext.data.TreeStore` class. First we need the `Ext.data.TreeStore` definition:

```
/**
 * @classApp.store.Files
 * @extends Object
 * This is the definition of our TreeStore
 */
Ext.define('App.store.Files', {
  extend: 'Ext.data.TreeStore',
  proxy: {
    type: 'ajax',
    url : 'data/files.json'
      }
});
```

Our `App.store.Files` class extends from the `Ext.data.TreeStore` class. We have set the proxy to get the data from our `files.json` file. Now let's see our tree panel class:

```
/**
 * @classApp.view.TreeStoreTreePanel
 * @extendsExt.tree.Panel
 * This is a tree panel with a tree store configuration.
 */
```

```
Ext.define('App.view.TreeStoreTreePanel', {
  extend: 'Ext.tree.Panel',
  xtype:'treestorepanel',
  store:'Files'
});
```

Our tree class configuration gets very simple. We just added a store and we now just need to tell our Ext.application file to render the panel:

```
/**
 * This is the main code of the application
 */

Ext.Loader.setConfig({
  enabled:true
});
Ext.application({
  name: 'App',

  requires:['App.view.BasicTreePanel','App.view.TreeStoreTreePanel'],
  stores:['Files'],//we import the store
  launch: function() {
  Ext.create('Ext.Window',{
      width:430,
      height:318,
      title:'ExtTreePanel',
      autoScroll:true,
      frame:false,
      layout:'fit',
      items:[{
        xtype:'treestorepanel'
      }]
    }).show();
    this.getFilesStore().load(); // load the TreeStore
    }
});
```

In the `Ext.application` code we just added the TreeStore and the tree panel to our window. The following screenshot shows the final result:

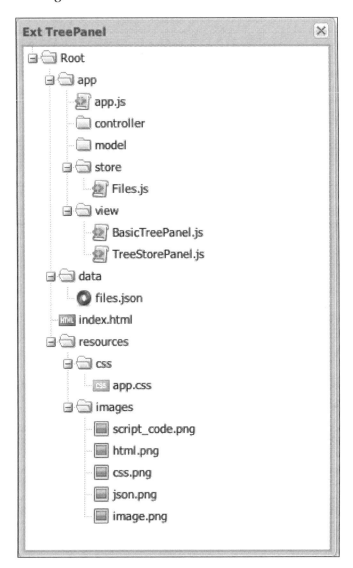

Tree nodes

The `Ext.data.NodeInterface` class is a set of methods that are applied to the model to decorate it with a node API. This means that when we use a model with a tree, the model will have all the tree-related methods. This class also creates extra fields on the model to help maintain the tree state and the UI.

Some of the field's configurations are as follows:

- `text`: This property configures the text to show on the node label.
- `root`: This property is true if this is the root node.
- `leaf`: If this property is set to true, it indicates that this child can have no children. The expand icon/arrow will not be rendered for this node.
- `expanded`: This property is true if the node is expanded.
- `iconCls`: This property configures the CSS class to apply for this node's icon.
- `children`: This property configures an array of child nodes.
- `checked`: This property is set to true or false to show a checkbox alongside this node.

Tree drag-and-drop

Adding additional functionality to the tree panel in Ext JS 4 is easy with the help of plugins.

We are going to use the `Ext.plugin.TreeViewDragDrop` plugin so our nodes can have the drag-and-drop behavior.

This plugin creates a specialized instance of **Drag Zone**, which knows how to drag out of a tree view and loads the data object which is passed to a cooperating Drag Zone's method with the following properties:

- `copy`: This property is true if the tree view was configured with `allowCopy:true`.
- `view`: This property configures the tree view from which the drag was originated.
- `ddel`: This is an HTML element which moves with the mouse.
- `item`: This is a tree view node upon which the `mousedown` event was registered.
- `records`: This is an array of models representing the data being dragged from the source tree view.

The plugin also creates a specialized Drop Zone, where the nodes are going to be dropped. When we add this plugin to the tree view, two new events may be fired from the client tree view: `beforedrop` and `drop`. Note that this plugin must be added to the tree view, not the panel itself.

Let's see how this plugin works, lets write some code:

```
/**
 * @classApp.view.TreeStoreTreePanel
 * @extendsExt.tree.Panel
 * This is a tree panel with a tree store configuration.
 */
Ext.define('App.view.TreeStoreTreePanel', {
  extend: 'Ext.tree.Panel',
  xtype:'treestorepanel',
  store:'Files',
  viewConfig:{ //the view config of our tree panel
    plugins:{
      ptype:'treeviewdragdrop' // adding the drag and drop
implementation
    }
  }
});
```

We only need to add some lines to our `App.view.TreeStoreTreePanel`
implementation and we are ready to see the drag-and-drop component in action!:

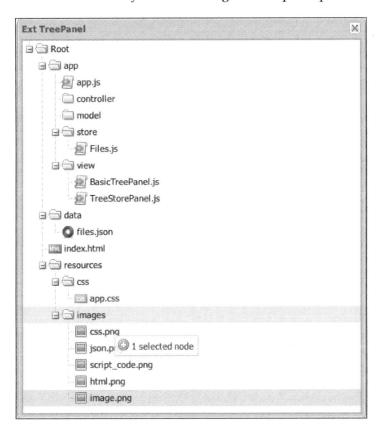

Now let's see what we need to do if we want to drag-and-drop between two
`Ext.tree.Panels`:

We are only going to change some code in our `Ext.application` definition:

```
/**
 * This is the main code for the application
 */
Ext.Loader.setConfig({
  enabled:true
});
Ext.application({
  name: 'App',

  requires:['App.view.TreeStoreTreePanel'],
  stores:['Files'],

launch: function() {
  Ext.create('Ext.Window',{
      width:630,
      height:318,
      title:'ExtTreePanel',
      autoScroll:true,
      frame:false,
      layout        : {
        type    : "hbox",
        align   : "stretch"
      },
      defaults:{
        flex:1
      },
      items:[{
        xtype:'treestorepanel'
      },{
        xtype:'treepanel',
        viewConfig:{ //the view config of our tree panel
          plugins:{
              ptype:'treeviewdragdrop' // adding the drag and drop
implementation
          }
        },
  root: {
        text:'Application',
          expanded:true
        }
      }]
    }).show();
    this.getFilesStore().load();
    }
});
```

First we need to change the window layout so it can render the two panels. Then we add the other `Ext.tree.Panel`. Note that both tree panels have the `Ext.tree. plugin.TreeViewDragDrop` plugin added on their `viewConfig` property.

Once we have made the appropriate changes we have the following result:

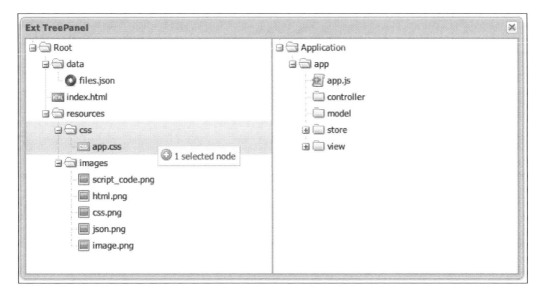

Adding and removing nodes

We can also add nodes dynamically to our tree panel. This is very handy because in most cases when we use the tree panel we will end up facing this requirement. Here, we will see how we can solve the problem in a fast and easy way.

In the following example we are going to add nodes dynamically to our tree panel taking advantage of our previous drag-and-drop example:

```
/**
 * @classApp.view.NodeForm
 * @extendsExt.form.Panel
 * @author Armando Gonzalez <iam@armando.mx>
 * The node form panel
 */
Ext.define('App.view.NodeForm', {
    extend: 'Ext.form.Panel',
    xtype:'nodeform',
    border:false,
    frame:true,
```

```
initComponent   : function(){
  var me = this;
  me.items = me.buildItems();
  me.buttons = me.buildButtons();
  me.callParent();
},
buildItems : function(){
  var store =  Ext.create('Ext.data.Store', {
  fields: ['value', 'name'],
  data : [
          {"value":true, "name":"File"},
          {"value":false, "name":"Folder"}
      ]
  });

  return [{
    fieldLabel  : 'Name',
    name      : 'text',
    xtype     : 'textfield',
  },{
    fieldLabel  : 'Type',
    xtype     : 'combo',
    name      : 'leaf',
    queryMode  : 'local',
    displayField: 'name',
    valueField  : 'value',
    store      : store
  }];
},
buildButtons:function(){
  return [{
text: 'Save',
      itemId: 'savebtn'
        }];
  }
});
```

In the previous code we have defined a form panel that will be used for adding nodes to our tree panel.

Once we have the form class definition we will make some changes to the `App.view.TreeStoreTreePanel` implementation so we can add the nodes:

```
/**
 * @classApp.view.TreeStoreTreePanel
 * @extendsExt.tree.Panel
 * @author Armando Gonzalez <iam@armando.mx>
```

```
 * This is a tree panel with a tree store configuration.
 */
Ext.define('App.view.TreeStoreTreePanel', {
  extend: 'Ext.tree.Panel',
  xtype:'treestorepanel',
  store:'Files',
  tbar:[{
    text:'Add',
    iconCls:'add',
    menu:{
      items:{
        xtype:'nodeform'
      }
    }
  },{
    text:'Delete',
    iconCls:'delete',
    itemId: 'deletebtn'
  }],
  viewConfig:{ //the view config of our tree panel
    plugins:{
      ptype:'treeviewdragdrop' // addigng the drag and drop
implementation
    }
  }
});
```

We just added a toolbar to our tree panel; in this toolbar we added two buttons,
the **Add** button and the **Delete** button. In the **Add** button we are going to add our
`App.view.NodeForm` property as a menu, so when the user clicks, the form panel
will appear.

Now we just need to add the `controller` class definition. Remember it's all
about MVC.

```
/**
 * @classMyApp.controller.Main
 * @extendsExt.app.Controller
 * @author Armando Gonzalez <iam@armando.mx>
 * The main controller, in here we define all the app logic
 */
Ext.define('App.controller.Main', {
  extend: 'Ext.app.Controller',
  refs: [{
  ref: 'treePanel',
```

```
selector: 'treestorepanel'
    }],
requires:['App.view.TreeStoreTreePanel','App.view.NodeForm'],
stores:['Files'],
init:function(){
  var me = this;
  me.control({
    'nodeform #savebtn' : {// we get the save button reference
      click :me.addTreeNode
    },
    'treestorepanel toolbar #deletebtn':{// we get the delete button
reference
      click :me.deleteTreeNode
    }
  });
  me.getFilesStore().load();
},
addTreeNode:function(btn){
  var me = this,
  node,
    tree = me.getTreePanel(),
    selectedNode = tree.getSelectionModel().getSelection()[0] ||
tree.getRootNode(); //get the root node if there is not selection

  node = btn.up('form').getValues();//get the form values

  if(selectedNode.isLeaf()){ //insert the node in the parent node
    selectedNode.parentNode.insertChild(0,node);
  }else{//inserting as a child
    selectedNode.insertChild(0,node );
  }
  btn.up('menu').hide();// hide the menu
},
deleteTreeNode:function(){
  var me = this,
    tree = me.getTreePanel(),
    node = tree.getSelectionModel().getSelection()[0];
  if(node){
    node.remove(true);//true to destroy the node
  }else{
    Ext.Msg.alert('Warning', 'Please select a node!');
  }

}
});
```

In the previous code we have our controller definition. Here we have two main methods: the `addTreeNode` and `deleteTreeNode` methods.

The `addTreeNode` method is where we do the logic for adding new nodes. We get the parent node where our new node is going to be. Note that we are using the `getSelectionModel` method, which is the same method we used in *Chapter 7, Gimme the Grid*.

The `deleteTreeNode` method is where we do the deletion logic of the tree nodes. We do a selection node validation and with the `node.remove()` method we destroy the node after removing it.

The following screenshot shows the adding and removing node example:

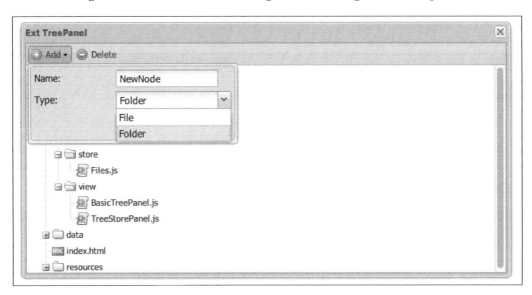

The check tree

The tree panel also has the ability to add checkboxes to its nodes. To do this we need to add one more property to each node in the data source that we are applying to the tree panel.

This is how the data source configuration must go:

```
{
    "text":"images",
    "checked":false,
    "children":[
      {
        "text":"script_code.png",
        "leaf":"true",
        "iconCls":"image",
        "checked":false
      },{
        "text":"html.png",
        "leaf":"true",
        "iconCls":"image",
        "checked":true
      },{
        "text":"css.png",
        "leaf":"true",
        "iconCls":"image",
        "checked":false
      },{
        "text":"json.png",
        "leaf":"true",
        "iconCls":"image",
        "checked":true
      },{
        "text":"image.png",
        "leaf":"true",
        "iconCls":"image",
        "checked":true
      }
    ]
}
```

As we can see in the previous code we added the checked property to our data source. Now our tree is ready to display a checkbox in each node.

The following screenshot shows the checked tree output:

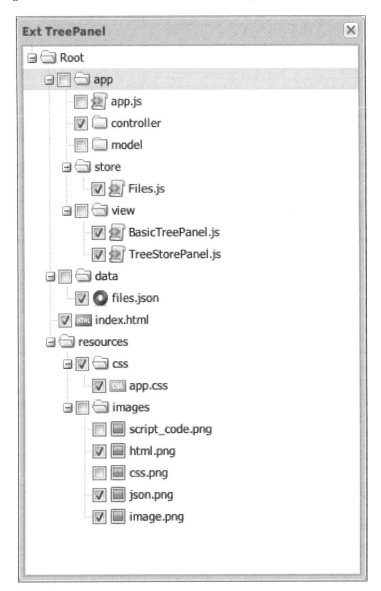

The grid tree

The grid tree panel has the power of the tree mixed with the flexibility of the grid panel; this tree configuration is very handy when we want to show more information in our tree panel.

We will need a model, a store, and some columns' definition to get our tree panel working. In this example we are going to list file properties, like file size, owner, and creation date.

First we are going to define the file model:

```
/**
 * @classApp.model.File
 * @extends Object
 * @author Armando Gonzalez <iam@armando.mx>
 * The file model definition
 */
Ext.define('App.model.File', {
  extend: 'Ext.data.Model',
  fields:[
    {name:'name', type:'string'},
    {name:'owner', type:'string'},
    {name:'created_at', type:'date', dateFormat: 'm/d/Y'},
    {name:'size', type:'string'}
  ]
});
```

Now let's change our data source configuration so that the model we had just defined can support it:

```
{
    "name":"images",
    "children":[
      {
        "name":"script_code.png",
        "leaf":"true",
        "owner":"Mark James",
        "created_at":"08/28/2012",
        "size":4,
        "iconCls":"image"
      },{
        "name":"html.png",
        "leaf":"true",
        "owner":"Mark James",
        "created_at":"08/28/2012",
        "size":4,
        "iconCls":"image"
      },{
        "name":"css.png",
        "leaf":"true",
```

        "owner":"Mark James",
        "created_at":"08/28/2012",
        "size":4,
        "iconCls":"image"
      },{
        "name":"json.png",
        "leaf":"true",
        "owner":"Mark James",
        "created_at":"08/28/2012",
        "size":4,
        "iconCls":"image"
      },{
        "name":"image.png",
        "leaf":"true",
        "owner":"Mark James",
        "created_at":"08/28/2012",
        "size":4,
        "iconCls":"image"
      }
    ]
  }
```

Next let's see the tree store definition:

```
/**
 * @classApp.store.Files
 * @extendsExt.data.TreeStore
 * @author Armando Gonzalez
 * This is the definition of our File store
 */
Ext.define('App.store.Files', {
  extend: 'Ext.data.TreeStore',
  requires: 'App.model.File',
  model: 'App.model.File',
proxy: {
  type: 'ajax',
  url : 'data/files.json'
}
});
```
```

In the previous store definition we added the file model. Once we have our model and store defined we are ready to define the file tree panel:

```
/**
 * @classApp.view.FilesTreePanel
 * @extendsExt.tree.Panel
 * @author Armando Gonzalez <iam@armando.mx>
 * This is a tree panel with a tree store configuration.
 */
Ext.define('App.view.FilesTreePanel', {
  extend: 'Ext.tree.Panel',
  xtype:'filestreepanel',
  store:'Files',
  columns:[{
    xtype:'treecolumn',
    text:'File name',
    flex:1,
    sortable:true,
    dataIndex:'name'
  },{
    text:'Owner',
    flex:1,
    dataIndex:'owner'
  },{
    text:'Creation date',
    flex:1,
    dataIndex:'created_at',
    renderer :Ext.util.Format.dateRenderer('m/d/Y')
  },{
    text:'Size',
    flex:1,
    dataIndex:'size',
    renderer:function(v){
      return  v ? v+ ' KB':'--';
    }
  }]
});
```

As the tree panel inherits from the same class as the grid panel does, we can add columns to our tree panel as we do with the grid panel. In the preceding code we have defined the columns that the tree panel will display.

Finally, we add the tree panel to our Ext.Window component in the Ext.application file:

```
/**
 * This is the main code for the application
 */

Ext.Loader.setConfig({
  enabled:true
});
Ext.application({
  name: 'App',

  requires:['App.view.FilesTreePanel'],
  stores:['Files'],

launch: function() {
  Ext.create('Ext.Window',{
      width:630,
      height:318,
      title:'ExtTreePanel',
      autoScroll:true,
      frame:false,
      layout:'fit',
      items:[{
        xtype:'filestreepanel'//adding the file tree panel to the
window
      }]
    }).show();
    this.getFilesStore().load();
    }
});
```

And the result is shown in the following screenshot:

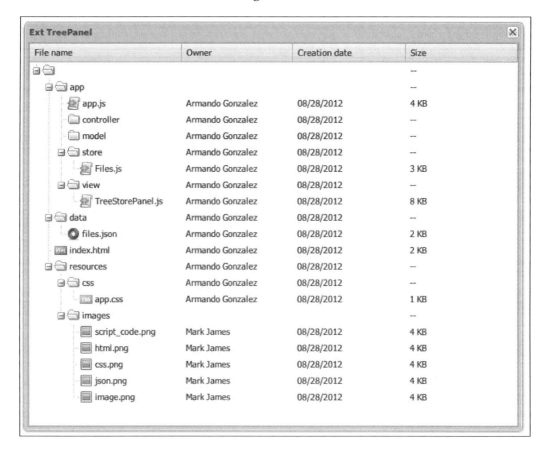

Adding an invoices' categories tree panel

Now that we have learned how the tree panel works, we are ready to add the invoices' categories tree panel to our application. We are going to make some changes to our previous mockup as shown in the following screenshot:

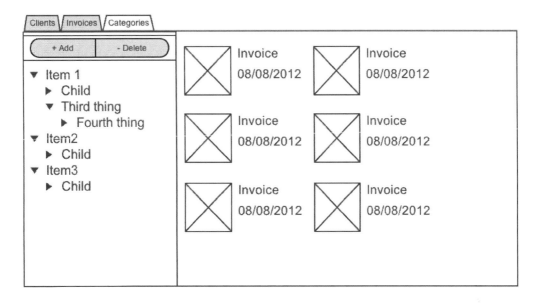

We are going to change the categories' UI, so we can have the categories' login to the left-hand side and an invoices' data view to the right-hand side of our main panel.

Let's start defining our category model:

```
/**
 * @classMyApp.model.categories.Category
 * @extendsExt.data.Model
 * @author Armando Gonzalez <iam@armando.mx>
 * The category model definition
 */
Ext.define('MyApp.model.categories.Category', {
  extend: 'Ext.data.Model',
  fields:[
    {name:'name', type:'string'},
    {name:'owner', type:'string'},
    {name:'created_at', type:'date', dateFormat: 'm/d/Y'}
  ]
});
```

In this model we have defined the `name`, `owner`, and `created_at` fields so we can keep track of our categories. Now let's see the store definition:

```
/**
 * @classMyApp.store.categories.Categories
 * @extendsExt.data.TreeStore
 * @author Armando Gonzalez <iam@armando.mx>
 * This is the definition of our Categories store
 */
Ext.define('MyApp.store.categories.Categories', {
  extend: 'Ext.data.TreeStore',
  requires: 'MyApp.model.categories.Category',
  model: 'MyApp.model.categories.Category',
proxy: {
  type: 'ajax',
  url : 'serverside/categories/list.json'
}
});
```

In the previous code we have the store definition for our categories' tree panel, now we are ready to define our form panel view:

```
/**
 * @classMyApp.view.categories.CategoriesForm
 * @extendsExt.form.Panel
 * @author Armando Gonzalez <iam@armando.mx>
 * The categories form panel
 */
Ext.define('MyApp.view.categories.CategoriesForm', {
  extend  : 'Ext.form.Panel',
  alias       : 'widget.categories.form',
  border   : false,
  frame    : true,
  initComponent   : function(){
    var me = this;
    me.items = me.buildItems();
    me.buttons = me.buildButtons();
    me.callParent();
  },
  buildItems : function(){
    return [{
      fieldLabel  : 'Name',
      name     : 'name',
      xtype    : 'textfield',
    }];
  },
  buildButtons:function(){
```

```
      return [{
   text: 'Save',
        itemId: 'savebtn'
           }];
   }
});
```

Our form panel has only one text field, which will be used to add the category name; we are going to add this form to the tree panel definition:

```
/**
 * @classMyApp.view.categories.TreePanel
 * @extendsExt.tree.Panel
 * @author Armando Gonzalez <iam@armando.mx>
 * This is the definition of the categories tree panel
 */
Ext.define('MyApp.view.categories.TreePanel', {
  extend     : 'Ext.tree.Panel',
  alias      : 'widget.categories.tree',
  requires   : [
    'Ext.tree.plugin.TreeViewDragDrop'
  ],
  store      :'categories.Categories',
  tbar       : [{
    text: 'Add',
    iconCls: 'new-icon16',
    menu:{
      items : {
        xtype:'categories.form'
      }
    }
  },{
    text:'Delete',
    iconCls:'delete-icon16',
    itemId: 'deletebtn'
  }],
  viewConfig      : {
    plugins:{
      ptype:'treeviewdragdrop'
    }
  },
  columns:[{
    xtype:'treecolumn',
    text:'File name',
    flex:1,
    sortable:true,
    dataIndex:'name'
  }]
});
```

The previous code is a tree grid definition, so if we want to display more of our categories' data, it will be easier to add those extra lines of code. Now we are going to define the main container for our categories:

```
/**
 * @classMyApp.view.categories.MainContainer
 * @extendsExt.container.Container
 * @author Armando Gonzalez <iam@armando.mx>
 *
 * The main container that uses a border layout.
 */

Ext.define('MyApp.view.categories.MainContainer',{
  extend        : 'Ext.container.Container',
  alias         : 'widget.categories.main',
  requires  : [
    'Ext.layout.container.Border',
    'Ext.resizer.BorderSplitterTracker'
  ],

  layout      : 'border',

  initComponent    : function(){
    var me = this;

    me.items = [{
      xtype : 'invoices.dataview',
      region: 'center'
    },{
      xtype : 'categories.tree',
      width : 300,
      region: 'west',
      split : true,
      collapsible : true
    }];

    me.callParent();
  }
});
```

Note that we are using a data view to display the invoices in each category; this data view is very similar to the one we defined in *Chapter 9, DataViews and Templates*. Let's do all the business logic of our categories module in the following controller:

```
/**
 * @classMyApp.controller.categories.Categories
 * @extendsExt.app.Controller
 * @author Armando Gonzalez <iam@armando.mx>
 *
```

```
 * This is the main controller for categories
 */

Ext.define('MyApp.controller.categories.Categories',{
  extend     : 'Ext.app.Controller',
  stores     : [
    'categories.Categories',
    'invoices.Invoices'
  ],
  views    : [
    'categories.CategoriesForm',
    'categories.TreePanel',
    'categories.MainContainer',
    'invoices.Dataview'
  ],
  refs: [{
  ref: 'treePanel',
  selector: '#categoriesmaintreepanel'
  }],
  init    : function(){
    var me = this;
    me.control({
        '#categoriesmaintreepanel #savebtn' : {// we get the save button
reference
          click :me.addTreeNode
        },
        '#categoriesmaintreepanel toolbar #deletebtn':{// we get the
delete button reference
          click :me.deleteTreeNode
        }
    });

    me.getCategoriesCategoriesStore().load();
    me.getInvoicesInvoicesStore().load();
  },
  addTreeNode:function(btn){
    var me = this,
    node,
      tree = me.getTreePanel(),
      selectedNode = tree.getSelectionModel().getSelection()[0] ||
tree.getRootNode(); //get the root node if there is not selection

    node = btn.up('form').getValues();//get the form values

    if(selectedNode.isLeaf()){ //insert the node in the parent node
      selectedNode.parentNode.insertChild(0,node);
    }else{//inserting as a child
      selectedNode.insertChild(0,node );
    }
```

```
        btn.up('menu').hide();// hide the menu
    },
    deleteTreeNode:function(){
      var me = this,
        tree = me.getTreePanel(),
        node = tree.getSelectionModel().getSelection()[0];
      if(node){
        node.remove(true);
      }else{
        Ext.Msg.alert('Warning', 'Please select a node!');
      }

    },
    addContent   : function(){
      this.container.add({
        xtype : 'categories.main',
        itemId: 'categoriesmain'
      });
    }
  });
```

The controller behavior is very similar to the controller we used, in the adding nodes example in the *Adding and removing nodes* section. We only need to update the refs property and add the views required by the categories' module. We also implemented the addContent method that is required by our main controller.

We are ready to see our categories' module implementation in our main application as shown in the following screenshot:

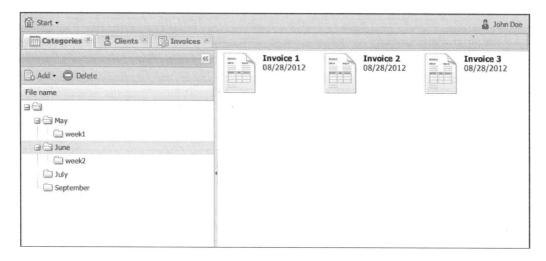

Summary

In this chapter we have learned the importance of the tree panels and how the Ext JS library has implemented a very robust component that supports all the common configurations we need while developing our applications. As with all components in the library it is very important to know in which situation we should use each component.

Remember when developing an Ext JS application we don't need to know all the properties of the classes by memory, we can always go and search the awesome API documentations the library has.

In the next chapter we are going to see how drag-and-drop works in Ext JS 4. This chapter will be very interesting because we can always enhance our applications, because some UIs work better and are more intuitive with drag-and-drop.

11
Drag and Drop

Drag and drop is a task that we humans do a lot in our day by day lives. That is why in user interfaces it is very helpful for accomplishing certain tasks. But not all the tasks can be accomplished that way. But when we face situations that do, Ext JS 4 offers a very complete set of classes to accomplish it.

Let's see the basic steps involved in drag-and-drop:

- Move the pointer to the object
- Press and hold the button of the pointing device, to grab the object
- Drag the object to the desired location
- Check if the desired location is a valid location to drop our object
- Drop the button in the desired location by releasing the button

Before starting our chapter, there are a few things we need to consider first, *not all situations that can be solved by drag-and-drop behavior must be solved that way*, because:

- Extended dragging and dropping can stress the hand
- It is not always clear to users when an item can be dragged and dropped, which can easily decrease usability
- Dragging requires more physical effort than just clicking on things

The most common situation for using drag-and-drop is ordering files between folders. Another useful situation is ordering items in a panel. Now that we know when to use the drag-and-drop operations, we are ready to learn how Ext JS helps us solve these situations.

We are going to cover the following topics in this chapter:

- Make an item draggable
- Hitting the drop zone
- Drag-and-drop between Ext JScomponents
- Enhancing our application with drag-and-drop

Make an item draggable

The first step we need to do when implementing drag-and-drop is make our object draggable, in Ext JS 4 this is very simple, let's see what we need to do to accomplish this.

Let's start by defining a container and rendering it to a window:

```
/**
 * @classMyApp.view.Container
 * @extendsExt.Container
 * @author Armando Gonzalez <iam@armando.mx>
 * This the container of the make it draggable example
 */
Ext.define('MyApp.view.Container', {
  extend  : 'Ext.Container',
  alias   : 'widget.dnd.container',
  style   : {
    backgroundColor:'white'
  },
  data    : [
    {"id":"1", "name":"Invoice 1", "date":"08/28/2012",},
    {"id":"2", "name":"Invoice 2", "date":"08/28/2012",},
    {"id":"3", "name":"Invoice 3", "date":"08/28/2012",}
  ],
  tpl     : [
    '<tpl for =".">',
      '<div class="invoice">',
        '<div class="content">',
          '<imgsrc="resources/images/invoice64.png"  height="60"
width="60">',
        '</div>',
        '<b>{name}</b></br>',
        '<span>{[Ext.util.Format.date(values.date)]}</span>',
        '</div>',
    '</tpl>'].join('')
});
```

The previous code has a container definition with some raw data and a template definition. This container is rendered in a window defined in our `app.js` file as follows:

```
/**
 * This is the main code for the application
 */

Ext.Loader.setConfig({
  enabled:true
});
Ext.application({
  name: 'MyApp',

  requires:['MyApp.view.Container'],
  stores:[],

launch: function() {
  Ext.create('Ext.Window',{
      width:630,
      height:318,
      title:'Drag and Drop',
      autoScroll:true,
      frame:false,
      layout:'fit',
      items:[{
          xtype : 'dnd.container',
      }]
    }).show();
    }
});
```

In the preceding code, we have defined a window that has the container definition. When we refresh our application we get the output, as shown in the following screenshot:

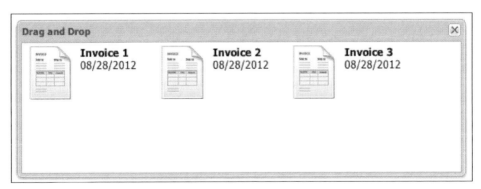

Now let's make our invoices' objects draggable, to accomplish that we need to add some behavior after the container renders:

```
/**
 * @classMyApp.view.Container
 * @extendsExt.Container
 * @author Armando Gonzalez <iam@armando.mx>
 * This the container of the make it draggable example
 */
Ext.define('MyApp.view.Container', {
  extend  : 'Ext.Container',
  alias   : 'widget.dnd.container',
  style   : {
    backgroundColor:'white'
  },
  data    : [
    {"id":"1", "name":"Invoice 1", "date":"08/28/2012",},
    {"id":"2", "name":"Invoice 2", "date":"08/28/2012",},
    {"id":"3", "name":"Invoice 3", "date":"08/28/2012",}
  ],
  tpl     : [
    '<tpl for =".">',
      '<div class="invoice" id="invoice-{id}">',
        '<div class="content">',
          '<imgsrc="resources/images/invoice64.png"  height="60"
width="60">',
        '</div>',
        '<b>{name}</b></br>',
        '<span{[Ext.util.Format.date(values.date)]}</span>',
        '</div>',
    '</tpl>'].join(''),
  afterRender:function(){
    var me = this,container;

    this.callParent(arguments);

    container = Ext.get(me.el.id).select('div.invoice'); //we get our
invoices objects

    Ext.each(container.elements, function(el) { // for each invoice
object
      vardd= Ext.create('Ext.dd.DD', el, 'invoicesDnDGroup', { //add
drag-and-drop functionallity and add it to de invoicesDnDGroup group
    isTarget  : false
          });
    });
  }
});
```

In the previous code, we do some extra logic in the `afterRender` method so each of the invoices' objects gets the drag behavior. First we need to get all of our invoice objects, then for each invoice object we have to create an `Ext.dd.DD` instance and add it to the group this object will belong to. The following output shows how the invoices objects can be dragged anywhere in the container:

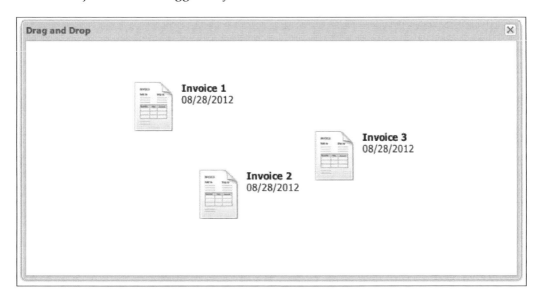

Hitting the drop zone

Once we have made our objects draggable we are ready to make them droppable. First, we need to define a valid drop zone, any zone that is not the valid one must return the selected object to its original state. Let's add some code to our objects so when it is not dropped in a valid zone it returns to its original state. To accomplish this, the `Ext.dd.DD` class has some abstract methods that can be overridden:

- `startDrag`: It is an abstract method that is called after a drag/drop object is clicked and the drag or mouse-down time thresholds have been met
- `onDrag`: It is an abstract method that is called during the `onMouseMove` event while dragging an object
- `onDragEnter`: It is an abstract method that is called when this element begins hovering over another DragDrop object
- `onDragOver`: It is an abstract method that is called when this element is hovering over another DragDrop object
- `onDragOut`: It is an abstract method that is called when we are no longer hovering over an element

- `onDragDrop`: It is an abstract method that is called when this item is dropped on another DragDrop object

- `endDrag`: It is an abstract method that is called when we are done dragging the object

We are going to define an extended implementation of the `Ext.dd.DD` class that will implement that invalid target validation:

```
/**
 * @class Ux.dd.DD
 * @extends Ext.dd.DD
 * @author Armando Gonzalez <iam@armando.mx>
 * This is a an extension of the Ext.dd.DD so we can implement a
personalized Drag-n-drop behavior
 */
Ext.define('Ux.dd.DD', {
  extend    : 'Ext.dd.DD',
  startDrag  : function(e){
    console.log('startDrag');
    if (!this.el) {
      this.el = Ext.get(this.getEl());
    }
    this.el.addCls('selected');
    this.initialPosition = this.el.getXY();
  },
  onDrag   : function(){
    console.log('onDrag');
  },
  onDragEnter : function(e, id) {
    console.log('onDragEnter');
  },
  onDragOver : function(e, id) {
    console.log('onDragOver');
  },
  onDragOut : function(e, id) {
    console.log('onDragOut');
  },
  onDragDrop : function(e, id) {
    console.log('onDragDrop');
if(this.initialPosition != this.el.getXY()){ //if the initial position
is diferent from the actual when finishing dragging
      this.onInvalidDrop();
    }
  },
  onInvalidDrop : function() {
    console.log('onInvalidDrop');
```

```
    this.el.removeCls('selected');
    this.el.moveTo(this.initialPosition[0], this.initialPosition[1]);
// return the object to its original position
  },
  endDrag : function() {
    console.log('endDrag');
    this.el.highlight();
  }
});
```

In the `startDrag` method, we get the initial position of our object so we can return it when it has been dropped on an invalid zone. In the `onInvalidDrop` method we set our object to the initial position. Sometimes, the object's final position is different from the initial position and the drop zone is not a valid one, so we need to validate these scenarios in the `onDragDrop` method and in the `endDrag` method, we do some fancy highlighting so the user knows when the drag ends.

To see this in action, we need to add an extra container in our window definition:

```
layout     : {
        type   : "hbox",
        align  : "stretch"
},
defaults:{
        margin:'3'
},
items:[{
        xtype   : 'dnd.container',
        flex    : 1
    },{
        xtype   : 'container',
        flex    : 1,
        style   : {
          backgroundColor:'white'
        },
    }]
```

Now we need to use our drag-and-drop implementation in our container definition:

```
vardd= Ext.create('Ux.dd.DD', el.id, 'invoicesDnDGroup', {
        isTarget  : true,
    });
```

The result is shown in the following screenshot:

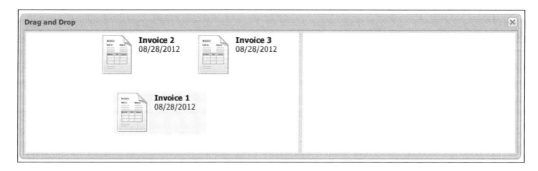

The console logs for the drag-and-drop behavior are shown in the following screenshot:

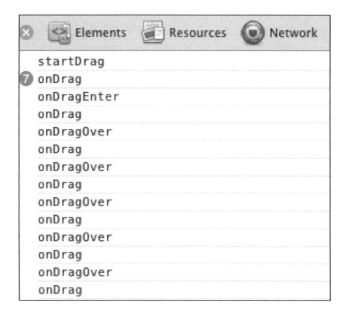

Now we are going to make the other container a valid drop zone, for this we are going to use the Ext.dd.DDTarget class, this class definition is an implementation that does not move, but can be a drop target.

We are going to define a custom container that has this drop behavior:

```
/**
 * @classMyApp.view.DropContainer
 * Ext.Container
 * @author Armando Gonzalez <iam@armando.mx>
 * This the container for the drop zone
 */
Ext.define('MyApp.view.DropContainer', {
  extend: 'Ext.Container',
  alias   : 'widget.drop.container',
  style   : {
    backgroundColor:'white'
  },
  dropGroup:undefined,
  afterRender:function(){
    var me = this;
    this.callParent(arguments);
    Ext.create('Ext.dd.DDTarget', me.el, me.dropGroup);
  }
});
```

In the previous code we have a generic container with a drop implementation, now we need to update the onDragDrop method of the Ux.dd.DD class so it adds the object when our target is in a valid drop zone:

```
onDragDrop : function(e, id) {
    var me = this;
    console.log('onDragDrop');
    vardropEl = Ext.get(id);

    if(this.initialPosition != this.el.getXY()){ //if the initial
position is different from the actual when finishing dragging
        this.onInvalidDrop();
    }
  if (me.el.dom.parentNode.id != id) {
    dropEl.appendChild(this.el);
    me.onDragOut(e, id);
      }
  else{
  this.onInvalidDrop();
      }
    }
```

The preceding code appends the object to the container when it is a valid drop target, once we have done this it updates to our code and we have output, as shown in the following screenshot:

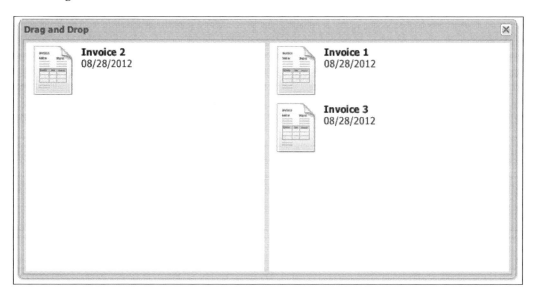

We have implemented a complete drag-and-drop example between two containers using the `Ext.dd package`, now we are ready to implement a more complex example using various Ext JS components.

Drag and drop between Ext JS components

Most of the Ext JS components can be added to a drag-and-drop group, this means that it is very easy to give them a drag-and-drop functionality. In the next example, we'll see how easily we can implement a complete drag-and-drop user interface using Ext JS components.

Let's start by defining our wireframe, so we can get an idea of what the UI should look like:

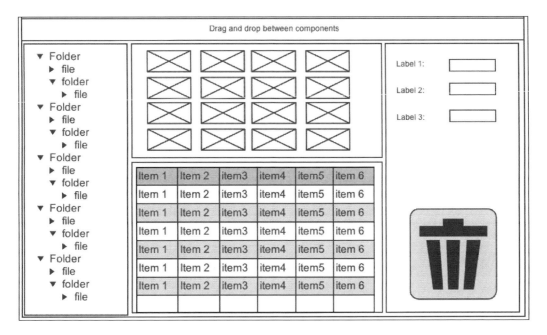

As we can see in the previous wireframe, we are going to use some Ext JS components, such as a tree panel, a data view, a grid panel, a form panel, and a container with a trash can icon so we can drag-and-drop the file object between them.

We are going to use a file model definition:

```
/**
 * @classMyApp.model.File
 * @extendsExt.data.Model
 * @author Armando Gonzalez <iam@armando.mx>
 * The file model definition
 */
Ext.define('MyApp.model.File', {
  extend: 'Ext.data.Model',
  fields:[
    {name:'name', type:'string'},
    {name:'owner', type:'string'},
    {name:'created_at', type:'date', dateFormat: 'm/d/Y'},
    {name:'size', type:'string'}
  ]
});
```

Then, we are going to define a **Files Tree** store:

```
/**
 * @classMyApp.store.TreeFiles
 * @extendsExt.data.TreeStore
 * @author Armando Gonzalez <iam@armando.mx>
 * This is the definition of our File store
 */
Ext.define('MyApp.store.TreeFiles', {
  extend: 'Ext.data.TreeStore',
  requires: 'MyApp.model.File',
  model: 'MyApp.model.File',
proxy: {
  type: 'ajax',
  url : 'serverside/tree-files.json'
}
});
```

And now we will define a **Files** store:

```
/**
 * @classMyApp.store.Files
 * @extendsExt.data.Store
 * @author Armando Gonzalez <iam@armando.mx>
 * This is the definition of our File store
 */
Ext.define('MyApp.store.Files', {
  extend: 'Ext.data.Store',
  requires: 'MyApp.model.File',
  model: 'MyApp.model.File',

proxy     : {
type   : 'ajax',
url    : 'serverside/files.json',
     reader   : {
        type   : 'json',
        root   : 'data'
      }
    }
});
```

Now we need our views; first we are going to define our **file form** panel:

```
/**
 * @classMyApp.view.FilesForm
 * @extendsExt.form.Panel
 * @author Armando Gonzalez <iam@armando.mx>
 * The files form
 */
```

```
Ext.define('MyApp.view.FilesForm', {
  extend: 'Ext.form.Panel',
  alias: 'widget.filesform',
  bodyPadding  : 5,
  defaultType  : 'textfield',
  initComponent:function(){
    var me = this;
    me.items = me.buildItems();
    this.callParent(arguments);
  },
  afterRender:function(){
    this.callParent(arguments);
    var me = this, dropTarget = me.body.dom;
    Ext.create('Ext.dd.DropTarget', dropTarget, {
    ddGroup: 'filesDDGroup',
    notifyEnter: function(ddSource, e, data) { //when the drag object
enters the form panel
    me.body.stopAnimation();
    me.body.highlight();
            },
    notifyDrop  : function(ddSource, e, data){

    //get the selected record
    varselectedRecord= ddSource.dragData.records[0];

// Load the record into the form
    me.getForm().loadRecord(selectedRecord);
    return true;
            }
        });
  },
  buildItems:function(){
    return [{
      fieldLabel  : 'Name',
  name         : 'name'
    },{
      fieldLabel  : 'Owner',
  name         : 'owner'
    },{
      xtype       : 'datefield',
      fieldLabel  : 'Created at',
      name       : 'created_at'
    }];
  }
});
```

The `afterRender` method was overridden so we can add the drop functionality to the panel using the `Ext.dd.DropTarget` class. The `notifyEnter` method is fired when a valid object defined in the `ddGroup` property enters the panel, the `notifyDrop` method fires when a valid object has been dropped in the panel.

Now we are going to define the grid panel:

```
/**
 * @classMyApp.view.FilesGrid
 * @extendsExt.grid.Panel
 * @author Armando Gonzalez <iam@armando.mx>
 * This is our files grid panel
 */
Ext.define('MyApp.view.FilesGrid', {
  extend  : 'Ext.grid.Panel',
  alias   : 'widget.filesgrid',

  store:'Files',
  viewConfig:{
    plugins: { //drag and drop configuration
      ptype: 'gridviewdragdrop',
      ddGroup: 'filesDDGroup'
    }
  },
  columns :[
    {text:'Name',dataIndex:'name',flex:1},
    {text:'Owner',dataIndex:'owner',flex:1},
    {text:'Created at',dataIndex:'created_at',flex:1, renderer:Ext.
util.Format.dateRenderer('m/d/Y')}
  ]
});
```

We only need to add the grid `Ext.grid.plugin.DragDrop` plugin with the correct `ddGroup` to the `viewConfig` of our grid and we are ready with our grid. Next we are going to define our tree panel:

```
/**
 * @classMyApp.view.FilesTreePanel
 * @extendsExt.tree.Panel
 * @author Armando Gonzalez <iam@armando.mx>
 * This is a tree panel with a tree store configuration.
 */
Ext.define('MyApp.view.FilesTreePanel', {
  extend: 'Ext.tree.Panel',
  alias   : 'widget.filestreepanel',
  store   : 'TreeFiles',
  columns:[{
```

```
      xtype:'treecolumn',
      text:'File name',
      flex:1,
      sortable:true,
      dataIndex:'name'
    }],
  viewConfig:{ //drag and drop configuration
    plugins:{
      ptype:'treeviewdragdrop',
      ddGroup: 'filesDDGroup'
    }
  }
});
```

The tree panel configuration is pretty similar to the grid panel, we just need to add our plugin to the `viewConfig` file with the correct drag-and-drop group and we are done with the tree panel configuration. Next we are going to define our data view configuration; here we are going to use `Ext.ux.Dataview.Draggable` mixin that comes in the `ux` folder of the Ext JS 4 library:

```
/**
 * @classMyApp.view.FilesView
 * @extendsExt.view.View
 * @author Armando Gonzalez <iam@armando.mx>
 * This is the definition of the files data view component
 */
Ext.define('MyApp.view.FilesView', {
  extend     : 'Ext.view.View',
  alias      : 'widget.filesview',
  store      : 'Files',
  emptyText  :'No files available',
  itemSelector: 'div.file',
  frame:false,
  ddGroup:undefined,
  style:{
    backgroundColor:'white'
  },
  mixins: { //drag an drop configuration mixin
    draggable   : 'Ext.ux.DataView.Draggable'
  },
  tpl:[
    '<tpl for =".">',
      '<div class="file">',
        '<div class="content">',
```

```
            '<imgsrc="resources/images/invoice64.png"  height="60"
width="60">',
            '</div>',
            '<b>{name}</b></br>',
            '<span>{[Ext.util.Format.date(values.created_at)]}</span>',
            '</div>',
        '</tpl>'].join(''),
    initComponent : function(){
      var me = this;
    this.mixins.draggable.init(this, {
    ddConfig: {
    ddGroup: 'filesDDGroup'
                }
        });
      this.callParent();
    }
});
```

We need to initialize our mixin, so we just need to override the initComponent method and initialize there the draggable mixin and pass it to the correct ddGroup. The final step is to configure our trash container:

```
/**
 * @classMyApp.view.TrashContainer
 * @extendsExt.Container
 * @author Armando Gonzalez <iam@armando.mx>
 * The trash container for the drag-and-drop operation
 */
Ext.define('MyApp.view.TrashContainer', {
  extend: 'Ext.Container',
  alias  : 'widget.trashcontainer',
  style  : {
    backgroundColor:'#EEE'
},
  padding:'50 0 0 70',
  html  :[
    '<div class = "file">',
      '<imgsrc="resources/images/recycle.png"  height="128"
width="128">',
    '</div>'
  ].join(),
  dropGroup:'filesDDGroup',
  afterRender:function(){
    this.callParent(arguments);
    var me = this, dropTarget = me.el.dom;
```

```
    Ext.create('Ext.dd.DropTarget', dropTarget, {
    ddGroup: 'filesDDGroup',
    notifyEnter: function(ddSource, e, data) {

//when the drag object enters the form panel
    me.el.stopAnimation();
    me.el.highlight();
            },
    notifyDrop  : function(ddSource, e, data){
        Ext.Msg.alert('Ext JS','Item deleted.');
        }
      });
  }
});
```

The drag-and-drop implementation of the data view is pretty similar to the form panel drag-and-drop implementation, but in `notifyDrop` we are sending some feedback to the user when he/she drops a file object in this container.

The main container definition of our example goes as follows:

```
/**
 * @classMyApp.view.Main
 * @extendsExt.Container
 * @author Armando Gonzalez <iam@armando.mx>
 * This is the main container of our application
 */
Ext.define('MyApp.view.main', {
  extend: 'Ext.Container',
  alias  : 'widget.maincontainer',

  layout  : {
    type  : "hbox",
    align : "stretch"
  },
items:[{
    title:'Files tree',
    xtype:'filestreepanel',
    flex  : 1
  },{
    xtype:'panel',
    title:'Files data view',
    flex  : 2,
    layout    : {
      type  : "vbox",
      align  : "stretch"
```

```
      },
      defaults : {
        flex : 1
      },
      items:[{
        xtype : 'filesview'
      },{
        xtype : 'filesgrid',
        title : 'Files grid'
      }]
    },{
      xtype : 'container',
      layout    : {
        type   : "vbox",
        align  : "stretch"
      },
      defaults : {
        flex : 1
      },
      items:[{
        title  : 'Files form',
        xtype  : 'filesform',
        flex   : 1
      },{
        xtype:'trashcontainer'
      }]
    }]
  });
```

Now we just need to configure the main app file definition (`app.js`):

```
/**
 * This is the main code for the application
 */

Ext.Loader.setConfig({
  enabled:true
});
Ext.Loader.setPath({
  'Ux':'app/ux'
});
Ext.Loader.setPath('Ext.ux.DataView', 'app/Ux/DataView'); // setting
the uxdataview path
Ext.application({
name: 'MyApp',
```

```
requires:['MyApp.view.main','MyApp.view.FilesTreePanel',
        'MyApp.view.FilesView','MyApp.view.FilesGrid',
        'MyApp.view.FilesForm','MyApp.view.TrashContainer'],
    stores:['TreeFiles','Files'],

launch: function() {
  Ext.create('Ext.Window',{
      maximized  : true,
      title      : 'Drag and Drop',
      autoScroll : true,
      layout     : 'fit',
      items:[{
        xtype:'maincontainer'
      }]
    }).show();
    //loading our stores
    this.getTreeFilesStore().load();
    this.getFilesStore().load();
    }
});
```

In the previous code, we first set the path for the `Ext.ux.Dataview` package, we then added our main container and when the window shows we just load our stores. The final result is a very nice UI with all the drag and drop behavior between our components:

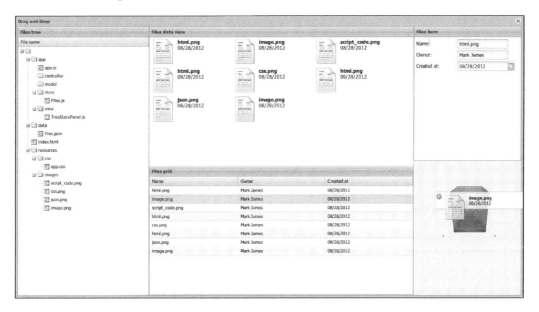

Enhancing our application with drag and drop

Now that we know how drag and drop works in Ext JS we are going to use these capabilities in our invoices' application.

In the categories module, we are going to add drag and drop to the invoices' data view, so we can add our invoices to different categories using the drag-and-drop operation.

In the `MyApp.view.invoices.Dataview` class, we need to add the methods so when an invoice item is selected we can drag it to the categories tree panel:

```
/**
 * @classMyApp.view.invoices.Dataview
 * @extendsExt.view.View
 * @author Armando Gonzalez <iam@armando.mx>
 * This is the definition of the invoices data view component
 */
Ext.define('MyApp.view.invoices.Dataview', {
  extend    : 'Ext.view.View',
  alias      : 'widget.invoices.dataview',
  store      : 'invoices.Invoices',
  emptyText  :'No invoices available',
  itemSelector: 'div.invoice',
  frame:false,
  style:{
    backgroundColor:'white'
  },
  mixins: { //drag an drop configuration mixin
    draggable    : 'Ext.ux.DataView.Draggable'
  },
  tpl:[
    '<tpl for =".">',
      '<div class="invoice">',
        '<div class="content">',
          '<imgsrc="resources/images/invoice64.png"  height="60"
width="60">',
        '</div>',
        '<b>{name}</b></br>',
        '<span>{[Ext.util.Format.date(values.date)]}</span>',
        '</div>',
    '</tpl>'].join(''),
  initComponent : function(){
    var me = this;
      this.mixins.draggable.init(this, {
      ddConfig: {
```

```
    ddGroup: 'invoicesDDGroup'
                }
        });
    this.callParent();
    }
});
```

In the previous code we are using the `Ext.ux.Dataview.Draggable` plugin as a mixin, then in the `initComponent` method we initialize our mixin. Next, we are going to add another field to our `MyApp.model.invoices.Invoice` so it behaves like a leaf in our categories tree:

```
/**
 * @classMyApp.model.invoices.Invoice
 * @extendsExt.data.Model
 * @author Armando Gonzalez <iam@armando.mx>
 * The invoice model definition
 */
Ext.define('MyApp.model.invoices.Invoice', {
  extend: 'Ext.data.Model',
  fields:[
    {name:'name', type:'string'},
    {name:'date', type:'date', dateFormat: 'm/d/Y'},
    {name:'leaf', type:'boolean'}
  ]
});
```

And the response should come like this:

```
{"id":"3", "name":"Invoice 3", "date":"08/28/2012",leaf:true}
```

Now we just need to set the path of our `Ext.ux.Dataview.Draggable` in the `app.js` file:

```
Ext.Loader.setConfig({
  enabled:true
});
Ext.Loader.setPath('Ext.ux.DataView', 'ux/DataView'); // setting the
us dataview path
Ext.application({
  name        : 'MyApp',
  appFolder       : 'app',
  controllers     : [
    'MyApp.controller.main.Main'
  ],
  autoCreateViewport  : true
});
```

Now we are ready to see our drag and drop in action:

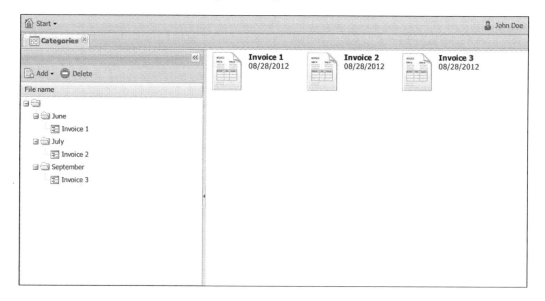

Summary

In this chapter, we have learned how the drag and drop works, now we can do very easy-to-use apps using this knowledge, we also keep enhancing our invoices' application and we are getting close to finishing.

Drag and drop is very useful but we need to know exactly when to use it, because if we are not sure we can make our application less usable.

In the next chapter, we are going to see how we can change the look and feel of our application using the powerful SASS framework.

12
Look and Feel

One of the biggest challenges of the Ext applications is to create a specific look and feel for our own products. It's very common to see many applications with the default light-blue theme. This is because in the previous version of Ext JS, there was not an easy way to customize or create themes that match our own branding colors and design guidelines.

With the latest version of Ext we are able to change the colors, gradients, fonts, and even dimensions of margins and padding of all the visual components. We can even create different styles for the same component using the `ui` property.

In this chapter we are going to learn how we can create our own themes. We will create a theme for our main application that we have been working on over the previous chapters. We will completely change the default theme to fit our needs.

We will be covering the following topics in this chapter:

- Compass and SASS
- Advanced theming
- Different styles on the same component
- Supporting legacy browsers

Setting up our environment

Before we start coding our new theme we need to install some tools. These tools will help us to write our first theme for Ext JS 4. We are going to use Compass and SASS to write our CSS code and bring some life to our application.

Compass (`http://compass-style.org/`) allows us to write easy and maintainable CSS code, we can use variables, conditional statements, mixins (similar to functions or macros), some basic math calculations, and many more awesome things. Once we have our Compass code we can compile it and generate a compressed CSS file with all the resulting CSS code.

In order to use Compass we need to install Ruby. Ruby is a very dynamic and popular language among web developers. Don't worry if you are not familiar with it, in fact we are not going to write any line of code at all, we are going to write only CSS code with the help of Compass.

Let's download and install Ruby. If you are using Windows, you can use the RubyInstaller. This is the easier way to get ready with Ruby. We can find the Ruby installer at http://www.ruby-lang.org/en/downloads/. If you are using Mac, you need to install XCode to install Ruby and all its dependencies. Also, you can use the RVM project to install any version of Ruby in the same machine, this also works for Linux systems.

At the time of this writing the latest version of Ruby is Version 1.9.3-p194, but Version 1.8.7 should work too. Once we have Ruby installed in our environment, we need to add it to the PATH, let's open a terminal and type the following command:

```
$ruby -v
```

This command should give us the version of our Ruby installation. We should see something as shown in the images of the following screenshot:

The previous screenshot shows the Ruby version on Mac and Windows platforms. As mentioned before the default version of Ruby on Mac should work for this chapter.

Ruby comes with a package management tool called **gem**. We are going to use this package manager to install Compass. In our terminal we only need to run the following command:

```
$gem install compass
```

This command downloads and installs the required software and its dependencies; in this case Compass uses SASS. We can see the version of the installed software by running the following commands:

```
$compass -v
$sass -v
```

If everything goes fine, we should see the version of the two gems installed in our system. Now we are ready to start working on our theme.

 Avoid using the SASS Version 3.1.4 because this version contains issues with performance and sometimes the compilation time takes minutes instead of seconds.

The resources folder

In *Chapter 1, The Basics*, we learned about the folders that come with the Ext library the first time we download and extract the framework. Inside the **resources** folder we have all the styles and images that are required for the default theme. We also have all the compass files to start creating our theme.

Before we start coding and modifying our styles we need to prepare our project to be able to compile the compass files. First we need to copy the **sass** folder located at extjs-4.1.0/resources/themes/templates/resources to our **resources** folder in our project. The folder structure for our project should look like the following screenshot:

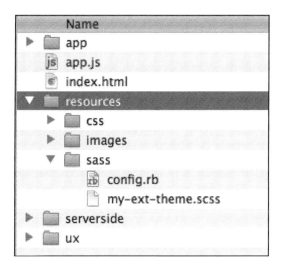

Inside the **sass** folder we have a Ruby configuration file and a Compass file. We are going to use these files a bit later.

We are almost ready to start, but before that we need to duplicate the **ext4** folder located at `extjs-4.1.0/resources/themes/stylesheets`. In this case we will set the name of the new folder to `mytheme`, but we can use any name as shown in the following screenshot:

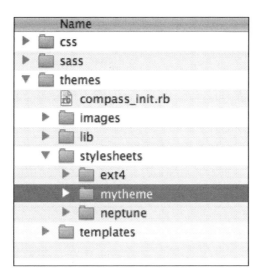

In this new folder we have all the required CSS code to generate a new theme. Now we need to start modifying the styles of this folder in order to create a new look and feel for our theme.

Finally, we need to configure the PATH where the files of our new theme are. Let's open the `resources/sass/config.rb` file and change the line number two for the correct path where the Ext library is located:

```
# $ext_path: This should be the path of the Ext JS SDK relative to this
file

$ext_path = "../../../extjs-4.1.0"


# sass_path: the directory your Sass files are in. THIS file should also
be in the Sass folder

# Generally this will be in a resources/sass folder

# <root>/resources/sass

sass_path = File.dirname(__FILE__)
```

```
# css_path: the directory you want your CSS files to be.
# Generally this is a folder in the parent directory of your Sass files
# <root>/resources/css
css_path = File.join(sass_path, "..", "css")


# output_style: The output style for your compiled CSS
# nested, expanded, compact, compressed
# More information can be found here http://sass-lang.com/docs/yardoc/
file.SASS_REFERENCE.html#output_style
output_style = :compressed


# We need to load in the Ext4 themes folder, which includes all its
default styling, images, variables and mixins
loadFile.join(File.dirname(__FILE__), $ext_path, 'resources', 'themes')
```

The `ext_path` variable contains the path where our Ext library is; we need to set this path accordingly. In our case Ext is located three levels above the `config` file, but this will depend on our folder structure.

Now we need to load our duplicated folder, the one that we are going to modify. Let's open the `resources/sass/my-ext-theme.scss` file and change the line number eight as follows:

```
// Unless you want to include all components, you must set $include-
default to false
// IF you set this to true, you can also remove lines 10 to 38 of this
file
$include-default: false;


// Insert your custom variables here.
// $base-color: #aa0000;
@import 'mytheme/default/all';
```

We use `mytheme` folder to hold all the Compass files for our new theme. If we use a different name for the folder that we duplicated previously, we just need to make sure this path is configured accordingly.

The `$include-default` variable allows us to include the styles of all components by setting it to `true`. This way we can remove all the mixin calls that we have in this file starting at line number 10.

Now let's compile our theme to check if everything is working. Let's open our terminal and go to the `resources/sass/` folder. In here we need to run the following command:

```
$compass compile my-ext-theme.scss
```

If everything goes fine, a `resources/css/my-ext-theme.css` file should be created when compiling our theme. This file contains a compressed version of our new theme.

We can also configure the output of this file to be expanded; this is a good idea for a development environment since we can read it easily. Let's modify our `resources/sass/config.rb` file at line number nine. In there we can set how we want the output of the resulting CSS file. We will expand this file only for development. For a production environment we need to compress this file.

In order to test our new theme we need to modify the HTML code to import the resulting CSS file instead of the default theme:

```
<!DOCTYPE HTML>
<html manifest="" lang="en-US">
<head>
<meta charset="UTF-8">
<title>Application</title>
<linkrel="stylesheet" href="resources/css/my-ext-theme.css" />
  <linkrel="stylesheet" href="resources/css/style.css"/>


<script type="text/javascript" charset="utf-8" src="http://cdn.sencha.
io/ext-4.1.0-gpl/ext-all-debug.js"></script>
<script type="text/javascript" src="app.js"></script>
</head>
<body>

</body>
</html>
```

Because we have replicated the default light-blue theme folder, our compiled theme is the same, but now we are ready to start modifying the code to create our new theme.

Variables

The new way to create themes is just awesome. There are a lot of variables that we can change to customize our theme, variables for colors, fonts, margins, borders, and many more things.

In Compass we can define variables using the dollar ($) sign. Every time we find a word that starts with the dollar sign it means that it's a variable that we can read or assign a value. The following lines of code are some examples of variables:

```
$background-color: #f3f3f3;
$font-size: 1.5em;
$header-height: 45px;
$custom-text: 'This is a text value';
```

As shown in the previous code we can assign a value using the colon (:), we can also use colors, sizes, or texts as values. We need to use a semicolon(;) every time we end a statement.

By default, Ext has defined a lot of variables for us, we can see all the available variables in the folder `extjs-4.1.0/resources/themes/stylesheets/mytheme/default/variables`. We have many files in here, you can see the name of some components in these files, that's because all the variables used for a component are in that respective file.

We are also going to find a file called `_core.scss`, this file contains many generic variables, for example the base color, base font, base type of gradient, and so on. We can change the value of each variable in here, but it's recommended to overwrite the value of every variable in our `my-ext-theme.scss` file, as follows:

```
// Insert your custom variables here.
$base-color: #4485ab;
```

Now, if we compile our theme again we will see that the base color of our components has changed as shown in the following screenshot:

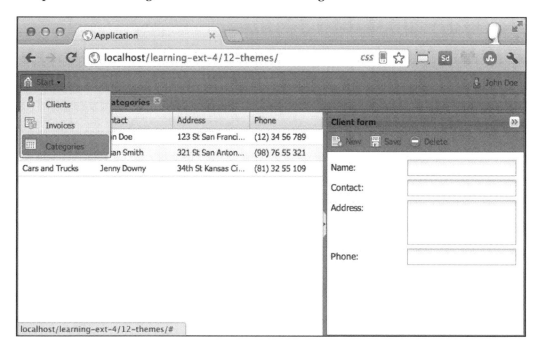

We have a different blue, just by changing a variable we have changed the color for all of our components. We can use any color we want depending on our design. We can start playing around with all the variables and see how our theme will change.

Advanced theming

In the rest of this chapter we are going to see common situations where we need to modify the original code from the original theme. We will create new gradients, change dimensions, paddings, colors, and custom UIs.

Adding new gradients

Let's start by defining a new gradient for the toolbar component. We already have a few available styles of gradients defined in the default theme, such as matte, glossy, and bevel. We can use any of the available gradients, but most of the time these gradients are not enough or maybe we need something different.

In order to create a new gradient we need to open the file located at `extjs-4.1.0/resources/themes/stylesheets/mytheme/default/mixins/_background-gradient.scss`. In here we have all the available gradients. Let's define a new gradient as follows:

```
//...

} @else if $type == glossy-button-pressed {
    @include background-image(linear-gradient($direction, color_stops(
        $bg-color,
adjust-color($bg-color, $hue: -1.839deg, $saturation: -2.18%,
$lightness: 2.157%) 48%,
adjust-color($bg-color, $hue: -2.032deg, $saturation: 37.871%,
$lightness: -4.706%) 52%,
adjust-color($bg-color, $hue: -1.641deg, $saturation: 36.301%,
$lightness: -2.549%)
    )));
} @else if $type == toolbar-blue{ //Step 1
    @include background-image(linear-gradient($direction,
#4486ac,#396e8e)); //Step 2
}
```

After the preceding gradient definition (`glossy-button-pressed`) we will add a new one called `toolbar-blue`.

First we use an `else if` condition to check if the `$type` variable is equal to `toolbar-blue`.

In the second step we use the `background-image` and `linear-gradient` mixins to define our new gradient. We use only two colors for our gradient hardcoding the two colors, but we can also use variables if we need. For now we will leave the hardcoded colors.

 We can use the `@if` statement to make a condition. We can also use the `@else if` statement to define the false actions of the previous conditions. This is Compass syntax for conditions and it is very useful.

Once we have defined our new gradient we need to use it as the background for our toolbar. If we go to the `_toolbar.scss` file located at `extjs-4.1.0/resources/themes/stylesheets/mytheme/default/variables`, we will find all the variables for the toolbar component. The variable that we need to modify with our own gradient is `$toolbar-background-gradient`. Let's assign a new value in our `my-ext-theme.scss` file:

```
// Unless you want to include all components, you must set $include-
default to false
// If you set this to true, you can also remove lines 10 to 38 of this
file
$include-default: false;

// Insert your custom variables here.
$base-color: #4485ab;

//Toolbar component
$toolbar-background-gradient:toolbar-blue;
```

Now let's compile our theme again using the command line:

```
$ compass compile my-ext-theme.scss
```

If we refresh our browser, we will see the changes applied in our main toolbar. The following screenshot shows the results of our modifications:

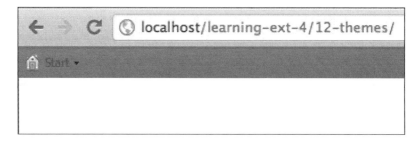

We have a nice gradient, now let's add one small detail to make it look really great. We are going to change the color of the border to a light blue color:

```
//Toolbar component
$toolbar-background-gradient:toolbar-blue;
$toolbar-border-color:#7caac4;
```

We have another variable that defines the color of the border for the toolbar called `$toolbar-border-color`. We can find this variable in the same file that we opened before. Let's compile our theme again and see the results in our browser as shown in the following screenshot:

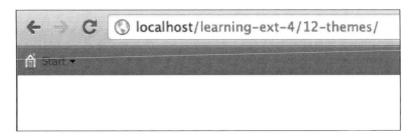

Adding this little pixel to our toolbar really improves the look and feel of our component; small details are always worthwhile and make a huge difference.

We are almost done with our main toolbar. Let's add more vertical space, this will make our toolbar a little bit larger vertically. In order to do this let's find the `right` variable in the `_toolbar.scss` file that we have already opened:

```
//margins
$toolbar-horizontal-spacing: 2px;
$toolbar-vertical-spacing: 4px;
$toolbar-footer-horizontal-spacing: 6px;
$toolbar-footer-vertical-spacing: 4px;

//border
$toolbar-border-color: $panel-body-border-color !default;
```

We are going to change the value of these variables in this file because they don't contain the `!default` rule. The `!default` rule allows us to override the original value, but if the variable doesn't have this rule, we can't override the value in our `my-ext-theme.scss` file.

If we compile our theme again, we will see how our toolbar height has increased a little bit more than before.

Styles for the tabs

Now, let's start working with the tabs. This will require a little more extra work, but the result will look really great. Let's start by creating two more gradients in the same file, where we already defined the gradient for the toolbar:

```
//...

} @else if $type == toolbar-blue{
    @include background-image(linear-gradient($direction,
#4486ac,#396e8e));

} @else if $type == tabbar-blue{
    @include background-image(linear-gradient($direction,
#55a7d5,#4d96c1));

} @else if $type == tab-active-white{
    @include background-image(linear-gradient($direction,
#fefefe,#e6e6e6));
}
```

The first gradient will be used for the background of the tab bar, and the second gradient will be used for the active tab background.

Once we define these two gradients let's open the _tabs.scss file located in the variables folder, where all the components' configurations are. This file contains all the available variables for the tab panel. We are going to use 12 variables from here. In our my-ext-theme.scss file we will override the following variables for the tab panel:

```
//...

//Toolbar component
$toolbar-background-gradient:toolbar-blue;
$toolbar-border-color:#7caac4;

//Tabs component
// Step 1 - define the background gradient for the tab bar
$tabbar-background-gradient:tabbar-blue;
$tabbar-border-color:#88c1e1;

//Step 2 - change the color for the border and the background
//          of the bottom strip of the tab bar
$tabbar-strip-border-color:#e6e6e6;
$tabbar-strip-background-color:#e6e6e6;

//Step 3 - define the styles for the inactive tab
$tab-height:22px;
$tab-background:null;
```

```
$tab-background-gradient:null;
$tab-inner-border:false;
$tab-border-color:transparent;
$tab-color:#fff;

//Step 4 - define the styles for the active tab
$tab-background-gradient-active:tab-active-white;
$tab-color-active:#000;
```

First we define the background gradient for the tab bar. We use the gradient that we already defined in the previous step. We will also add a light-blue color to the border; this small detail will make the bar stand out and it will make it look beautiful.

In the second step we change the color for the border and the background of the bottom strip of the tab bar. We use a gray color because our active tab will be a gray gradient.

In the third step we define the styles for the inactive tab. When the tab is not active, we will remove the background and make it transparent. We will also remove the borders and set the color of the font to white.

In the last step we define the styles for the active item. We set the background of the tab to use the gray gradient, which we already defined before, and we set the font color to black:

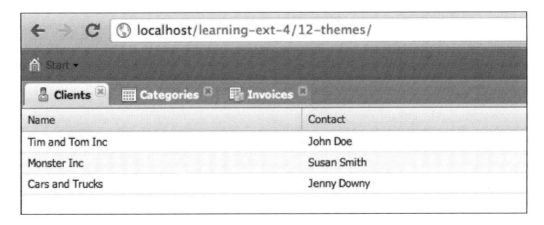

The previous screenshot shows the result of the changes that we made to our theme. It's looking good, but there are a few issues that we need to fix.

Even if we define the background color as null, the background of the tab is getting some ugly blue color. We need to remove that, but unfortunately, we don't have another way to do it but changing the code from the source.

We already know where the variables are located; in that same folder we will find another folder called `widgets`. In here we will find all the code for each of the available widgets on the framework. Each component is in a file, this allows us to modify the CSS code for each component easily. Let's open the `_tab.scss` file:

```
/**
 * @classExt.Tab
 */
@mixinextjs-tab {
    @include x-frame(
        $cls: 'tab',
        $ui: 'default-top',
        $border-radius: $tab-top-border-radius,
        $border-width: $tab-top-border-width,
        $background-color: null,//$tab-base-color,
        $background-gradient: $tab-background-gradient,
        $background-direction: top,
        $table: true
    );
```

On line number nine we can see that the background for the tab is getting the value of the `$tab-base-color` variable. If we want to make it transparent, we should pass a `null` value in this configuration of the `x-frame` mixin. We can also try to set a transparent value to the variable, but we will get some errors when compiling our theme because one of the mixins will try to calculate a lighter color based on this value. So the only way to solve this is by setting a null value.

Let's compile our theme and see the result in our browser; the following screenshot shows the results of our changes, as we can see the issues are solved:

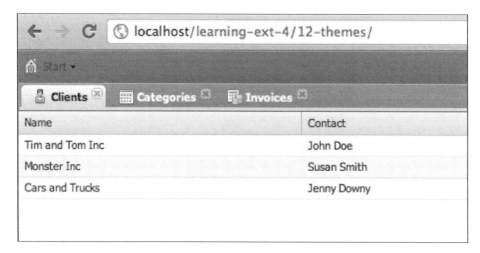

Now our tabs are looking really good. We are almost done, but before moving forward let's add a box shadow to the active tab and hide the close button of the inactive tabs. We are going to show the close button only in the active tab.

In order to hide the close button we need to find the rule where the style for this element is being set, around the line number 366, in the _tab.scss file, located at extjs-4.1.0/resources/themes/stylesheets/mytheme/default/widgets. We will find the class that sets the styles. In here we are going to hide the element as follows:

```
.#{$prefix}tab-close-btn {
position: absolute;
top: $tab-closable-icon-top;
right: $tab-closable-icon-right;
width: $tab-closable-icon-width;
height: $tab-closable-icon-height;
font-size: 0;
line-height: 0;
text-indent: -999px;
background: no-repeat;
background-image: theme-background-image($theme-name, $tab-closable-
icon);
        @include opacity(.6);
display:none;
    }
```

 Use the DOM inspector to find the CSS class that is adding the styles to the element that we want to modify. Google Chrome is great for this; we can also use Firebug if we use Firefox to develop.

By using the display:none rule we hide the close button; now we need to show this button only for the active tab. Let's add the following code that will follow our previous example:

```
.#{$prefix}tab-active{
.#{$prefix}tab-close-btn{  //step 1
display:block;
        }
        @include box-shadow(rgba(0,0,0,0.8) 0px 0px 5px); //Step 2
    }
```

Inside the active tab we show the close button using the display:block rule, this will show the element.

In the second step we use the `box-shadow` mixin to add a shadow to the active tab.

Let's compile our theme again and see the results in our browser. The following screenshot shows our latest changes:

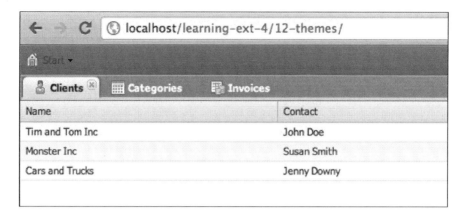

Now our tabs are looking really good. We have been changing some variables, we have also added and modified some CSS code to achieve this beautiful look and feel.

There's still one small detail that we need to fix. There's a blue line at the bottom of the tabs. This line looks really bad, we need to remove that line from there! If we inspect the DOM using the developer's tool from Google Chrome or Firebug, if we are in Firefox, we will notice that that line is on the body content of the tabs. We will see that specific DOM node doesn't contain any CSS class related to the tab panel, it is just a node with a few classes that are very generic. If we modify one of those CSS classes, we will change the look for all of our panels and container components and we don't want to do that, we only need to affect that specific element.

The easiest way to do it is to modify our JavaScript file and remove the border for that specific component. We will do this because we can't do it without changing everything that uses this stylesheet. Let's open our main `Viewport` class and add the following lines of code:

```
Ext.define('MyApp.view.Viewport',{
extend       : 'Ext.container.Viewport',

    //...

initComponent    : function(){
var me = this;

me.items = [{
```

```
            //...

        items : {
            xtype : 'tabpanel',
            itemId: 'maintabs',
            border: false,
            hidden: true,
    bodyBorder:false
        }
            }];

    me.callParent();
        }
    });
```

Just by adding the `bodyBorder` property and setting it to `false`, we can get rid of that ugly border. If we refresh our browser, we will see how nice our tabs are looking as shown in the following screenshot:

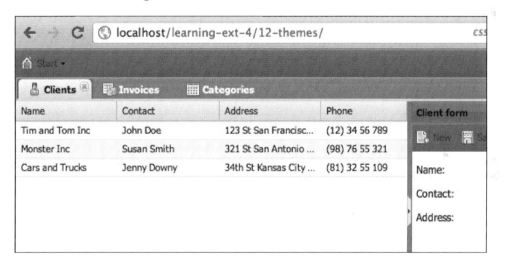

Styling the panel

Let's change the styles of our panels. We are going to define a gray header. We will use the same gray color that we have in our tab panel. We are also going to remove the gradient and use a plain gray.

If we open the file where all the variables for the panel are, we will find the variables that we need to modify. Let's redefine their value in our main theme file by adding the following code:

```
//Panel
$panel-header-background-gradient:null;
$panel-header-background-color:#e6e6e6;
$panel-header-color:#000;
$panel-header-border-color:null;
```

First we remove the gradient of the header by setting a `null` value to the `right` variable, then we set a flat color as the background of the header. We are using the same gray color from the tab component.

We are also setting the font color to black and removing the borders from the header by setting the border color property to `null`.

If we compile our changes, we will notice that there's still a border showing up and it looks really bad, it breaks our design. In order to get rid of it we need to make some changes in the original CSS code. Let's open the `_panel.scss` file located at `extjs-4.1.0/resources/themes/stylesheets/mytheme/default/widgets`. In here we have all the CSS code that is used in the panel component.

If we scroll down to line number 244, we will find the following code:

```
@if $ui-header-inner-border-color == null and $ui-header-background-
color != null {
    $ui-header-inner-border-color: lighten($ui-header-background-color,
10);
}
```

The inner border color is getting its value from the background color. To get rid of the border we need to set the color of this variable to `transparent`. Let's change the code as follows:

```
@if $ui-header-inner-border-color == null and $ui-header-background-
color != null {
        $ui-header-inner-border-color: transparent;
}
```

Now, if we compile our Compass code again, we will see the following screenshot as a result:

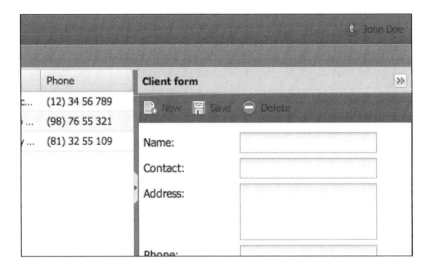

That's all for the panels! Now let's change the color of the blue spacebar that divides the grid and form. If we inspect the DOM, we will find out that the color is not being set on the bar, this bar is transparent. So if we want to change the color, we need to change the background color of the main container. Let's open the `_layout.css` file to see if we can find a variable to change the background color of the container in an easy way.

```
$border-layout-ct-background:#e6e6e6;
```

Unfortunately, this is just the way it is right now. It might be easier with a fully developed theme, but even the one that comes with Ext JS 4 does not have complete SASS coverage so that leaves some work to get things just as you might want them. It is possible to add your own SASS rules and variables in the CSS code also, if you are interested in expanding it yourself.

By adding the previous line of code to our main theme we can change the background color of the border layout that we are using, this is all we need to do. Let's compile our project again and we will see the results as shown in the following screenshot:

Now we have a good looking theme. We have changed the default colors and created a completely different theme.

Different styles for the same component

It's very common to have different styles of buttons, windows, panels, or any other component. For example, in our application we can define a different style for the main top toolbar and different styles for the other toolbars that are inside the panels in our forms or anywhere else.

In such cases the ui property shines. Every widget defines a ui property, which contains a prefix for the CSS classes. This way we can define specific classes for every component. Let's modify our JavaScript code and define a ui property for our main toolbar. The main toolbar is defined in the Viewport class. Let's open that file and add the following code:

```
Ext.define('MyApp.view.Viewport',{

    //...

    initComponent   : function(){
    var me = this;

    me.items = [{
        xtype : 'panel',
```

```
        layout: 'fit',
        dockedItems : [{
          xtype : 'toolbar',
          docked: 'top',
          itemId: 'mainmenu',
ui      : 'maintoolbar',
          items : [

                //...

          ]

        }],
        items : {
          xtype : 'tabpanel',
          itemId: 'maintabs',
          border: false,
          hidden: true,
bodyBorder:false
        }
        }];

    me.callParent();
        }
});
```

Once we define the new `ui` property for our main toolbar we need to create that `ui` in our CSS code. Let's open the `_toolbar.scss` file located at `extjs-4.1.0/resources/themes/stylesheets/mytheme/default/widgets`.

In this file we will find around line number 116 a call to a mixin called `extjs-toolbar-ui`. A mixin is like a function to which we can pass parameters and generate different results. In this case the mixin receives four parameters, but other components such as panels or buttons receive a bunch of parameters because we can modify a lot of things.

For this example we will call the mixin again but with different parameters for our specific `ui`. Let's add the following code after the first call of the mixin that is already defined:

```
@includeextjs-toolbar-ui(
    'maintoolbar',
    $background-color: $main-toolbar-background-color,
    $background-gradient: $main-toolbar-background-gradient,
    $border-color: $main-toolbar-border-color
);
```

In Compass we call a mixin using the `@include` word. In this case we called an Ext mixin, but Compass comes with many more mixins for creating gradients, shadows, and many more CSS3 goodies.

The first parameter will define the `ui` name; this parameter will be the prefix for the resulting CSS classes. We are using the same text that we use in the JavaScript file.

The other parameters define the background color, the gradient that we are going to use, and the border color. It's important to note that we are defining new variables in here, so let's define those variables in our main theme file:

```
//Toolbar component UI
$main-toolbar-background-gradient:toolbar-blue;
$main-toolbar-background-color:null;
$main-toolbar-border-color:#7caac4;

$toolbar-background-gradient:null;
$toolbar-background-color:#e6e6e6;
$toolbar-border-color:#e6e6e6;
```

The previous code defines the styles for our new toolbar `ui`. We are also setting a gray color for the default toolbars. If we compile our theme, we will get some warnings because the new `ui` is looking for some images that don't exist yet. For now we will ignore it. Let's refresh our browser to see the changes as shown in the following screenshot:

Now we have two toolbars with really different looks! We can create as many UIs as we need. Some components require a lot more variables, but the process of creating a new UI is the same as we did here.

Supporting legacy browsers

So far we have created our theme that looks perfect on most of the modern browsers such as Google Chrome, Firefox, Opera, and Safari, but the chances are that we want to support Internet Explorer, maybe from version 7 or 6. If at this moment we open our application using IE, the theme won't work well because IE doesn't support many of the new goodies of CSS3:

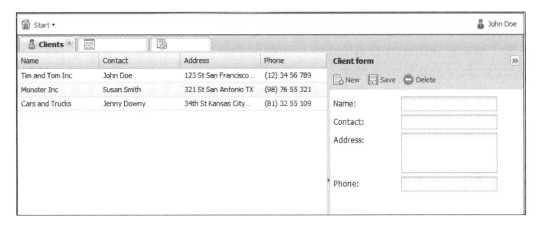

In order to make our theme work on IE we need to use images instead of CSS3 gradients. We can create all the required images manually using our favorite image editor software or we can create them automatically using the Sencha tools.

 Even if we create the images automatically using the Sencha command, we usually need to retouch some of those images to make it look right.

Let's download and install the Sencha SDK Tools (http://www.sencha.com/products/sdk-tools/). With these tools we can generate all the required images automatically.

Before we generate the images let's copy all the images from `extjs-4.1.0/resources/themes/images/gray` to `resources/images`. We also need to configure the location of where the images will be taken; right now the images are taken from the default Ext theme library. If we want to change that, we need to open the `utils.rb` file located at `extjs-4.1.0/resources/themes/lib`. Now let's replace line number 62 as shown in the following code:

```
#images_path = File.join($ext_path, 'resources', 'themes', 'images',
theme)
images_path = relative_path
```

We are just commenting out the URL for the images and setting a relative path. This relative path contains the `resources/images` URL from our main project.

If we again compile our CSS code, we will have a new CSS file that uses the images that we have in our own project instead of the default Ext theme. Now let's run the following command in the root folder of our application to generate the images for our new theme:

```
$ sencha slice theme -d ../extjs-4.1.0 -c resources/css/my-ext-theme.css
-o resources/images -v
```

The `-d` parameter defines the location of the Ext library. We need to make sure to point to the right path where the Ext is located, otherwise we will get some errors.

The `-c` parameter defines the CSS file of our new theme.

The `-o` parameter is the output folder, where the generated images will be placed. Keep in mind that the images that already exist in this directory will be replaced.

The `-v` parameter allows us to see the progress of process while generating the images. This parameter is optional.

If everything goes fine, we will get a success message telling us that the images are getting generated correctly. We are almost done with the theme, but since we define a new `ui` property for the main toolbar we need to generate those images too.

In order to generate the images for all the UIs defined, we need to create a `manifest` file, where we define all the UIs that we have in our theme. In our example the `manifest` file will contain the following code:

```
Ext.onReady(function() {
Ext.manifest = {
widgets: [
            {
xtype: 'widget.toolbar',
ui   : 'maintoolbar'
            }
        ]
    };
});
```

We are using the `onReady` method, then we set the `manifest` object with all the widgets that have defined a new `ui` property. In this example we only have one for the toolbar component, but if we have more, we can add them to the array.

Save this file at the root folder of our application, and then we only need to run the following command to generate the images for our new UIs:

```
$ sencha slice theme -d ../extjs-4.1.0 -c resources/css/my-ext-theme.css
-o resources/images -v -m manifest.json
```

We have added a new parameter called −m, which defines the location of the `manifest` file. When finished all the images for the UIs will be generated. Now let's refresh Internet Explorer and see how our new theme looks in this old browser as shown in the following screenshot:

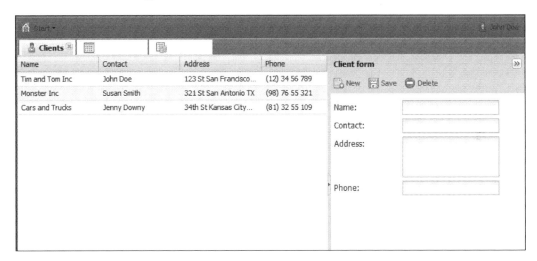

We are having some issues with the tabs, this is because we set the borders to transparent and the images are not getting generated correctly. We need to use an image editor to fix these images, unfortunately these are just some of the kinks we have to work through with the way Ext JS theming is set up right now. Overall it's still far easier to do it this way than theming by hand.

We can use the DOM inspector to see exactly the images that we need to fix. The DOM elements that are rendered on Internet Explorer are different from the nodes on the modern browsers; this is because we need to place the images at specific locations.

Once we finish fixing the required images we will be able to see our beautiful theme across all the browsers. The final theme should look as shown in the following screenshot:

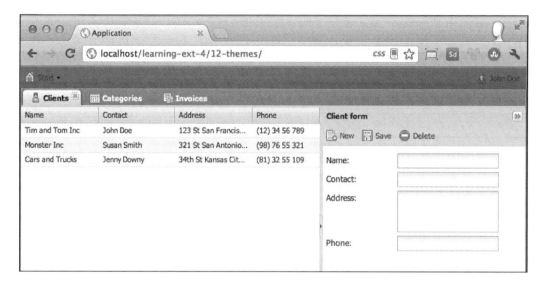

 We can find a great post in the Sencha's blog about the slicer tool at http://www.sencha.com/blog/using-CSS3-in-every-browser/.

Summary

In this chapter we learned how to create beautiful themes. We can create very complex designs and even completely change the default look and feel of the default Ext library. We shouldn't be afraid to modify the original Compass files to fit our needs, we can create our own mixins or define new variables, we are free to change all that we need.

One of the greatest things about this version is the way we can create a theme, using the `ui` property we can have as many different components as we need.

In the next chapter we will learn about the drawing package of the library and how to create awesome charts to visually represent reports to our users.

13
From Drawing to Charting

The Ext JS 4 framework offers a complete drawing library used on the chart components. However, the Sencha team did not only focus on the charting components, they decided to implement a more versatile set of tools that are the core of the charting library.

This means that we can use the drawing package to implement cross-browser custom graphics. The drawing package contains a `Surface` class that abstracts the graphics implementation and enables the developer to create arbitrarily shaped sprites that respond to the user; it also provides a rich set of animations.

The topics we are going to cover in this chapter are as follows:

- Basic drawing
- Adding interactions
- Charts
    - Legend
    - Axis
    - Gradients
    - Series
    - Theming

- Series examples
  - Area
  - Bar
  - Line
  - Pie
  - Radar
  - Scatter
  - Gauge

- Enhancing our application with charts

Basic drawing

First we need to know that the implementations of the `Surface` class are SVG (for SVG capable browsers) and VML (for the Internet Explorer family that does not support SVG). Most of the methods and ways to create sprites are inspired by the SVG standard.

In the following example we are going to draw some shapes inside `Ext.Window` and will learn how the drawing package works.

First we are going to define our view:

```
/**
 * @class MyApp.view.DrawingSurface
 * @extends Ext.draw.Component
 * @author Armando Gonzalez <iam@armando.mx>∫
 * This is the drawing component of the basic drawing example
 */
Ext.define('MyApp.view.DrawingSurface', {
  extend  : 'Ext.draw.Component',
    alias  : 'widget.drawingsurface',
    items  : [{
     type: 'circle', //this will draw a circle
      fill: 'blue',
      radius: 50, //the radius of our circle
      x: -150, //the x position of the circle
      y: 60 //the y position of the circle
    },{
      type: 'rect', //this will draw a rectangle
      width: 100,
      height: 100,
      radius: 10, //border radius
      fill: 'green', //the fill color of the shape
```

```
                opacity: 0.5,
                x: -120,
                y: 0,
                stroke: 'red', //the stroke color
                'stroke-width': 2
            },{
                type: "ellipse",
                radiusX: 80,
                radiusY: 50,
                opacity: 0.8, //the opacity of the sprite
                x: 50,
                y: 60,
                fill: 'red'
            },{
                type: "path",//svg
                path: "M 230 0 L 300 0 L 265 100 z", //a triangle
                opacity: 0.9,
                fill: "green"
            },{
                type: "text",
                text: "Text!",
                fill: "black",
                x: -50,
                y:-50,
                font: "18px monospace"
            },{
                type: "image", //this will sprite an image
                src: "http://www.sencha.com/img/apple-touch-icon.png",
                width: 200,
                opacity: 0.9,
                x: 120,
                y: 0,
                height: 100,
                width: 100
            }]
    });
```

In the previous code we are defining Ext.draw.Component that contains the six
Ext.draw.Sprite available classes in the Ext JS library:

- **Circle**: To draw circles, you can set the radius in the radius
  property configuration.

- **Rect**: To draw rectangles, the width and height configurations are set in the
  width and height properties.

- **Text**: To render text as sprite, the font/fontsize can be set using the
  font property.

- **Path**: This is the most powerful sprite type. With this type you can create arbitrary shapes by using the SVG path syntax.

- **Image**: This type renders an image as sprite; you can set the source path of the image in the `src` property.

- **Ellipse**: To draw ellipses, you can set the radius in the `radiusX` and `radiusY` properties.

A sprite is an object that is rendered in a drawing surface. The object properties' configurations are as follows:

- **type**: This property is used to define the type of the sprite. Possible options for the `type` property are circle, path, rect, text, ellipse, image.

- **width**: This property is used in rectangle and image sprites for defining the width of the rectangle or image.

- **height**: This property is used in rectangle and image sprites for defining the height of the rectangle or image.

- **radius**: This property is used in circle sprites for defining the radius of the circle.

- **radiusX**: This property is used in ellipses for defining the x-axis radius of the ellipse.

- **radiusY**: This property is used in ellipses for defining the y-axis radius of the ellipse.

- **x**: This property defines the position along the x-axis.

- **y**: This property defines the position along the y-axis.

- **path**: This property is used in path sprites for defining the path of the sprite written in SVG-like path syntax.

- **opacity**: This property is used to define the opacity of the sprite.

- **fill**: This property defines the fill color.

- **stroke**: This property defines the stroke color.

- **stroke-width**: The width of the stroke.

- **font**: This property is used with text type sprites. This gives the full font description. It uses the same syntax as the CSS `font` parameter.

- **text**: This property is used with text type sprites. It defines the text itself.

Now we just need to render the component in a window:

```
/**
 * This is the main code for the application
 */

Ext.Loader.setConfig({
  enabled:true
});
Ext.application({
  name: 'MyApp',
  requires:['MyApp.view.DrawingSurface'],
  launch: function() {
    Ext.create('Ext.Window',{
      width:630,
      height:318,
      title:'Drawing and charting',
      autoScroll:true,
      frame:false,
      layout:'fit',
      items:[{
        xtype:'drawingsurface'
      }]
    }).show();
  }
});
```

The following screenshot is the result of the previous basic drawing example:

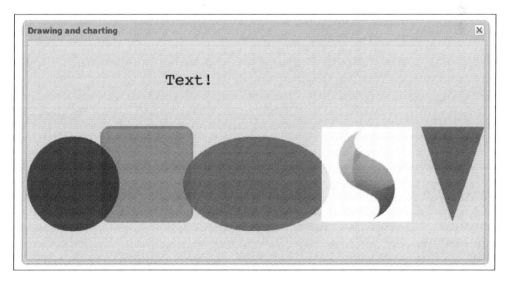

Adding interaction

The `Ext.draw.Sprite` class is a very versatile class. We can add events, animation, and add custom behavior to the sprites. The main feature of this class is that we aren't tied to a specific shape or structure, and it is browser and device agnostic.

In the following example we are going to code a bouncing ball, using the `Ext.Draw.Sprite` class power:

```
/**
 * @class MyApp.view.BouncingBall
 * @extends Ext.draw.Component
 * @author Armando Gonzalez <iam@armando.mx>
 * This is the bouncing ball component
 */
Ext.define('MyApp.view.BouncingBall', {
  extend    : 'Ext.draw.Component',
    alias  : 'widget.bouncingball',
style:{
  backgroundImage:"url('resources/images/court.jpeg')"
},
    width: 700,
    height: 350,
    ballSize :30,
    afterRender : function(){
      varball,dx = 5, dy = 5, x = 20, y = 100,
      me = this, sound ;

      //Adding some sound to the bouncing ball
      sound = new Audio("resources/sounds/toing.mp3");


      this.callParent(arguments);


      ball = new Ext.draw.Sprite({
        type: 'image',
        src: "resources/images/ball.png",
        height: me.ballSize,
        width: me.ballSize
      });

      me.surface.add(ball); // adding the ball
```

```
        var runner = new Ext.util.TaskRunner(); //create a runner to
    loop the ball
        var task = runner.newTask({ //start a task
        run: function () {
          ball.setAttributes({ //change the ball position
              y : y,
              x : x
          }, true); // the true value redraws tha ball

          if( x < 0 || x >me.width - me.ballSize ) { // validation to
    change the x direction
              dx = -dx;
              sound.play(); // play the sound
          }
          if( y < 0 || y >me.height - me.ballSize ) { // validation to
    change the y direction
            dy = -dy;
          }
          y += dy; // change the ball´s position
          x += dx;
        },
        interval: 10 // this goes every 10 milliseconds
      });
      task.start(); // start the task

      ball.addListener('mouseover', function() {
          dx = -dx;//changing the ball direction
        });
      }
    });
```

We have added a Tennis court background image to our drawing surface component, then we set the size of our drawing surface and the ball size. All the logic to make the ball bounce goes in the `afterRender` method. We added some audio object to produce a bouncing sound when the ball reaches any of the sides, then we add our ball sprite to the drawing surface.

We are going to use `Ext.util.TaskRunner` to move the ball around the drawing surface at an interval of 10 milliseconds. The use of a task is useful for pausing the bouncing ball. The final step is to add a listener to the ball so when the mouse is over, the ball changes direction.

Once we have the code, we run it and will have the following result, try it!:

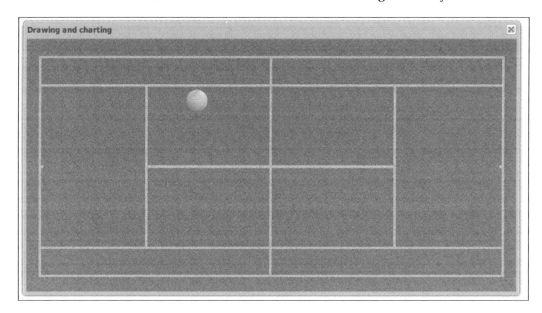

Charts

Now that we know how the drawing package works, we are ready to see how the Ext JS library uses the package capabilities in the chart package.

The chart package is a set of classes that define a chart container to manage axes, legends, series, labels, tips, cartesian and radial coordinates, and specific series like Pie, Area, Bar, Radar, Gauge, and so on.

The Ext.chart.Chart class is the main drawing surface for series. It manages the rendering of each series and also manages how axes are defined and drawn.

Legend

The chart configuration object accepts a legend parameter to enable legend items for each series and to set the position of the legend as follows:

```
legend: {
  position: 'left' // possible values are left, top, bottom, right
}
```

Axis

The axis package contains an abstract axis class that is extended by the `Axis` and `Radial` classes. There are axes for categorical information (**Category axis**) and also axis for quantitative information like **Numeric axis**. There is a **Time axis** that is used for rendering information over a specific period of time.

Gradients

The charting package also has the power to create linear gradients. The gradients can be defined as an array of gradient configurations in the `Chart` object. The following is a valid configuration:

```
gradients: [{
     id: 'gradient1',
  angle: 45,
  stops: {
     0: {
          color :'#333'


  },
  100:{
          color :'#DDD'
     }
  }
},{
  id: 'gradient2',
  angle: 0,
  stops: {
     0: {
color: '#587'
  },
  20: {
          color: '#FFF'
     },
     100: {
       color: '#333'
}}
}]
```

Series

A `series` class is an abstract class extended by Line or Scatter visualizations. This class contains code that is common to these series, like event handling, animation, shadows, gradients, common offsets, and so on. A `series` class will contain an array of items with information about the positioning of each element; it also contains a shared `drawSeries` method that updates all positions for the series and then renders the series.

Theming

We can add custom themes to the charts using the `theme` property, as shown in the following example:

```
Ext.create('Ext.chart.Chart',{
    theme :'custom_theme'
})
```

A `Theme` class defines the style of the shapes, color, font, axes, and background of a chart. The easiest way to create a theme is to create a base set of colors that will base the theme. This is done in the `color` property configuration.

```
{
colors: ['#aaa', '#bcd', '#eee']
}
```

Another way of creating a theme is setting a base color; the theme will generate an array of colors that match the base color:

```
{
baseColor: '#bce'
}
```

Now that we have seen the main concepts of the chart package, we are going to see the different series types Ext JS has.

Series examples

The Ext JS charting system is one of the most complete systems for charting; we have a variety of series we can choose from to use in our applications like area, bar, line, pie, radar, scatter, gauge, and mixed type series.

Area

The stacked area chart is useful when displaying multiple layers of information. In the following example we are going to see how to use this series type. First we need to configure a set of data that we'll be using with this example.

All of the series types are populated using stores, so let's start by defining the data store:

```
/**
 * @class App.store.Data
 * @extends Ext.data.Store
 * This our data store definition
 * @authore Armando Gonzalez <iam@armando.mx>
 */
Ext.define('MyApp.store.Data', {
  extend: 'Ext.data.Store',
    fields: ['month', 'data1', 'data2', 'data3', 'data4', 'data5',
'data6', 'data7', 'data9'],
    autoLoad: true,
    proxy: {
      type: 'ajax',
      url : 'serverside/data.json',
      reader:{
          type:'json',
          root:'data'
      }
    }
});
```

The store definition has the field's definition and the proxy definition from where the data will be requested. Once we have the store definition we are going to define the stacked area chart component:

```
/**
 * @class MyApp.view.Area
 * @extends Ext.chart.Chart
 * @author Armando Gonzalez <iam@armando.mx>
 * The Area chart definition
 */
Ext.define('MyApp.view.Area', {
  extend: 'Ext.chart.Chart',
    alias: 'widget.areachart',
  store: 'Data',
  style: 'background:#fff',
  animate: true,
```

```
legend: {
position: 'right'
},
axes: [{
    type: 'Numeric',
    grid: true,
    position: 'left',
    fields: ['data1', 'data2', 'data3', 'data4', 'data5', 'data6',
    'data7'],
title: 'Number of Invoices',
    minimum: 0
},{
type: 'Category',
position: 'bottom',
fields: ['month'],
title: 'Month of the Year',
label: {
  rotate: {
  degrees: 315
}
}
}],
series: [{
type: 'area',
axis: 'left',
xField: 'month',
yField: ['data1', 'data2', 'data3', 'data4', 'data5', 'data6',
'data7'],
style: {
  opacity: 0.93
}
}]
});
```

In the previous code we have the stacked chart definition. First we configure the data store, then we set the legend position to the right. The axes configuration comes next, here we are setting two axes, a Numeric and a Category axis. The Numeric axis is our y axis aligned to the left of the drawing surface and has the data it is going to control. The Category axis renders the months on the bottom of the drawing surface.

Next we have the series definition. Here we have the series type definition and how the data will be rendered. We have defined the data for yField and the data for xField.

The previous class definition produces the following result:

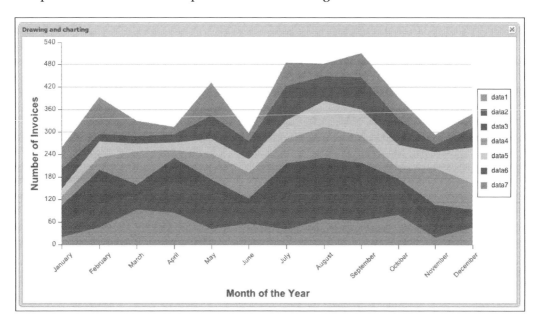

Bar

The bar chart configuration is very similar to the area chart configuration. These type of charts are easy to understand, that is why they are commonly used for displaying categorical data:

```
/**
 * @class MyApp.view.Bar
 * @extends Ext.chart.Chart
 * @author Armando Gonzalez <iam@armando.mx>
 * The Bar chart definition
 */
Ext.define('MyApp.view.Bar', {
  extend: 'Ext.chart.Chart',
    alias: 'widget.barchart',
  store: 'Data', //store definition
style: 'background:#fff',
animate: true,
legend: {
position: 'right'
},
```

```
axes: [{
  type: 'Numeric',
  grid: true,
  position: 'bottom', // the axe position
  fields: ['data1', 'data2'], // the mapping data axe
  title: 'Number of Invoices',
  minimum: 0
  },{
  type: 'Category',
  position: 'left', // the axe position
  fields: ['month'], // the mapping data for this axe
  title: 'Month of the Year'
  }],
series: [{
  type: 'bar',
  axis: 'bottom',
  xField: 'month',
  yField: ['data1', 'data2'],
  style: {
  opacity: 0.93
},
    tips: { // adding a tooltip to the chart
    trackMouse: true,
    width: 140,
    height: 48,
    renderer: function(storeItem, item) {
    this.setTitle(storeItem.get('month') + '</br> data1 : ' +
  storeItem.get('data1') + ' views</br>' + ' data2 : ' +
  storeItem.get('data2') + ' views');
    }
    }
  }]
});
```

In the previous code we have changed the axis positions and are only rendering two sets of data (`data1` and `data2`). The series type has changed to `bar` type and we just added a tool tip configuration. So when the user sets the mouse over any bar, it shows a tooltip with some useful information:

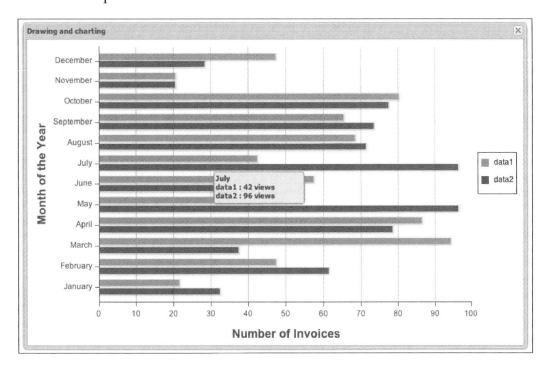

Line

The line chart is very useful when we want to see progression or regression in our data; in the chart configuration we need to configure the series correctly so we can get the correct visualization of our data.

```
/**
 * @class MyApp.view.Line
 * @extends Ext.chart.Chart
 * @author Armando Gonzalez <iam@armando.mx>
 * The Line chart definition
 */
Ext.define('MyApp.view.Line', {
  extend: 'Ext.chart.Chart',
  alias: 'widget.linechart',
  store: 'Data',
```

```
style: 'background:#fff',
animate: true,
legend: {
  position: 'right'
},
axes: [{
  type: 'Numeric',
  grid: true,
  position: 'left',
  fields: ['data1', 'data2', 'data3'], //the mapping data for
    this axis
  title: 'Number of Invoices',
  minimum: 0
    },{
    type: 'Category',
    position: 'bottom',
    fields: ['month'],//the mapping data for this axe
    title: 'Month of the Year',
    label: {
     rotate: {
       degrees: 315
     }
   }
  }
}],
series: [{ //define a serie for each line
    type: 'line',
    axis: 'left',
    xField: 'month',
    yField: 'data1', // the mapping data
    highlight: { // the highlight behavior
      size: 7
    },
      fill: true, // this line is fill
    markerConfig: {
      type:'cross', //cross type marker
      size: 4,
    radius: 4,
      'stroke-width': 0
  }
},{
type: 'line',
axis: 'left',
xField: 'month',
yField: 'data2',
highlight: {
  size: 7
},
```

```
markerConfig: {
  type: 'circle', //circle type marker
  size: 4,
  radius: 4,
    stroke-width': 0
  }
}, {
  type: 'line',
  axis: 'left',
  xField: 'month',
  yField: 'data3',
  highlight: {
    size: 7
  },
  markerConfig: {
    type: 'circle',//circle type marker
  size: 4,
  radius: 4,
    'stroke-width': 0
  }
    }]
});
```

In the previous code we are rendering three sets of data, and now we are using a `line` type series. The line series configuration has highlight property to add some highlight behavior when the user selects a line, we have also configured a `markerconfig` property that sets some nice markers to our lines' peaks. The marker configuration has some attributes configurations that enhance the markers.

The following image shows the line chart in action:

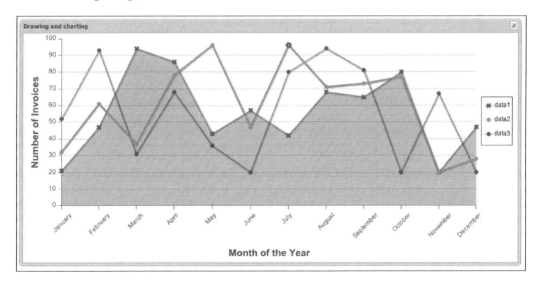

Pie

The pie chart visualization is a very common visualization to display quantitative information for different categories. Like other charts in Ext JS 4, configuring a pie chart is very fast and simple, we only need to know how the series work in this type of chart:

```
/**
 * @class MyApp.view.Pie
 * @extends Ext.chart.Chart
 * @author Armando Gonzalez <iam@armando.mx>
 * The Pie chart definition
 */
Ext.define('MyApp.view.Pie', {
    extend: 'Ext.chart.Chart',
    alias: 'widget.piechart',
    store: 'Data',
    style: 'background:#fff',
    animate: true,
    legend: {
    position: 'right'
  },
    series: [{
    type: 'pie', // pie chart type
    field: 'data1', // the mapping data for this pie
    showInLegend: true,
    highlight: {
     segment: {
      margin: 20
     }
    }
  },
    label: { // show the months names inside the pie
    field: 'month',
    display: 'rotate',
    contrast: true,
    font: '18px Arial'
    }
}]
});
```

As we can see, configuring a pie chart is very simple. The `label` property is where the month's name configuration goes so each slice of the pie has a label. The pie configuration code produces the following result:

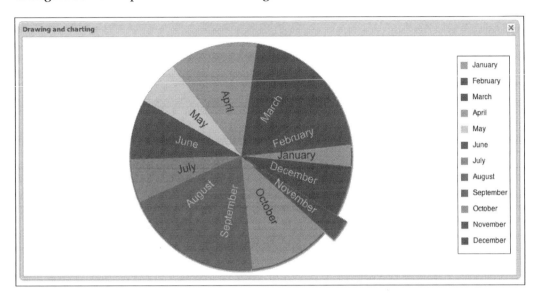

Radar

The radar chart is very useful when you want to compare different quantitative values for a constrained number of categories; with this type of chart you can see the gaps each category has in an interval. Using this type of chart in the Ext JS 4 library is very straightforward because it's very similar to the line chart. We only need to change the series type, add the radial axes, and we will have the radar chart working:

```
/**
 * @class MyApp.view.Radar
 * @extends Ext.chart.Chart
 * @author Armando Gonzalez <iam@armando.mx>
 * The Radar chart definition
 */
Ext.define('MyApp.view.Radar', {
    extend: 'Ext.chart.Chart',
    alias: 'widget.radarchart',
    style: 'background:#fff',
    insetPadding: 20,
    animate: true,
    store: 'Data',
```

```
legend: {
  position: 'right'
},
axes: [{ // setting the radial axe
  type: 'Radial',
  position: 'radial',
  label: {
    display: true
  }
}],
series: [{
  showInLegend: true,
  type: 'radar', // setting the series type
  xField: 'month',
  yField: 'data1',
  style: {
    opacity: 0.4
  }
    },{
    showInLegend: true,
    type: 'radar', // setting the series type
  xField: 'month',
  yField: 'data2',
  style: {
    opacity: 0.4
  }
}, {
  showInLegend: true,
  type: 'radar', // setting the series type
  xField: 'month',
  yField: 'data3',
  style: {
    opacity: 0.4
  }
}]
});
```

Once we have configured the chart with the radial axe and the series with a radar type, we have the following result:

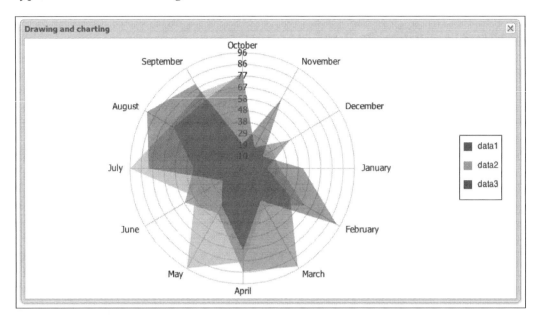

Scatter

The scatter chart is a little more complex chart. It is useful when trying to display and compare more than two variables in the same visualization. These variables can be mapped into x and y coordinates and also to an element's radius/size, color, and so on.

```
/**
 * @class MyApp.view.Scatter
 * @extends Ext.chart.Chart
 * @author Armando Gonzalez <iam@armando.mx>
 * The Scatter chart definition
 */
Ext.define('MyApp.view.Scatter', {
    extend: 'Ext.chart.Chart',
    alias: 'widget.scatterchart',
    style: 'background:#fff',
    animate: true,
    store: 'Data',
    axes: false,
```

```
      series: [{
       type: 'scatter',
        markerConfig: {
            type: 'circle',
   radius: 40,
   size: 20
        },
        axis: 'left',
         xField: 'data1',
         yField: 'data2',
         color: '#a00'
     }]
  });
```

We only need to configure the series to scatter type and set the marker configuration object with the attributes we want in the marker. The scatter example result is the following:

Gauge

Gauge charts are used to show where certain values fall within a given range. We can configure the `maximum` and `minimum` values, and in how many steps we want to split the label intervals along the gauge.

```
/**
 * @class MyApp.view.Gauge
 * @extends Ext.chart.Chart
 * @author Armando Gonzalez <iam@armando.mx>
 * The Gauge chart definition
 */
Ext.define('MyApp.view.Gauge', {
  extend: 'Ext.chart.Chart',
  alias: 'widget.gaugechart',
  style: 'background:#fff',
  animate: true,
  store: 'Data',
  axes: [{
      type: 'gauge', // gauge type axe
      position: 'gauge',
      minimum: 0, //minimum value for the gauge
      maximum: 100, //maximum value for the gauge
  steps: 10, // the steps the gauge will have
  margin: -10 // setting a margin to the axe
    }],
  series: [{
  type: 'gauge', // gauge series type
  field: 'data1', // the data we are mapping
      donut: 50, // setting a donut radius
    colorSet: ['#3AA8CB', '#ddd'] // the char color
    }]
});
```

When using Ext JS Gauge charts, it's important to configure the axes correctly with a minimum value and a maximum value that are directly related with the possible values the data has; in the previous code we have set a `donut` property in the `series` property so the gauge area render in a donut shape type:

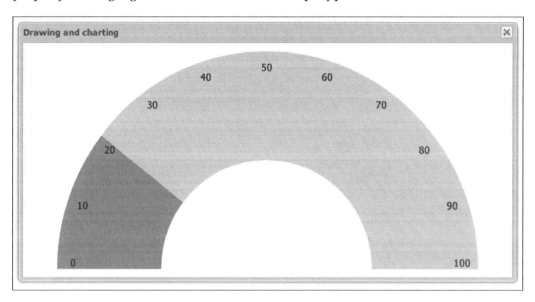

Now that we know how charts and series work in the Ext JS 4 library, we are ready to add some charts to our invoices application.

Enhancing our application with charts

We are going to add some charts to our invoices application to see how the invoices are doing each month. First we need to define the store that will populate our chart:

```
/**
 * @class MyApp.store.invoices.Summaries
 * @extends Ext.data.Store
 * @author Armando Gonzalez <iam@armando.mx>
 * This is the definition of our Invoices summary store
 */
Ext.define('MyApp.store.invoices.Summaries', {
  extend: 'Ext.data.Store',
    fields: ['invoice', 'data1', 'data2', 'data3', 'data4', 'data5',
'data6', 'data7', 'data9'],
    autoLoad: true,
proxy    : {
  type  : 'ajax',
```

```
url   : 'serverside/invoices/summary.json',
        reader   : {
                type   : 'json',
                root   : 'data'
            }
        }
});
```

Once we have defined the `summaries` store, we define the line chart:

```
/**
 * @class MyApp.view.invoices.LineChart
 * @extends Ext.chart.Chart
 * @author Armando Gonzalez <iam@armando.mx>
 * The Line chart definition for the invoices summary
 */
Ext.define('MyApp.view.invoices.LineChart', {
    extend: 'Ext.chart.Chart',
        alias: 'widget.invoices.linechart',
    store: 'invoices.Summaries',
    style: 'background:#fff',
    animate: true,
    legend: {
        position: 'right'
    },
    axes: [{
     type: 'Numeric',
     grid: true,
     position: 'left',
     fields: ['data1', 'data2', 'data3'],
     title: 'Invoices data',
     minimum: 0
     },{
     type: 'Category',
     position: 'bottom',
     fields: ['invoice'],
      title: 'Invoices'
    }],
    series: [{
     type: 'line',
     axis: 'left',
     xField: 'invoice',
      yField: 'data1',
     highlight: {
      size: 7
    },
```

```
        fill: true,
         markerConfig: {
         type: 'cross',
         size: 4,
         radius: 4,
         'stroke-width': 0
        }
       },{
       type: 'line',
        axis: 'left',
        xField: 'invoice',
        yField: 'data2',
        highlight: {
        size: 7
       },
       markerConfig: {
        type: 'circle',
         size: 4,
        radius: 4,
         'stroke-width': 0
       }
       },{
       type: 'line',
        axis: 'left',
        xField: 'invoice',
        yField: 'data3',
       highlight: {
        size: 7
       },
       markerConfig: {
        type: 'circle',
         size: 4,
        radius: 4,
        'stroke-width': 0
       }
       }]
     });
```

We need to configure the series of the line chart with the invoices data of our previous store. Now we are going to add the line chart to the main categories container:

```
/**
 * @class MyApp.view.categories.MainContainer
 * @extends Ext.container.Container
 * @author Armando Gonzalez <iam@armando.mx>
 *
 * The main container that uses a border layout.
 */
```

```
Ext.define('MyApp.view.categories.MainContainer',{
    extend     : 'Ext.container.Container',
    alias      : 'widget.categories.main',
    requires : [
    'Ext.layout.container.Border',
    'Ext.resizer.BorderSplitterTracker'
    ],

    layout     : 'border',

    initComponent    : function(){
      var me = this;

      me.items = [{
          xtype : 'container',
          region: 'center',
          style: 'background:#fff',
          layout: 'border',
          items:[{
            xtype : 'invoices.dataview',
            region: 'center'
        },{
            region: 'south', // adding a panel that will contain our
line chart component
            height: 300,
            collapsible : true,
            collapsed:'true',
            itemId: 'sumaries',
            xtype : 'panel',
            title:'Invoices Summaries',
            layout:'fit',
            items:{ // adding the line chart component
              xtype : 'invoices.linechart',
            }
        }]
        },{
          xtype : 'categories.tree',
          width : 300,
          region: 'west',
          split : true,
          collapsible : true
      }];

    me.callParent();
  }
});
```

Now we just need to add the new panel logic to the categories controller. So we can make our chart component work.

```
/**
 * @class MyApp.controller.categories.Categories
 * @extends Ext.app.Controller
 * @author Armando Gonzalez <iam@armando.mx>
 *
 * This is the main controller for categories
 */

Ext.define('MyApp.controller.categories.Categories',{
  extend : 'Ext.app.Controller',
    stores : [//the store of our controller
      'categories.Categories',
      'invoices.Invoices',
        'invoices.Summaries'
    ],
    views : [//the views of our controller
      'categories.CategoriesForm',
      'categories.TreePanel',
      'categories.MainContainer',
      'invoices.Dataview',
      'invoices.LineChart'
    ],
    refs: [{
      ref: 'treePanel',
      selector: '#categoriesmaintreepanel'
    },{
      ref: 'invoicesSummaries',
  selector: '#categoriesmain #sumaries'
  }],
    init  : function(){
      var me = this;
      me.control({
          '#categoriesmaintreepanel #savebtn' : {// we get the save
button reference
            click :me.addTreeNode
          },
          '#categoriesmaintreepanel toolbar #deletebtn':{// we get the
delete button reference
            click :me.deleteTreeNode
          },
        '#categoriesmaintreepanel':{// when a folder is selected
            itemclick :me.onNodeClick
        }
      });
```

```
    me.getCategoriesCategoriesStore().load();
    me.getInvoicesInvoicesStore().load();
  },
  addTreeNode:function(btn){
    //add tree node logic

  },
  deleteTreeNode:function(){
    //delete tree node logic

  },
  addContent      : function(){
    this.container.add({
      xtype : 'categories.main',
      itemId: 'categoriesmain'
    });
  },
  onNodeClick : function(){
    var me = this;
    me.getInvoicesSummaries().expand();
    me.getInvoicesSummariesStore().load();//loading the chart store
  }
});
```

In the categories controller code we added the `summaries` panel reference, then defined the listeners that will fire when the user clicks on a folder node. The logic when the user selects a node comes next, here we load the `summaries` store and expand the chart panel.

When we run the application we get the following result:

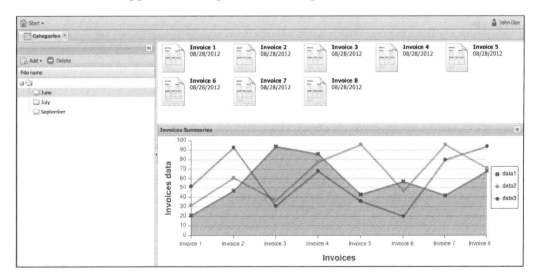

Summary

The drawing package of the Ext JS 4 library is very powerful. We can do amazing stuff with it; charts are a clear example of what can be done with it. In this chapter we have learned how charts, series, and the drawing works in the Ext JS 4 library. We can now add some nice charts to our enterprise applications, and enhance the usability of the reports our applications have.

In the next chapter we are going to finish our application and will see the process of deploying an Ext JS 4 to a production environment. The following chapter is very important because we are going to see what steps you need to perform when releasing an Ext JS 4 application in a production environment.

Index

Symbols

$include-default variable 355
01-basics folder
  app.js file, creating 13
  creating 13
  installation.html file, creating 13

A

accordion layout 102, 103
addEvents method 140
addListener method 143, 150
addTreeNode method 313
advanced theming
  about 358
  new gradients, adding 358-361
  panel, styling 367-370
  tabs, styling 362-366
Ajax
  about 106
  used, for acquiring data 106
Ajax proxy
  about 126
  defining 126
Ajax request 106
alert method 16
alias 53
append method 67
application
  dataview, defining for 285, 286
application, Ext JS 4
  building 26
  data structure 30
  enhancing, with charts 400-405

file structure 31
planning 26
wireframes, using 27
App.view.UsersView class 295
Aptana editor
  about 20
  autocomplete functionality 20
  Bundles 20
  CSS and HTML validator 20
  JavaScript debugger 20
  JavaScript validator 20
area chart 387, 388
autocomplete class 19

B

bar chart 389-391
basic drawing
  about 378
  circles 379
  ellipses 380
  image 380
  path 380
  rectangles 379
  text 379
bbar property 90
beforerender event 75
border layout 101, 102
build folder 11
builds folder 11
Bundles 20
button
  creating 145-147
  icons 148

C

callParent method 141
card layout 93, 94
categories module 29
CellSelectionModel class 219
charts
  about 384
  axis class 385
  gradients 385
  legend parameter 384
  series class 386
  theme property 386
  used, for enhancing application 400
checkbox
  adding, to tree panel 313, 314
Checkbox class 199
checkbox field 196-198
checked property 306
children property 306
class system
  about 33-36
  alias 53
  classes, mixing 42-49
  configurations, handling 49
  Jump class, defining 42
  post-processors 39
  pre-processors 39
  simple inheritance 37
  singleton class 52
  Spin class, defining 43
  statics methods 51
  statics properties 51
click event 139
client model
  defining 208
client module 28
closable property 91
code
  writing, for dataview 286, 287
column renderers
  about 216, 217
  arguments 216
columns 213-215
columns property 161 213
combination method 48
combobox field 188-192

Compass 8, 352
  URL 8, 352
  using 352
compete method 45
competition program 42
complex dataview 294, 295
components lifecycle
  about 71
  children, adding to component 82-85
  creation phase 72
  destruction phase 78
  executing 79-82
  phases 72
  rendering phase 72, 75
config object 34
configurations
  about 49
  handling, with pre-processors 49-51
confirm method 17
constructor method 34, 44, 140
container property 76
containers
  about 82
  panel 86
  window component 90
Content Delivery Network (CDN) 10
contentEl property 76
controller 253
controller layer 246
control method 255
copy property 306
count method 120
creation phase, components lifecycle
  about 72
  diagrammatic representation 73
  steps 72-75
creditcard function 116
creditcardMessage function 116
CSS and HTML validator 20
CSS file
  URL 10

D

data
  acquiring, Ajax used 106-110
  sending 134-137

submitting 204-206
data connection
  about 208, 283
  model, defining for store 208
  store, defining 285
  store, defining for grid 209, 210
  user model, defining 284
data structure 30
dataview
  about 283
  code, writing for 286, 287
  defining, for application 285, 286
  events, handling on 287, 288
  listeners, adding to 288
dataview file 285
date field 192-195
dateFormat property 111
dateIssued field 111
dateIssued property 134
ddel property 306
define method 34
deleteTreeNode method 313
destroy method 79
destruction phase, components lifecycle
  about 78
  diagrammatic representation 78
  steps 78, 79
different styles, for same components 370, 371, 372
dockedItems property 157
docs folder 11
documentation 9
DOM
  about 33
  elements, obtaining 62, 63
  manipulation 66-69
  query 63
  working with 61
DomHelper object 67
DomQuery class 64
drag and drop
  about 329
  application, enhancing with 348
  drop zone, hitting 333-337
  implementing, between Ext JS components 338-347
  object, making draggable 330-333

Drag Zone
  about 306
  copy property 306
  ddel property 306
  item property 306
  records property 306
  view property 306
drawSeries method 386
drop zone
  hitting 333, 334, 335, 336, 337, 338

E

Eclipse editor
  about 19
  web tools plugin 19
editors, Ext JS 4
  Aptana editor 20
  Eclipse editor 19
  Sencha Architect 22
  Sublime Text 2 editor 18
  Textmate editor 21
employee class 142
endDrag method 334
event driven development 139, 140, 141, 142, 144
events
  handling, on dataview 287, 288
  listening 255, 256
examples folder 11
expanded property 306
Ext.AbstractComponent class 71
Ext.Ajax 106
ext-all-debug.js file 12
ext-all-dev.js file
  about 12
  importing 14, 15
ext-all.js file 12
Ext.button.Button class 145
Ext.Class class 39
Ext.ClassManager object 34
Ext.Component class 71
Ext.container.Container class 82
Ext.container.Viewport component 163
Ext Core layer 10
Ext.createis 34
Ext.create method 250 39

Ext.data.Connection class 106
Ext.data.Model class 39, 111
Ext.data.reader.Json class 129
Ext.data.reader.Xml class 130
Ext.data.Store class 119
Ext.data.validations object 114, 115
Ext.dd.DD class
 about 333
 endDrag method 334
 onDragDrop method 334
 onDragEnter method 333
 onDrag method 333
 onDragOut method 333
 onDragOver method 333
 startDrag method 333
Ext.dd.DDTarget class 336
ext-debug.js file 12
Ext.define 34
ext-dev.js file 12
Ext.draw.Sprite class 382
Ext.Element class 62
Ext.form.field.Base class 182
Ext Foundation layer 10
Ext.getCmp method 74
Ext.grid.column.Action type 216
Ext.grid.column.Boolean type 215
Ext.grid.column.Date type 215
Ext.grid.column namespace 213
Ext.grid.column.Number type 215
Ext.grid.column.Template type 215
Ext.grid.Feature class 223
Ext.grid.feature.Grouping 223-227
Ext.grid.feature.GroupingSummary 227-229
Ext.grid.feature.RowBody 230, 231
Ext.grid.feature.Summary 232, 233
Ext.grid.plugin.CellEditing 234-236
Ext.grid.plugin.DragDrop plugin 342
Ext.grid.plugin.Editing 234
Ext.grid.plugin.RowEditing 236, 238
Ext.grid.RowNumberer column 215
Ext JS
 about 8
 data, submitting 204
 Ext Core layer 10
 Ext Foundation layer 10
 Ext JS 4 layer 10

field container 201
fields 182
form component 173
layers 10
MVC pattern 245
Ext JS 4
 about 8
 basic drawing 378
 CDN, using 10
 charts 384
 class system 33
 commercial license 9
 components lifecycle 71
 containers 82
 data, acquiring using Ajax 106
 data, sending 134-137
 DOM, working with 61
 downloading 9
 editors 17
 event driven development 139
 features 8, 9
 GPLv3 license 9
 layout system 91
 learning-ext-4 folder, creating 12
 loader system 54
 look and feel 351
 main menu, invoice management
  application 162
 menus, adding 151
 simple button 145
 toolbars 156
Ext JS 4 layer 10
Ext JS application
 appFolder configuration 247
 controller 253, 254
 controller folder 249
 controllers configuration 247
 creating 246-249
 enhancing, with drag and drop 348, 349
 events, listening 255-257
 model folder 249
 modules, opening 257-262
 view folder 249
 views 250-253
ext.js file 12
Ext.menu.Item class 152

Ext.menu.Menu class 152
Ext.Msg object 15
Ext.onReady function 14
Ext.panel.Panel class 86
Ext.panel.Tool class 88
ext_path variable 355
Ext.selection.CellModel model 218
Ext.selection.RowModel model 218
Ext.Template 289
Ext.toolbar.Fill class 168
Ext.tree.Panel class 299
Ext.util.Observable base class 140
Ext.view.View class 283
Ext.widget 34
Ext.XTemplate class 283, 291

F

fadeOut method 63
fail event 140
Field class 182
field configurations, tree nodes
  about 305
  checked 306
  children 306
  expanded 306
  iconCls 306
  leaf 306
  root 306
  text 306
field container 201-203
field property 114
field structure 182
files, Ext JS 4
  ext-all-debug.js file 12
  ext-all-dev.js file 12
  ext-all.js file 12
  ext-debug.js file 12
  ext-dev.js file 12
  ext.js file 12
file structure 31
fireEvent method 141
Firefox 373
firstChild.data property 109
fit layout 92, 93

folders, Ext JS 4
  build folder 11
  builds folder 11
  docs folder 11
  examples folder 11
  jsbuilder folder 11
  locale folder 11
  resources folder 12
  src folder 11
  welcome folder 12
form component
  about 173
  Address field, adding 178-181
  HTML file, creating 175, 176
  JavaScript file, creating 174
  working on 174, 175

G

gauge charts 399, 400
gem 352
getCmp method 74
getSelection method 219
getSelectionModel method 313
Google Chrome 373
grid
  about 207, 283
  store, defining for 209, 210
grid features
  about 223
  Ext.grid.feature.Grouping 223-227
  Ext.grid.feature.GroupingSummary
    227-229
  Ext.grid.feature.RowBody 230, 231
  Ext.grid.feature.Summary 232, 233
grid listeners 220-223
grid panel
  labout 208-212
  paging 239, 240
grid tree panel 315, 318

H

hasMany property 117
hbox layout 95-98
hidden property 77

I

iconCls property
  about 306
  using 147, 149
idInvoice field 111
idInvoice property 134
infinite scrolling grid 241-243
inheritance 37-39
initComponent function 74, 344
installation.html file
  about 13, 14
  creating 13
interaction
  adding 382
Internet Explorer 373
Invoice class 111
invoice management application
  main menu 162
invoices' categories
  adding, to tree panel 320-326
itemclick event 139
itemId property 251
item property 306
items array 87
itemSelector property 288

J

JavaScript debugger 20
JavaScript file
  URL 10
JavaScript Lint plugin
  using 18
JavaScript validator 20
jsbuilder folder 11
JSON reader 128, 129
Jump class
  defining 42

L

Labelable class 182
launch method 247
layout system
  about 91
  accordion layout 102, 103
  border layout 101, 102
  card layout 93, 94
  fit layout 92, 93
  hbox layout 95-99
  vbox layout 99, 100
leaf property 306
learning-ext-4 folder
  01-basics folder, creating 12
  creating 12
  extjs-4.1.1 folder, creating 12
legacy browsers
  supporting 373-375
lenghtMessage property 115
line chart 391, 393
listeners
  adding, to dataview 288
loader system
  about 54
  dependencies 57-59
  loader, enabling 55, 56
  synchronous loading 60
  using 54
locale folder 11
look and feel
  advanced theming 358
  different styles, for same
    component 370-372
  environment, setting up 351, 352
  legacy browsers, supporting 373-375
  resources folder 353-355
  variables 357

M

main menu, invoice management
    application
  about 162
  creating 163-170
mapping property
  about 132
  using 132-134
maximizable property 90
menu property 151
menus
  adding 151-155
model
  about 111
  creating 111, 112

defining, for store 208
relationships 117
validations 113
model layer 246
Model-View-Controller pattern. *See* **MVC**
modules
creating 263-271
functionality, adding 272-279
opening 257-262
references 279, 280
msg property 107
MVC pattern
about 7, 245, 283
controller layer 246
model layer 246
view layer 246
MySQL database
URL 126

N

nodes
adding 309, 310
removing 311-313
number field
about 185-188
Numeric axis 385

O

object properties configurations, sprite
fill 380
font 380
height 380
opacity 380
path 380
radius 380
radiusX 380
radiusY 380
stroke 380
stroke-width 380
text 380
type 380
width 380
x 380
y 380
Observable class 44

onDestroy method 79
onDragDrop method 334
onDragEnter method 333
onDrag method 333
onDragOut method 333
onDragOver method 333
on method 143
onReady event 56
onReady method 58, 108, 374
Opera 373
overCls property 76

P

pageSize property 239
paging, grid panel 239, 240
PagingToolBar item 239
panel 86-89
Panel class 87
params property 109
paths property 55
pie chart 394
plugins
about 233
Ext.grid.plugin.CellEditing 234-236
Ext.grid.plugin.Editing 234
Ext.grid.plugin.RowEditing 236-238
post-processors
about 40
alias 41
alternateClassName 41
creating 41
singleton 41
uses 41
pre-processors
about 39
alias 41
className 41
config 41
creating 40, 41
extend 41
inheritableStatics 41
loader 41
mixins 41
statics 41
xtype 41

proxy
  about 126
  JSON reader 128
  types 126
  XML reader 130

Q

querying, DOM 63-65

R

radar chart 395-397
radio button 198-201
Radio class 199
raw value 182
record property 131
records property 306
relationships, model 117, 118
remote data
  retrieving 126
remote data, retrieving
  Ajax proxy used 126
  JSON reader used 128
  mapping property used 132
  XML reader used 130
rendering phase, components lifecycle
  about 75
  diagrammatic representation 75
  rsteps 75-77
renderTo property 74, 90, 146
request method 106
require method 56
resources folder
  about 12, 353
  config.rb file 354
  ext4 folder 354
  mytheme folder 355
  sass folder 354
responseText property 108
responseXML property 109
Rich Internet Applications (RIAs) 7
root property 130, 306
RowSelectionModel class 218
rowspan property 161
Ruby
  about 352

downloading 352
gem 352
installing 352

S

Safari 373
scatter chart 397, 398
selection models 218, 219
Sencha
  URL 9
Sencha Architect desktop application
  about 22, 25
  creating 23-25
Sencha blog
  URL 376
Sencha SDK Tools
  downloading 373
  installing 373
series class 386
series examples
  about 386
  area chart 387, 388
  bar chart 389-391
  gauge charts 399, 400
  line chart 391-393
  pie chart 394
  radar chart 395-397
  scatter chart 397, 398
setConfig method 55
setPath method 56
setStyle method 62
show method 90
singleton class
  defining 52
Skater class 44
Spin class
  defining 43
Spke tplugin
  URL 19
sprite
  interaction, adding 382, 383
src folder 11
startDrag method 333
statics methods
  alias 51

statics properties
  alias 52
store
  about 119
  creating 119
  defining 285
  defining, for grid 209, 210
  elements, adding 120, 121
  elements, looping through 122
  records, removing 125
  records, retrieving 122, 123
  remote data, retrieving 126
style tag 158
Sublime Text 2 editor
  about 18
  plugins, adding 18
success event 140
success function 107
synchronous loading 60

T

taxtId property 115
tbar property 89
templates
  about 289
  working 290, 291, 293
Textfield class 183-185
Textmate editor
  about 21
  bundles 21
text property 146, 306
Theme class 386
Time axis 385
timeout property 110
toolbars
  about 156
  components, adding 157
  creating 156-162
tree nodes 305
tree panel
  about 300, 301, 302
  checkbox, adding 313, 314
  grid tree 315, 317, 319

invoices' categories, adding 320-326
nodes, adding 309, 310, 311
tree drag-and-drop 306-309
tree nodes 305
TreeStore 303-305
TreeStore 303-305
type property 114, 127

U

url property 127
user model
  defining 284

V

validations, model 113, 114
variables 357
viewConfig property 309
view layer 246
Viewport class 163, 164
view property 306
views 250-253
views folder 285

W

WAMP server
  URL 126
welcome folder 12
window component 90, 91
wireframes
  about 27
  categories module 29
  client module 28
  using 27

X

XAMP
  URL 126
XML reader 130, 131
xtype 152

Thank you for buying
Learning Ext JS 4

About Packt Publishing

Packt, pronounced 'packed', published its first book "*Mastering phpMyAdmin for Effective MySQL Management*" in April 2004 and subsequently continued to specialize in publishing highly focused books on specific technologies and solutions.

Our books and publications share the experiences of your fellow IT professionals in adapting and customizing today's systems, applications, and frameworks. Our solution based books give you the knowledge and power to customize the software and technologies you're using to get the job done. Packt books are more specific and less general than the IT books you have seen in the past. Our unique business model allows us to bring you more focused information, giving you more of what you need to know, and less of what you don't.

Packt is a modern, yet unique publishing company, which focuses on producing quality, cutting-edge books for communities of developers, administrators, and newbies alike. For more information, please visit our website: www.packtpub.com.

About Packt Open Source

In 2010, Packt launched two new brands, Packt Open Source and Packt Enterprise, in order to continue its focus on specialization. This book is part of the Packt Open Source brand, home to books published on software built around Open Source licenses, and offering information to anybody from advanced developers to budding web designers. The Open Source brand also runs Packt's Open Source Royalty Scheme, by which Packt gives a royalty to each Open Source project about whose software a book is sold.

Writing for Packt

We welcome all inquiries from people who are interested in authoring. Book proposals should be sent to author@packtpub.com. If your book idea is still at an early stage and you would like to discuss it first before writing a formal book proposal, contact us; one of our commissioning editors will get in touch with you.

We're not just looking for published authors; if you have strong technical skills but no writing experience, our experienced editors can help you develop a writing career, or simply get some additional reward for your expertise.

Ext JS 4 First Look

ISBN: 978-1-849516-66-2   Paperback: 340 pages

A practical guide including examples of the new features in Ext JS 4 and tips to migrate from Ext JS 3

1. Migrate your Ext JS 3 applications easily to Ext JS 4 based on the examples presented in this guide

2. Full of diagrams, illustrations, and step-by-step instructions to develop real word applications

3. Driven by examples and explanations of how things work

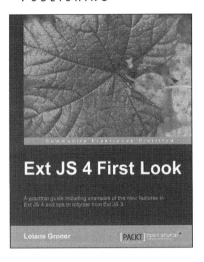

Ext JS 4 Web Application Development Cookbook

ISBN: 978-1-849516-86-0   Paperback: 488 pages

Over 110 easy-to-follow recipes backed up with real-life examples, walking you through basic Ext JS features to advanced application design using Sencha's Ext JS

1. Learn how to build Rich Internet Applications with the latest version of the Ext JS framework in a cookbook style

2. From creating forms to theming your interface, you will learn the building blocks for developing the perfect web application

3. Easy to follow recipes step through practical and detailed examples which are all fully backed up with code, illustrations, and tips

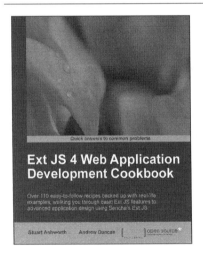

Please check **www.PacktPub.com** for information on our titles

Learning Ext JS 3.2

ISBN: 978-1-849511-20-9   Paperback: 432 pages

Build dynamic, desktop-style user interfaces for your data-driven web applications using Ext JS

1. Learn to build consistent, attractive web interfaces with the framework components

2. Integrate your existing data and web services with Ext JS data support

3. Enhance your JavaScript skills by using Ext's DOM and AJAX helpers

4. Extend Ext JS through custom components

Learning Vaadin

ISBN: 978-1-849515-22-1   Paperback: 412 pages

Master the full range of web development features powered by Vaadin-built RIAs

1. Discover the Vaadin framework in a progressive and structured way

2. Learn about components, events, layouts, containers, and bindings

3. Create outstanding new components by yourself

4. Integrate with your existing frameworks and infrastructure

Please check **www.PacktPub.com** for information on our titles

Made in the USA
Lexington, KY
31 July 2014